T0155762

Communications
in Computer and Information Science   900

Commenced Publication in 2007
Founding and Former Series Editors:
Phoebe Chen, Alfredo Cuzzocrea, Xiaoyong Du, Orhun Kara, Ting Liu,
Krishna M. Sivalingam, Dominik Ślęzak, Takashi Washio, and Xiaokang Yang

More information about this series at http://www.springer.com/series/7899

Stefano Cagnoni · Monica Mordonini ·
Riccardo Pecori · Andrea Roli ·
Marco Villani (Eds.)

Artificial Life and Evolutionary Computation

13th Italian Workshop, WIVACE 2018
Parma, Italy, September 10–12, 2018
Revised Selected Papers

 Springer

Editors
Stefano Cagnoni ⓘ
University of Parma
Parma, Italy

Monica Mordonini ⓘ
University of Parma
Parma, Italy

Riccardo Pecori ⓘ
Università degli Studi eCampus
Novedrate, Italy

Andrea Roli ⓘ
University of Bologna
Cesena, Italy

Marco Villani ⓘ
University of Modena and Reggio Emilia
Modena, Italy

ISSN 1865-0929   ISSN 1865-0937 (electronic)
Communications in Computer and Information Science
ISBN 978-3-030-21732-7   ISBN 978-3-030-21733-4   (eBook)
https://doi.org/10.1007/978-3-030-21733-4

This Springer imprint is published by the registered company Springer Nature Switzerland AG
The registered company address is: Gewerbestrasse 11, 6330 Cham, Switzerland

Preface

This volume of *Communication in Computer and Information Science* contains the proceedings of WIVACE 2018, the XIII Workshop on Artificial Life and Evolutionary Computation. The event was successfully held on the Sciences Campus of the University of Parma, Italy, during September 10–12, 2018. WIVACE aimed to bring together researchers working in the field of artificial life and evolutionary computation to present and share their research in a multidisciplinary context. The workshop provided a forum for the discussion of new research directions and applications in different fields, where different disciplines effectively meet. Some examples of these interdisciplinary topics are: Bioinformatics and Computational Biology, Bioinspired Algorithms and Robotics, Complex Systems, Evolutionary Computation, Genetic Algorithms, Modeling and Simulation of Artificial, Biological, Social and Business Intelligence Systems, Synthetic and Systems Biology and Chemistry, Theories and Applications of Artificial Life, Quantum Computing.

WIVACE 2018 received 30 total submissions, 24 of which were selected for presentation at the workshop as either long or short talks. We accepted 12 high-quality papers (40% of the original submissions) for publication in an extended version in this proceedings volume, after a single-blind review round performed by at least three Program Committee members. Submissions and participants in WIVACE 2018 came from 13 different countries making WIVACE an increasingly international event despite its origins as an Italian workshop. Following this ever-increasing international spirit, future WIVACE editions are expected to be held also outside Italy. Many people contributed to this successful edition. We express our gratitude to the authors for submitting their works, to the members of the Program Committee for devoting so much effort to reviewing papers despite a tight schedule, and finally to the invited speakers of both WIVACE and the special session on quantum computing.

Our gratitude also goes to the University of Parma for offering the venue for the event, Centro Santa Elisabetta, which allowed the workshop to be held in a peaceful and green atmosphere, and to SPECIES, the Society for the Promotion of Evolutionary Computation in Europe and its Surroundings, and, in particular to its administrator and president, Jennifer Willies and Marc Schoenauer, for giving their support to the workshop administration. We would also like to mention Roberto Serra for being a constant source of fruitful inspiration and ideas for WIVACE itself and Michele Amoretti, Stefano Carretta, and Paolo Villoresi for successfully organizing the special session on quantum computing.

We also thank Laura Sani, Michele Tomaiuolo, Paolo Fornacciari, Gianfranco Lombardo, and Giulio Angiani for their precious help before and during the conference.

And finally, we acknowledge the helpful advice of the staff at Springer, who provided their professional support through all the phases that led to this volume.

September 2018

Stefano Cagnoni
Monica Mordonini
Riccardo Pecori
Andrea Roli
Marco Villani

Organization

General Chairs

Stefano Cagnoni   University of Parma, Italy
Monica Mordonini   University of Parma, Italy

Program Committee Chairs

Riccardo Pecori   eCampus University, Italy
Andrea Roli   University of Bologna, Italy
Marco Villani   University of Modena and Reggio Emilia, Italy

Program Committee

Antonia Azzini   C2T Consortium, Italy
Vito Antonio Bevilacqua   Polytechnic University of Bari, Italy
Leonardo Bich   Universidad del Pais Vasco, Spain
Leonardo Bocchi   University of Florence, Italy
Matteo Borrotti   CNR-IMATI, Italy
Michele Braccini   University of Bologna, Italy
Marcello Antonio Budroni   University of Sassari, Italy
Timoteo Carletti   University of Namur, Belgium
Mauro Castelli   Universitade Nova de Lisboa, Portugal
Antonio Chella   University of Palermo, Italy
Chiara Damiani   University of Milan Bicocca, Italy
Luca Di Gaspero   University of Udine, Italy
Pietro Ducange   eCampus University, Italy
Alessandro Filisetti   Explora Biotech Srl, Italy
Francesco Fontanella   University of Cassino, Italy
Paolo Fornacciari   University of Parma, Italy
Mario Giacobini   University of Turin, Italy
Alex Graudenzi   University of Milan Bicocca, Italy
Giovanni Iacca   University of Trento, Italy
Gianfranco Lombardo   University of Parma, Italy
Roberto Marangoni   University of Pisa, Italy
Francesco Masulli   University of Genoa, Italy
Giancarlo Mauri   University of Milan Bicocca, Italy
Sara Montagna   University of Bologna, Italy
Giuseppe Nicosia   University of Catania, Italy
Stefano Piotto   University of Salerno, Italy
Clara Pizzuti   CNR-ICAR, Italy
Irene Poli   European Centre for Living Technology, Italy

Riccardo Righi	European Commission, Joint Research Center, Spain
Simone Righi	MTA Tk Lendület Research Center for Educational and Network studies, Hungary
Federico Rossi	University of Salerno, Italy
Laura Sani	University of Parma, Italy
Gael Sentis	University of Siegen, Germany
Debora Slanzi	European Centre for Living Technology, Italy
Giandomenico Spezzano	CNR-ICAR and University of Calabria, Italy
Pasquale Stano	University of Salento, Italy
Thomas Stuetzle	Université Libre de Bruxelles, Belgium
Pietro Terna	University of Turin, Italy
Andrea Tettamanzi	University of Nice, France
Leonardo Vanneschi	Universitade Nova de Lisboa, Portugal
Olli Yli-Harja	Tampere University of Technology, Finland

Sponsor

SPECIES, Society for the Promotion of Evolutionary Computation in Europe and its Surroundings.

Contents

Boolean Networks and Complex Systems

An Improved Relevance Index Method to Search Important Structures in Complex Systems

Laura Sani[1], Alberto Bononi[1], Riccardo Pecori[1,4(✉)],
Michele Amoretti[1], Monica Mordonini[1], Andrea Roli[2], Marco Villani[3],
Stefano Cagnoni[1], and Roberto Serra[3]

[1] Dip. di Ingegneria e Architettura, Università di Parma, Parma, Italy
[2] Dip. di Informatica - Scienza e Ingegneria, Università di Bologna - Sede di Cesena, Cesena, Italy
[3] Dip. di Scienze Fisiche, Informatiche e Matematiche, Università degli Studi di Modena e Reggio Emilia, Modena, Italy
[4] SMARTEST Research Centre, Università eCAMPUS, Novedrate (CO), Italy
riccardo.pecori@uniecampus.it

Abstract. We present an improvement of a method that aims at detecting important dynamical structures in complex systems, by identifying subsets of elements that show tight and coordinated interactions among themselves, while interplaying much more loosely with the rest of the system. Such subsets are estimated by means of a Relevance Index (RI), which is normalized with respect to a homogeneous system, usually described by independent Gaussian variables, as a reference. The strategy presented herein improves the way the homogeneous system is conceived from a theoretical viewpoint. Firstly, we consider the system components as dependent and with equal pairwise correlations, which implies a non-diagonal correlation matrix of the homogeneous system. Then, we generate the components of the homogeneous system according to a multivariate Bernoulli distribution, by exploiting the NORTA method, which is able to create samples of a desired random vector, given its marginal distributions and its correlation matrix. The proposed improvement on the RI method has been applied to three different case studies, obtaining better results compared with the traditional method based on the homogeneous system with independent Gaussian variables.

Keywords: Complex systems analysis · Information theory · Relevance Index · NORTA

1 Introduction

The identification of functional structures in dynamical systems composed of many interacting parts is a major challenge in science. In particular, the formation of intermediate-level structures is of particular interest for what concerns

S. Cagnoni et al. (Eds.): WIVACE 2018, CCIS 900, pp. 3–16, 2019.
https://doi.org/10.1007/978-3-030-21733-4_1

biological as well as artificial systems. These structures come from the dynamics of small-scale processes, but possess peculiar characteristics and are able to deeply influence the system they belong to.

Several measures have been proposed to describe the organization of these dynamical complex systems, many of which are based on information theory [10, 19]. Some of the most relevant results of the application of such metrics can be found in the domain of neuroscience [25, 27].

Starting from these results, Villani et al. [31] introduced a method to identify relevant structures in dynamical complex systems, based on a dataset including samples of the system status at different times. In particular, the Relevance Index (RI) quantifies how much the behavior of these relevant structures deviates from the behavior of a reference (homogeneous) system, in which the variables have, individually, the same marginal distributions as in the dataset, and all have the same pairwise correlation. In particular, a system characterized by independent Gaussian variables, i.e., with zero pairwise correlation, was originally taken as a reference [31].

In previous works, we improved the aforementioned RI method by applying some metaheuristics, in order to deal with the curse of dimensionality in computing the index [22, 26], and a GPU-based parallelization scheme, in order to speed up the overall computation [30].

In this paper we propose a further improvement to the RI method, by imposing that the variables in the homogeneous system all have the same nonzero pairwise correlation, matching the average pairwise correlation estimated from the system under analysis. This is achieved by using the NORTA method [6]. The introduction of this pairwise correlation value has allowed us to identify particularly interesting groups of variables, undetected in previous experiments.

The rest of the paper is structured as follows: in Sect. 2 we summarize some previous applications of the relevance index and of the NORTA method; in Sect. 3 we describe the most significant theoretical steps underlying the RI computation and the NORTA method; in Sect. 4 we assess the improvements obtained by applying the proposed modification to some relevant use cases; finally, in Sect. 5, we draw some conclusions.

2   Background

In this section we summarize previous works that take advantage either of the RI method or of the NORTA method, which we are going to combine in the proposed technique.

2.1   The Relevance Index Method

Much research has been already focused on the search for particularly informative groups in dynamical complex systems. Because of the emphasis on the (nonlinear) relationships among their constituents, many efforts have been based on the analysis of their representation through either networks [14] (for example community detection [4,16]), multigraphs [1,13] or hypergraphs [11]. Nevertheless, often the interactions across these informative groups are not known; in addition, the interaction topology could turn out not to be sufficient by itself to determine the behavior of the whole system, since it is often necessary to consider also the dynamical movements of the constituents. Besides this, it has been shown that relevant information about emergent structures in dynamical systems can be extracted by observing the system behavior "from the outside", by means of information-theoretical and statistical techniques [2,3,18], sometimes combined with dynamical systems analyses [8]. Some previous works have documented the use of these information-theoretical measures for studying complexity [10,19] and criticality [5,20,34,37]. However, none of the existing methods has all the following desirable properties:

- ability to identify groups of variables that change in a coordinated fashion;
- ability to identify critical states;
- direct applicability to data, without any need to resort to models;
- robustness with respect to sampling effort and system size.

The RI method, which is based on Shannon's entropy, appears to be a step towards obtaining all the aforementioned requirements. Indeed, the RI is a method based on the Cluster Index (CI), introduced by Edelman and Tononi in 1994 and 1998 [28,29], which detects functional groups of brain regions, assuming system fluctuations around a steady state. The RI method extends the applicability of the CI to a broad range of non-stationary dynamical systems, such as abstract models of gene regulatory networks and simulated chemical [31], biological [32], as well as social [9,23] systems. Moreover, the experimental analysis concerning two prominent models that exhibit two different kinds of criticality, namely the Ising model for phase transition and the Random Boolean Network (RBN) for dynamical criticality, demonstrated that the RI can be effectively used to identify critical states [21].

2.2 The NORTA Method

NORTA ("NORmal To Anything") is a method devised to generate specifically correlated random vectors [6]. This is a mathematical procedure that solves the issue of creating random vectors of correlated samples, given the set of their marginal distributions (marginals) and a measure of the dependence among them.

This is a good choice in our scenario, since, usually, the majority of complex systems components experience a certain degree of mutual dependence [35]. Some recent examples, where NORTA has been successfully employed in different fields, include wind power generation in renewable power supply systems [17], and the modeling of probabilistic load flows, based on Latin Hypercube Sampling [36]. Indeed, NORTA presents some degrees of uncertainty in the estimation of the marginal distributions and of the correlation matrix [35], since it is not always guaranteed that its samples have exactly the desired correlation matrix. However, we found it useful to overcome some issues encountered in applying the original RI method to some simple systems described by a moderate number of variables.

3   Theoretical Approach

The RI can be used to study data from a wide range of dynamical system classes, with the purpose of identifying sets of variables that behave in a somehow coordinated way, i.e., the variables belonging to the set are integrated with each other much more than with the other variables not pertaining to the set itself. These subsets can be used to describe the whole system organization, thus they are named Relevant Subsets (RSs).

The computation of the RI, which is an information-theoretical measure based on Shannon's Entropy (H in the following) [7], is usually based on observational data, and probabilities are estimated as the relative frequencies of the values observed for each variable. The theoretical definition of the RI is summarized in the following.

Let us consider a system U composed of n random variables $X_1, X_2, ..., X_n$ (e.g., agents, chemicals, genes, artificial entities) and suppose that S_k is a subset composed of k elements, with $k < n$. The RI of S_k is defined as:

$$RI(S_k) = \frac{I(S_k)}{MI(S_k; U \backslash S_k)} \tag{1}$$

where $I(S_k)$ is the integration, which measures the mutual dependence among the k elements in S_k, and $MI(S_k; U \backslash S_k)$ is the mutual information, which quantifies the mutual dependence between subset S_k and the remaining part of the system $U \backslash S_k$.

The integration, in turn, is defined as:

$$I(S_k) = \sum_{s \in S_k} H(s) - H(S_k) \tag{2}$$

while the mutual information is formalized as follows:

$$MI(S_k; U \backslash S_k) = H(S_k) + H(U \backslash S_k) - H(S_k, U \backslash S_k) \tag{3}$$

The integration can be shown to be the Kullback-Leibler Distance [7] between the joint distribution of the system variables and the product distribution of their marginals. Hence the integration is zero whenever the system variables are independent.

Trivially, the RI is undefined if $MI(S_k; U \backslash S_k) = 0$. However, a vanishing MI is a sign of independence (i.e., physical separation) of the subset under exam from the rest of the system, and therefore the subset has to be studied separately.

Since the RI increases with the subset size, a normalization method is required to compare RI values of subsets of different sizes. Moreover, the statistical significance of RI differences should be assessed by means of an appropriate test. For these reasons, a statistical significance index was introduced as [28]:

$$T_c(S_k) = \frac{\nu RI(S_k) - \nu \langle RI_h \rangle}{\nu \sigma(RI_h)} = \frac{RI(S_k) - \langle RI_h \rangle}{\sigma(RI_h)} \tag{4}$$

where $\langle RI_h \rangle$ and $\sigma(RI_h)$ are, respectively, the average and the standard deviation of the RI of a sample of subsets of size k extracted from a reference homogeneous system U_h, and $\nu = \langle MI_h \rangle / \langle I_h \rangle$ is its normalization constant.

A post-processing sieving algorithm [33] is used to select the most relevant sets, reducing the list of Candidate Relevant Sets (CRSs) to the most representative ones, i.e., those having the highest T_c values. The sieving algorithm is based on the criterion by which, if a CRS is a proper subset of another CRS and ranks higher than this, then it should be considered more relevant than this. Therefore, the algorithm keeps only those CRSs that are not included in or do not include any other CRS with higher T_c: this "sieving" action stops when no more eliminations are possible and the remaining groups of variables are the elementary RSs.

The generation of the homogeneous system is critical, as stated also in [31], and often, in the past, a simple but general and easy to compute solution was preferred. This solution encompassed the computation of the frequency of occurrence of each variable, given the available observations, and the generation of a new random series of samples, where each variable had a prior probability equal to the frequency of the original observations. The homogeneity required by Tononi was achieved by considering the components of the random vector U_h to be Gaussian and independent. This caused:

1. the correlation matrix of the homogeneous system to be a diagonal matrix, i.e., with pairwise correlations set to zero;
2. the integration $I(S_k)$ to be zero for all subsets of the homogeneous system.

The improved version of the method we propose in this paper consists in taking the pairwise correlation between variables describing the homogeneous system into account, requiring that it be not null, which seems a more realistic assumption. In this way, we remove a hypothesis (the independence of the variables) that is not true in general. Moreover, we maintain the homogeneity required by Tononi, by forcing all off-diagonal elements of the correlation matrix to have the same constant value ρ:

$$CORR(U_h) = \begin{bmatrix} 1 & \rho & \cdots & \rho \\ \rho & \ddots & \ddots & \vdots \\ \vdots & \ddots & \ddots & \rho \\ \rho & \cdots & \rho & 1 \end{bmatrix}.$$

while we normalize all variances to 1. The value of ρ is computed, in a first approximation, as the average value of all pairwise correlations of the observed variables.

In order to generate a homogeneous system with the aforementioned features, we take advantage of the NORTA method [6]. The measure of dependence we used in NORTA is the usual *product-moment* correlation matrix, based on the linear Pearson correlation coefficient with entries defined according the following formula:

$$\rho(X_i, X_j) = \frac{COV(X_i, X_j)}{\sigma_{X_i} \sigma_{X_j}}. \tag{5}$$

The NORTA method creates independent and identically distributed replicas of a random vector $\mathbf{X} = (X_1, X_2, ..., X_n)$, based on its (known) marginal distributions $F_i(x) = P(X_i \leq x)$, $i = 1, ..., n$ and the correlation matrix $CORR(\mathbf{X})$.

In summary, the NORTA procedure performs the following steps:

1. generates a normal random vector $\mathbf{Z} = (Z_1, Z_2, ...Z_n)$ with zero mean and covariance matrix $COV(\mathbf{Z})$, with 1s on the main diagonal;
2. obtains the prescribed marginal distributions by computing the replica $\mathbf{X}' = (X_1', X_2', ..., X_n')$ according to the following equation:

$$X_i' = F_i^{-1}(\Phi(Z_i)) \ i = 1...n, \tag{6}$$

where Φ is the distribution function of a standard Gaussian random variable and F_i^{-1} is the inverse of F_i, defined as:

$$F_i^{-1}(u) = \inf\{x : F_i(x) \geq u\}. \tag{7}$$

3. chooses $COV(\mathbf{Z})$ in order to induce the requested correlation matrix $CORR(\mathbf{X})$. In this case there is no closed-form solution and the method often relies on an efficient numerical search, by solving a number of one-dimensional root-finding problems. In some cases the procedure does not lead to the exact desired correlation matrix, failing to produce a positive semidefinite matrix, which is a requirement for a valid correlation matrix. However, NORTA can often get very close to the desired correlation matrix, even in very high dimensions.

In this work, NORTA is used to generate the homogeneous system based on the R implementation known as NORTARA[1]. This package generates n-dimensional random vectors with given marginal distributions and correlation matrix. The NORTA algorithm, which generates a standard normal random vector and then transforms it into a random vector with specified marginal distributions, is combined with the RA (Retrospective Approximation) algorithm, which is a generic stochastic root-finding algorithm.

4   Experimental Evaluation

In order to test the presented methodology, we analyzed three different systems whose dynamics are precisely known. In particular, we studied the consequences

---

[1] http://cran.r-project.org/web/packages/NORTARA/.

of using different homogeneous systems: the one produced with the method proposed in this work (where we "inject" the average correlation which characterizes the system under study - H_{wiC}, where wiC means "with correlation") and the one produced with the original method (H_{noC}). In the following, we focus on the application of the RI analysis, possibly applying the sieving algorithm in order to simplify the results. The binary nature of the variables of the test systems we used allows one to apply the H_{wiC} approach with simple Bernoulli distributions to all situations.

The three case studies we considered are representative of valuable research fields, that is, (i) the dynamics of Boolean networks, (ii) dynamical simulations of autocatalytic reaction systems happening within a Continuous-flow Stirred-Tank Reactor (CSTR for short) and (iii) simplified models of the dynamics of opinion diffusion.

The **Boolean network framework**, despite its apparent simplicity, has obtained remarkable results in simulating several aspects of real gene regulatory networks [12, 24]. In particular, here we present a collection of 5 different Boolean systems (denoted as RBN1, ..., RBN5) composed of 12 nodes, synchronously updated on the basis of either a Boolean function or a random Boolean value generator.

In each analysis considered in this paper, instead of juxtaposing different states belonging to the different attractors of each system [31], we follow single trajectories, perturbed every 20 steps by temporarily changing a randomly chosen variable from 0 to 1 (or vice versa).

The **CSTR** case study simulates a collection of molecules able to collectively self-replicate [12], a situation frequently studied in researches about the origin of life [15]; very similar assemblies could play an important role also in future bio-technological systems.

In this research, we tested a simple system featuring two distinct reaction pathways, a Linear reactions CHain (LCH) and an AutoCatalytic set of molecular Species (ACS). The reactions occur only in the presence of a specific catalyst, since spontaneous reactions are assumed to occur too slowly to affect the system behavior. Both LCH and ACS pathways occur in an open CSTR with a constant influx of feed molecules and a continuous outgoing flux of all the molecular species proportional to their concentration (see [31] for a more detailed description of the model). The problem we address in this paper is the detection of the groups of chemicals that participate in distinct dynamical organizations, by simply observing their concentration in time.

The asymptotic behavior of this kind of systems is a single fixed point [31], due to the system feedback structure. In order to apply our analysis, we need to observe the feedbacks in action; so, we perturb the concentration of some molecules in order to trigger a response in the concentration of (some) other species. We temporarily set to zero the concentration of some species after the system has reached its stationary state. In order to analyze the system response to perturbations we discretize its trajectory by observing it within equally-sized, non-overlapping time windows and by classifying the behavior of the chemical concentrations within this interval as "chemical concentration changing" ("1" tag) and "no change in chemical concentration" ("0" tag).

Finally, we compare the results of the application of the RI to different homogeneous systems on a simple model, in which the integration among variables in a subsystem under observation and its mutual information with the remaining part of the system can be tuned by acting on few parameters. The model abstracts from specific functional relationships among elements of the system and could resemble a basic **Leader-Followers model** (LF), used in opinion dynamics studies.

The system is composed of a vector of n binary variables $\{X_1, X_2, ..., X_n\}$ representing, for example, the opinion in favor of or against a given proposal. The model generates independent observations of the system state, i.e., each observation is a binary n-vector generated independently of the others, based on the following rules:

- Variables are divided into three groups, G1 = $\{L_a, F1_a, F2_a, F3_a\}$, G2 = $\{L_b, F1_b, F2_b\}$, and G3 = $\{L_c, F1_c, ... , F8_c\}$.
- L_a, L_b, L_c are the leaders of their groups[2], and they have a probability p_{lcpy} to copy the value of another leader, and a probability of 1-p_{lcpy} to independently assume a random value in $\{0,1\}$ (with probability of obtaining a "1" equal to 0.4, 0.3, and 0.3, respectively).
- The values of the followers of the three groups are set as a copy (or negation) of their leaders with probability p_{copy} and randomly (according to a Bernoulli distribution with probability 0.5) otherwise.
- The three groups are submerged into a "sea" of random variables following a Bernoulli distribution with $P(x = 0) = P(x = 1) = 0.5$.

It is possible to tune the integration among elements within groups and the mutual information between groups by changing p_{lcpy} or p_{copy}. In our examples, we fixed for simplicity p_{lcpy}=0.0 (non-interacting groups) with p_{copy}=1.00 (perfect followers) and p_{copy}=0.98 (imperfect followers).

4.1   Results

In Fig. 1, we report the relevant subsets identified by the RI analysis performed on RBNs using the H_{noC} or H_{wiC} homogeneous systems as a reference for the T_c computation. The RBN systems are relatively simple, and the most interesting relevant subsets are evident also without applying the sieving algorithm (see Table 1).

Figure 1 reports the two groups that rank highest according to the T_c value (the first four ranks for case RBN5).

Both approaches find the same solutions in cases RBN1, RBN2 and RBN3. In particular, the two methods directly identify the two correct solutions of RBN1, the two fundamental groups composing the correct solution of RBN2, and the correct solution of case RBN3. In RBN2, the simple iteration of the

---

[2] In details, $L_b(t) = L_a(t - 1)$ and $L_c(t) = L_b(t - 1)$.

Table 1. Table showing the relationships among nodes of the considered RBNs.

Node	Node rule				
	RBN 1	RBN 2	RBN 3	RBN 4	RBN 5
A	RND(0.5)	RND(0.5)	RND(0.5)	RND(0.5)	RND(0.5)
B	RND(0.5)	RND(0.5)	RND(0.5)	RND(0.5)	RND(0.5)
C	(D⊕E)	(D⊕E)	L^(D⊕E)	(D⊕E)	(D⊕E)
D	(C⊕E)	(C⊕E)	(C⊕E)	(C⊕E)	(C⊕E)
E	(C⊕D)	(C⊕D)	(C⊕D)	(C⊕D)	(C⊕D)
F	RND(0.5)	RND(0.5)	RND(0.5)	(E⊕H)	(E⊕H)
G	RND(0.5)	RND(0.5)	RND(0.5)	(G+H+I+L)≥2	RND(0.5)
H	(I⊕L)	E^(I⊕L)	E^(I⊕L)	(C⊕L)	(I⊕L)
I	(H⊕L)	(H⊕L)	(H⊕L)	(D+E+G+H)≥2	(H⊕L)
L	(H⊕I)	(H⊕I)	(H⊕I)	F⊕(E⊕I)	(E⊕I)
M	RND(0.5)	RND(0.5)	RND(0.5)	RND(0.5)	RND(0.5)
N	RND(0.5)	RND(0.5)	RND(0.5)	RND(0.5)	RND(0.5)

RI method after the application of the sieving algorithm is able to identify the correct big group (formed of variables C, D, E, H, I and L)[3]. In RBN3, the slightly preeminent position of the first triplet in Fig. 1 is due to the particular set of samples that has been chosen; indeed, by analyzing several sets of samples both triplets are equally represented.

The structure in case RBN4 is highly heterogeneous and comprises loosely integrated parts: the H_{noC} approach (though identifying correct nodes) is not able to spot out most variables composing the groups acting within the system, whereas the H_{wiC} approach identifies almost all the correct nodes. The variables not detected are just nodes G and I, which indeed have a very low coupling with the other variables (see Table 1 for details): so, the H_{wiC} approach seems to be more accurate than the H_{noC} approach. In other words, the T_c rank orders obtained by the two approaches are different, but often the H_{wiC} approach identifies larger groups, which are also the correct ones. In case RBN5, for example, the most relevant group is composed of eight nodes and it is immediately identified by the H_{wiC} approach, whereas the H_{noC} approach identifies in the first positions only the small subsets composing the largest group of variables.

This hypothesis is supported by the analysis of the CSTR case: the H_{noC} approach is able to identify merely small subsets of the ACS system, whereas the H_{wiC} approach directly identifies in its first iteration almost all the members of the ACS. At the same time, this approach identifies also the largest part of the LCH structure. In this case, we repeated the RI analysis several times, by using different H_{noC} and H_{wiC} homogeneous systems: all these analyses consistently confirmed these results. Figure 2, which, for simplicity, shows only the relevant

---

[3] data not shown.

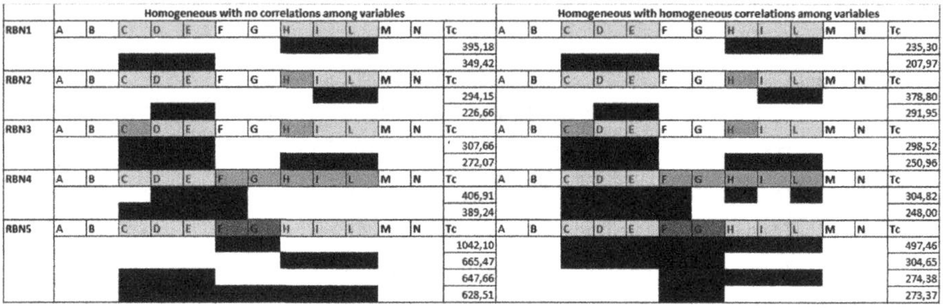

Fig. 1. The first two candidate relevant sets for each RBN case (four candidate relevant sets in the RBN5 case) and their T_c values, computed by using the "classical" homogeneous system (H_{noC}, left) and by using the homogeneous system built using NORTA (H_{wiC}, right). In each row, a black cell indicates that the corresponding variable is selected in the candidate relevant set, whereas white cells denote the variables not belonging to the candidate relevant set. For each RBN case, we also report the correct solution, in which the different colors denote particular nodes or subdivisions of the dynamical structure of the systems. In particular: (i) case RBN1 hosts two dynamically-independent structures, (ii-iii) which in cases RBN2 and RBN3 are linked through the orange nodes; (iv) in case RBN4, a structure, observable also in case RBN1, is providing signals to other 5 nodes (highlighted in orange, and in turn exchanging messages among each other in various ways); (v) in case RBN5, the two structures, present also in case RBN1, are both sending signals to the blue nodes F and G. For a more detailed description see Table 1. (Color figure online)

sets selected by the application of the sieving algorithm (two sets using H_{noC} and two sets using H_{wiC}) which have a much higher value than the other possible sets, strongly supports these observations.

The LF scenario described in the previous part of the section is a particularly difficult case for the RI analysis. Indeed, the addition to a group of size N_v of a variable, which is an almost perfect function of a variable already present within the group itself, leads to a new group of size $N_v + 1$ with a normalized integration very similar to the normalized integration of the initial group. Indeed, the integration of the group of size N_v subtracted from the integration of the group of size $N_v + 1$ is equal to the entropy of the added variable: the same holds for the homogeneous system if the difference between the average integrations of groups of size $N_v + 1$ and of size N_v is taken into consideration.

In the case of $p_{copy}=1$ (perfect followers) the H_{noC} approach ranks in the top 130 positions almost all subsets of group G3 (of sizes 7, 6 and 8, in frequency order)[4], before identifying the correct G3 group, whereas the H_{wiC} approach identifies the correct G3 group (with $T_c= 522.803$) immediately after its 8 subsets composed of 8 variables (with T_c values slightly lower than 524). Figure 3 shows the superposition of these subsets, which highlights the presence of the G3 group,

---

[4] Notice that, in case of a perfect copy, the action of excluding a particular variable and including another one leads to groups having the same T_c value.

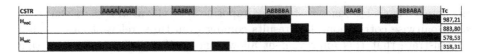

Fig. 2. The two candidate relevant sets - obtained by applying the sieving algorithm to the results of the RI analysis - of the CSTR case and their T_c values, computed using the "classical" homogeneous system (H_{noC}, first two rows) and using the homogeneous system built with NORTA (H_{wiC}, last two rows). The groups of variables remaining after the application of the sieving algorithm have T_c values by far lower than those shown here. The blue and yellow colors indicate the chemical species belonging to LCH and ACS structures, respectively; darker colors indicate the chemical species produced by the reactions happening within the CSTR reactor (for these species the names are also reported). The constant species are not included in the table reported in this figure; the colored nodes without name indicate substrates or intermediate complexes. (Color figure online)

and the corresponding T_c values range: indeed, the H_{wiC} approach is able to discriminate among all the possibilities in a sophisticated way, thereby effectively identifying the correct G3 position.

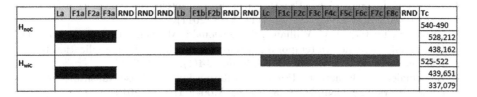

Fig. 3. The candidate relevant sets identified by using the "classical" homogeneous system (H_{noC}) and by using the homogeneous system built with NORTA (H_{wiC}), related with the Leader-Followers case analyzed in this paper (different colors highlight different LF groups). The variable sets reported in the top line (in light grey for H_{noC} and in dark grey for H_{wiC}) actually represent the top-ranked 130 (H_{noC}) and 8 (H_{wiC}) sets, all subsets of the same variables, that were detected; in this case the T_c column shows the range of the subsets' T_c values. Notice that the T_c range identified by the H_wiC approach is significantly smaller than the range identified by the H_{noC} approach. (Color figure online)

Eventually, both systems correctly identify the G1 and G2 groups. Similar results hold for $p_{copy} = 0.98$ (data not shown).

5   Conclusion

In this paper, we have proposed an improvement to the RI method for identifying relevant subsets in complex systems. In particular, we have introduced a constant nonzero degree of statistical dependence in the variables composing the homogeneous reference system, by imposing that all variable pairs share the same pairwise correlation. The results coming from three relevant case studies demonstrate that this improvement allows one to identify sets of interacting variables of larger size compared with the previous way of generating the homogeneous system. Actually, because the analyzed systems and the H_{wiC} approach feature the same integration values, we suspect that this fast identification of larger groups might be related to their total amount of integration more than to their size. As future work we plan to verify this hypothesis by analyzing systems where dynamical structures of different size exhibit similar integration levels. Other possible future developments may regard the application of the new method of computing the homogeneous system to complex systems with many more variables and to verify its performance, also by applying some meta-heuristics or an iterative version of the sieving procedure, in order to identify hierarchical relations among RSs.

References

1. Balakrishnan, V.: Graph Theory. McGraw Hill, New York (1997)
2. Balduzzi, D., Tononi, G.: Integrated information in discrete dynamical systems: motivation and theoretical framework. PLOS Comput. Biol. **4**(6), 1–18 (2008)
3. Barrett, A.B., Seth, A.K.: Practical measures of integrated information for time-series data. PLOS Comput. Biol. **7**(1), 1–18 (2011)
4. Bazzi, M., Porter, M.A., Williams, S., McDonald, M., Fenn, D.J., Howison, S.D.: Community detection in temporal multilayer networks, with an application to correlation networks. Multiscale Model. Simul. **14**(1), 1–41 (2016)
5. Bossomaier, T., Barnett, L., Harré, M.: Information and phase transitions in socioeconomic systems. Complex Adapt. Syst. Model. **1**(1), 9 (2013)
6. Cario, M.C., Nelson, B.L.: Modeling and generating random vectors with arbitrary marginal distributions and correlation matrix. Technical report (1997)
7. Cover, T., Thomas, A.: Elements of Information Theory, 2nd edn. Wiley, New York (2006)
8. Cross, M.C., Hohenberg, P.C.: Pattern formation outside of equilibrium. Rev. Mod. Phys. **65**, 851–1112 (1993)
9. Filisetti, A., Villani, M., Roli, A., Fiorucci, M., Poli, I., Serra, R.: On some properties of information theoretical measures for the study of complex systems. In: Pizzuti, C., Spezzano, G. (eds.) WIVACE 2014. CCIS, vol. 445, pp. 140–150. Springer, Cham (2014). https://doi.org/10.1007/978-3-319-12745-3_12
10. Gershenson, C., Fernandez, N.: Complexity and information: measuring emergence, self-organization, and homeostasis at multiple scales. Complex **18**(2), 29–44 (2012)
11. Johnson, J.: Hypernetworks in the Science of Complex Systems. Imperial College Press, London (2013)
12. Kauffman, S.: The Origins of Order. Oxford University Press, Oxford (1993)
13. Kivelä, M., Arenas, A., Barthelemy, M., Gleeson, J.P., Moreno, Y., Porter, M.A.: Multilayer networks. J. Complex Netw. **2**(3), 203–271 (2014)
14. Lewis, T.G.: Network Science: Theory and Applications. Wiley, Hoboken (2009)
15. Mansy, S., Schrum, J., Krishnamurthy, M., Tobe, S., Trecol, D., Szostak, J.: Template-directed synthesis of a genetic polymer in a model protocell. Nature **454**, 122 (2008)

16. Newman, M.E.J., Girvan, M.: Finding and evaluating community structure in networks. Phys. Rev. E **69**, 026113 (2004)
17. Nuño, E., Cutululis, N.: A heuristic for the synthesis of credible operating states in the presence of renewable energy sources. In: 2016 International Conference on Probabilistic Methods Applied to Power Systems (PMAPS), pp. 1–7, October 2016
18. Pearl, J.: Causality: Models, Reasoning, and Inference. Cambridge University Press, New York (2000)
19. Prokopenko, M., Boschetti, F., Ryan, A.J.: An information-theoretic primer on complexity, self-organization, and emergence. Complexity **15**(1), 11–28 (2009)
20. Prokopenko, M., Lizier, J.T., Obst, O., Wang, X.R.: Relating fisher information to order parameters. Phys. Rev. E **84**, 041116 (2011)
21. Roli, A., Villani, M., Caprari, R., Serra, R.: Identifying critical states through the relevance index. Entropy **19**(2), 73 (2017)
22. Sani, L., et al.: Efficient search of relevant structures in complex systems. In: Adorni, G., Cagnoni, S., Gori, M., Maratea, M. (eds.) AI*IA 2016. LNCS (LNAI), vol. 10037, pp. 35–48. Springer, Cham (2016). https://doi.org/10.1007/978-3-319-49130-1_4
23. Sani, L., Lombardo, G., Pecori, R., Fornacciari, P., Mordonini, M., Cagnoni, S.: Social relevance index for studying communities in a facebook group of patients. In: Sim, K., Kaufmann, P. (eds.) EvoApplications 2018. LNCS, vol. 10784, pp. 125–140. Springer, Cham (2018). https://doi.org/10.1007/978-3-319-77538-8_10
24. Serra, R., Villani, M., Semeria, A.: Genetic network models and statistical properties of gene expression data in knock-out experiments. J. Theor. Biol. **227**(1), 149–157 (2004)
25. Shalizi, C.R., Camperi, M.F., Klinkner, K.L.: Discovering functional communities in dynamical networks. In: Airoldi, E., Blei, D.M., Fienberg, S.E., Goldenberg, A., Xing, E.P., Zheng, A.X. (eds.) ICML 2006. LNCS, vol. 4503, pp. 140–157. Springer, Heidelberg (2007). https://doi.org/10.1007/978-3-540-73133-7_11
26. Silvestri, G., et al.: Searching relevant variable subsets in complex systems using k-means PSO. In: Pelillo, M., Poli, I., Roli, A., Serra, R., Slanzi, D., Villani, M. (eds.) WIVACE 2017. CCIS, vol. 830, pp. 308–321. Springer, Cham (2018). https://doi.org/10.1007/978-3-319-78658-2_23
27. Sporns, O., Tononi, G., Edelman, G.: Theoretical neuroanatomy: relating anatomical and functional connectivity in graphs and cortical connection matrices. Cereb. Cortex **10**(2), 127–141 (2000)
28. Tononi, G., McIntosh, A., Russel, D., Edelman, G.: Functional clustering: identifying strongly interactive brain regions in neuroimaging data. Neuroimage **7**, 133–149 (1998)
29. Tononi, G., Sporns, O., Edelman, G.M.: A measure for brain complexity: relating functional segregation and integration in the nervous system. Proc. Natl. Acad. Sci. **91**(11), 5033–5037 (1994)
30. Vicari, E., et al.: GPU-based parallel search of relevant variable sets in complex systems. In: Rossi, F., Piotto, S., Concilio, S. (eds.) WIVACE 2016. CCIS, vol. 708, pp. 14–25. Springer, Cham (2017). https://doi.org/10.1007/978-3-319-57711-1_2
31. Villani, M., Filisetti, A., Benedettini, S., Roli, A., Lane, D., Serra, R.: The detection of intermediate-level emergent structures and patterns. In: Miglino, O. et al. (ed.) Advances in Artificial Life, ECAL 2013, pp. 372–378. The MIT Press (2013). http://mitpress.mit.edu/books/advances-artificial-life-ecal-2013

32. Villani, M., et al.: A relevance index method to infer global properties of biological networks. In: Pelillo, M., Poli, I., Roli, A., Serra, R., Slanzi, D., Villani, M. (eds.) WIVACE 2017. CCIS, vol. 830, pp. 129–141. Springer, Cham (2018). https://doi.org/10.1007/978-3-319-78658-2_10

33. Villani, M., et al.: An iterative information-theoretic approach to the detection of structures in complex systems. Complexity **2018**, 15 (2018). https://doi.org/10.1155/2018/3687839. Article ID 3687839

34. Wang, X., Lizier, J., Prokopenko, M.: Fisher information at the edge of chaos in random boolean networks. Artif. Life **17**(4), 315–329 (2011)

35. Xie, W., Nelson, B.L., Barton, R.R.: Statistical uncertainty analysis for stochastic simulation with dependent input models. In: Proceedings of the Winter Simulation Conference, pp. 674–685 (2014)

36. Xu, X., Yan, Z.: Probabilistic load flow evaluation with hybrid Latin hypercube sampling and multiple linear regression. In: 2015 IEEE Power Energy Society General Meeting, pp. 1–5, July 2015

37. Zubillaga, D., et al.: Measuring the complexity of self-organizing traffic lights. Entropy **16**(5), 2384–2407 (2014). http://www.mdpi.com/1099-4300/16/5/2384

Evolving Critical Boolean Networks

Salvatore Magri[1(✉)], Marco Villani[1,2(✉)] iD, Andrea Roli[3] iD,
and Roberto Serra[1,2,4] iD

[1] Department of Physics, Informatics and Mathematics,
University of Modena and Reggio Emilia, Modena, Italy
salvamagri95@gmail.com,
{marco.villani, roberto.serra}@unimore.it
[2] European Centre for Living Technology, Venice, Italy
[3] Department of Computer Science and Engineering,
University of Bologna, Bologna, Italy
andrea.roli@unibo.it
[4] Institute for Advanced Study, University of Amsterdam,
Amsterdam, The Netherlands

Abstract. Random Boolean networks are a widely acknowledged model for cell dynamics. Previous studies have shown the possibility of achieving Boolean networks with given characteristics by means of evolutionary techniques. In this work we make a further step towards more biologically plausible models by aiming at evolving networks with a given fraction of active nodes along the attractors, while constraining the evolutionary process to move across critical networks. Results show that this path along criticality does not impede to climb the mount of improbable, yet biologically realistic requirements.

Keywords: Random Boolean networks · Genetic algorithms · Criticality · Evolutionary path

1 Introduction

Random Boolean networks (RBNs for short) are discrete-time models of gene regulatory networks, which have been subject of extensive research concerning their dynamical properties (reviewed e.g. in (Kauffman 1993, 1995; Aldana et al. 2003; Bastolla and Parisi 1998a, b; Aldana 2003), their evolvability (Aldana et al. 2007; Gershenson 2012; Benedettini et al. 2013) and their capability to describe real biological phenomena (Raeymaekers 2002; Kauffman et al. 2003; Serra et al. 2004a; Shmulevich et al. 2005; Ramo et al. 2006; Serra et al. 2007b; Bornholdt 2008; Serra et al. 2008, Villani et al. 2018), including differentiation (Serra et al. 2010; Villani et al. 2011). Various modifications of the original models have been proposed, concerning, among others, the way in which network nodes are updated (Shmulevich et al. 2002; Gershenson 2002), the interactions among networks (Serra et al. 2007a; Damiani et al. 2010; Damiani et al. 2011; Cheng et al. 2012), the network topology (Serra and Villani 2002; Aldana 2003; Serra et al. 2004b), the use of continuous activation values (Serra et al. 2001) or the explicit introduction of proteins (Graudenzi et al. 2011a; Graudenzi et al. 2011a;

© Springer Nature Switzerland AG 2019
S. Cagnoni et al. (Eds.): WIVACE 2018, CCIS 900, pp. 17–29, 2019.
https://doi.org/10.1007/978-3-030-21733-4_2

Sapienza et al. 2018]. In this paper we will consider the original Kauffman model, with Boolean values and synchronous updating, where the number of incoming links is the same for every node.

In RBNs two different dynamical regimes can be identified (Kauffman 1993; Bastolla and Parisi 1998a, b): (i) an ordered one, where the length of the attractors grows as a power of network size, and the basins of attraction are reasonably regular and (ii) a disordered one, often called "chaotic", although the attractors of finite RBNs are cycles of finite length. In these latter networks the typical length of attractor cycles depends upon the network size in a very steep way, and nearby initial states often evolve to different attractors (a kind of sensitive dependence upon initial conditions).

The two regimes are usually associated to statistical ensembles of networks, which are built by fixing the values of some parameters, like e.g. the average number of links per node, while some other features (like e.g. the initial conditions, or the precise association of a Boolean function to a specific node) are left free to vary at random. Note that a single network realization can behave in a way that is markedly different from the typical behaviour of the ensemble it belongs.

A particularly intriguing feature of RBNs is that their dynamical regime, considered at the ensemble level, can be tuned from ordered to disordered by modifying a single parameter, which depends upon the average number of connections per node and upon the choice of the Boolean functions. In this paper, following Kauffman, it will be called the "Derrida parameter" λ (Derrida and Pomeau 1986): briefly, it determines whether the distance between two states which are close at time t will increase or decrease at the following time step. In a chaotic ensemble, where $\lambda > 1$, such distance will increase on average, while in ordered ensembles, where $\lambda < 1$, it will decrease. Networks with $\lambda = 1$ are called (dynamically) critical and they are supposed to have major advantages, so that it has been suggested that biological organisms are likely to be found in those regimes, under the action of evolution (Kauffman 1993; Kauffman 1995) (or perhaps in ordered regimes, but close to the critical boundary (Shmulevich et al. 2005; Serra et al. 2007a, b; Di Stefano et al. 2016).

The reason why critical systems may have an edge is that a system that is deeply ordered might be unable to respond to changes in the environment, while a chaotic system might be very hard to control. Several papers have addressed the issue of determining the actual regime of biological genetic networks (Harris et al. 2002; Raeymaekers 2002; Kauffman et al. 2003; Serra et al. 2004a; Moreira and Amaral 2005; Serra et al. 2007b). Moreover, dynamical criticality has also been proposed as a useful guideline for building artificial systems, like e.g. robots, able to cope with a changing environment (Roli et al. 2011a; Roli et al. 2015; Roli et al. 2018).

On the other hand, a property of RBNs that does not seem biologically sound is their symmetry with respect to the transformation $1 \rightarrow 0$ and vice versa. If node value "1" means that the corresponding gene is active, then one has to consider the fact that, in most biological cells, the number of active and inactive nodes is different. In this paper we study whether some networks with a large number of "1"s in their attractor states can be evolved, starting from an initial population of random networks, under the action of genetic algorithms (GAs).

Indeed, Random Boolean networks had already been evolved to solve some tasks (Benedettini et al. 2013) or to display some peculiar features, like e.g. short transient periods, large distances between attractors (Roli et al. 2011b), cell differentiation lineages (Braccini et al. 2017) or robustness (Szejka and Drossel 2007). In these studies, the evolved populations are no longer random as in the beginning, although they still preserve some randomness.

In the case we consider here, the desired result can quite easily be achieved by a standard GA. The evolved networks, e.g. those with a large fraction of active nodes, turn out to be of the ordered type, even if the initial population is composed by critical networks. Given that criticality is supposed to be also an important property, it is particularly interesting to consider whether networks can be evolved which (i) have a large fraction of active nodes in their asymptotic states and (ii) are dynamically critical. Moreover, it is also interesting to constrain the whole evolutionary process to proceed through critical networks, and to see whether the result can be achieved.

The paper is organized as follows. In Sect. 2 the model of RBNs will be briefly reviewed. In Sect. 3 a standard GA will be introduced, alongside with two modified versions, which limit the evolutionary process to critical (or almost critical) networks only. In Sect. 4 the results of the three GAs will be presented. The results are definitely positive, in the sense that it is possible to achieve critical networks with the desired fraction of nodes with a given activation value – a non obvious result, which was not expected a priori. Moreover, these networks can be reached by constraining the evolutionary process to critical (or almost critical) networks only. Finally, in Sect. 5 some indications for further work will be summarized.

2   Random Boolean Networks

In this section a synthetic description of the main properties of the model is presented, referring the reader to (Kauffman 1993, 1995, Aldana et al. 2003) for a more detailed account. Several variants of the model have been presented and discussed, but we will restrict our attention here to the "classical" model. A classical RBN is a dynamical system composed of N genes, or nodes, which can take either the value 0 (inactive) or 1 (active).

The relationships between genes are represented by directed links and Boolean functions, which model the response of each node to the values of its input nodes. In a classical RBN each node has the same number of incoming connections k_{in}, and its k_{in} input nodes are chosen at random with uniform probability among the remaining N-1 nodes: in such a way the distribution of the outgoing connections per node tends to a Poissonian distribution for large N. The Boolean functions can be chosen in different ways (Aldana et al. 2003): in this paper we will only examine the case where the Boolean functions are generated by assigning, to each set of input values, a value "1" with probability p (called the bias of the Boolean function), and a value "0" with probability 1-p.

We will study the so-called quenched model, where both the topology and the Boolean function associated to each node do not change in time, since this choice resembles the way in which real gene regulatory networks operate much closer than the alternative annealed approach (Derrida and Pomeau 1986; Drossel 2008), in which the topology and the Boolean functions associated to the nodes change at each time step. The network dynamics is discrete and synchronous, so fixed points and cycles are the only possible asymptotic states in finite networks (a single RBN can have, and usually has, more than one attractor).

A very important aspect concerns how to determine and measure the RBNs' dynamical regime: while several procedures have been proposed, an interesting and well-known method directly measures the spreading of perturbations through the network. This measure involves two parallel runs of the same system, whose initial states differ for just a small fraction of the units (Derrida and Pomeau 1986). Their difference is measured by the Hamming distance h(t), defined as the number of units that have different activations on the two runs at the same time step t (the measure is performed on many different initial conditions, so one actually considers the average value < h(t) > , but we will omit the brackets for ease of reading). If the two runs converge to the same state, i.e. h(t) → 0, then the dynamics of the system is robust with respect to small perturbations (a signature of the ordered regime), while if h(t) initially grows in time then the system is in a disordered state. The critical states are those where h(t) remains initially constant (Derrida and Pomeau 1986; Bastolla and Parisi 1998a; Villani et al. 2017). A Derrida plot represents h(1) vs h(0) for different values of the initial distance h(0); the Derrida parameter λ, already mentioned in Sect. 1, is then the slope of this curve in the limit of small initial distances.

For the sake of the discussion of the following sections, it is useful to introduce also the notion of the "grey level" of an attractor of a network, defined as the fraction of nodes that are active (i.e. "on") in that state. If an attractor is not a fixed point, an oscillating node is counted as "on" if its value is 1 in a fraction of states $\geq 1/2$. The grey level of an attractor should of course not be confused with the bias of a Boolean function, although in randomly generated BN these values tend to coincide.

3   Evolving RBNs

Genetic algorithms, introduced by John Holland a long time ago (Holland 1975), are well known and their properties will not be reviewed here, as we assume that the reader is familiar with these techniques. Let us only recall that have been successfully applied in order to evolve RBNs which are able to solve some tasks (Roli et al. 2011a; Roli et al. 2015) or endowed with particular properties, like robustness (Szejka and Drossel 2007; Mihaljev and Drossel 2009). It seems therefore appropriate to apply a GA also to the task of finding attractors with a predefined fraction of nodes with a given activation value; for the sake of definiteness let θ be the fraction of "1"s in the system asymptotic states (i.e. their average grey level) we wish these attractors exceed.[1] There are different versions of a "standard" GA; the one that has been used here is described in Table 1. Note that we chose to modify only the Boolean functions associated to each node, without changing its inputs: since the numbering of nodes is arbitrary (i.e. the number

---

[1] In other words, we aim to obtain a divergence between the grey level and the Boolean functions' bias, being not interested in reaching a particular final grey level

of a node does not carry any intrinsic meaning, like e.g. any reference to a specific biological gene), this does not limit the set of actually different networks that can be generated.

The fitness of each network (step 4 of Table 1) is computed using the recipe detailed in Table 2.

We run a series of experiments using networks with two inputs per node. In this case the critical networks are those with bias equal to ½, and we generated the initial population using precisely this bias. The "grey level" of the attractors of randomly generated networks with this bias typically is equal to 0.5; on the contrary, our desired "grey level" was markedly different, and in many experiments it equals 0.8.

Table 1. The standard GA (#G denotes the number of elements in set G)

Step	Step description
1	Create network topology (it will be the same for all the networks for all generations)
2	Create the first population G of networks (Boolean functions are generated at random with bias p)
3	For each network in G, compute its fitness (see Table 2)
4	Select the set E of the individuals with the highest fitness, which will be passed unaltered in the next generation (elitism)
5	Select parents for the individuals of the new generation, with probability proportional to their fitness (their number being equal to #G-#E)
6	Generate the set G' by applying single-point crossover to the selected parents in G with a given probability (otherwise parents pass unmodified in the new population)
7	Generate the set G" by applying single-point mutation to individuals in G' with a fixed (small) probability
8	Generate the new population of networks G = E∪G"
9	If termination condition has not been met, return to step 3
10	End

It is worthwhile to observe that the GA rapidly "discovers" networks with a grey level close to the threshold (i.e. the desired value). As it might be expected, this result is achieved by modifying the bias of the Boolean functions (see Fig. 1). It can also be checked (see Sect. 4) that the networks that have been evolved in this way are typically ordered, i.e. with $\lambda < 1$.

As remarked in Sect. 1, it is believed that critical networks may have an advantage with respect to networks that are in other dynamical regimes. Therefore, we looked for critical networks with the desired grey level. Moreover, since it seems unlikely that a spontaneous process like natural evolution can pass through states that are far from critical, we also tried to determine whether such "critical networks with the desired grey level" could be achieved by passing only close to critical states. Note that this is far from trivial, since random networks with a high bias are typically in the ordered regime.

Table 2. Computing the fitness of a network (in most simulations, it was chosen $\theta = 0.8$ – other thresholds have been tested without finding significant qualitative differences)

Step	Step description
1	For each network in G
2	Simulate its evolution for a number of initial conditions and find its attractors
3	For each attractor, compute its grey level, i.e. the fraction of nodes that are "on" (if the attractor is a cycle, a node is counted as "on" if its value is 1 in a fraction of time steps $\geq 1/2$)
4	Compute the average f of the fraction of nodes which are "on" in the attractors
5	Compute the fitness ϕ of that network, defined as follows (θ is a fixed threshold value): $\phi = f$ if $f < \theta$ $\phi = \theta$ otherwise
6	End

The scientific question is then whether it is possible to reach a critical network with a high fraction of 1 s by passing through intermediate states that are also critical, or almost critical. To this aim, two variants of the standard GA have been introduced, which have been called a *blocked* and a *balanced* GA.

The *blocked* GA differs from the standard one in that, after step 7 in the algorithm of Table 1, i.e. after generating the individuals by crossover and mutation, further

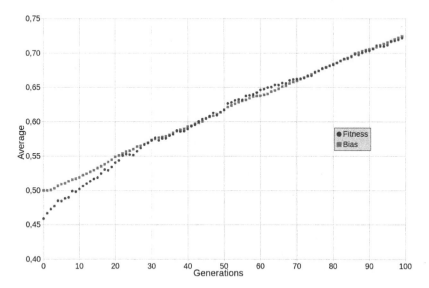

Fig. 1. The evolution of the average fitness and of the average bias under the action of a standard GA. 100 generations are not enough to reach an average fitness level close to FI; nevertheless the best individuals reach this threshold, as shown in Fig. 3.

random mutations are introduced if their average bias differs from the critical value ½.[2]

Indeed, starting from two individual networks with bias ½, random crossing easily generates individuals with a markedly different bias. This is avoided "by brute force" in the case of the blocked GA. As it can be expected, the wider use of random point mutations raises the variance among individuals in this algorithm with respect to the standard case.

The *balanced* GA aims to reach a similar result without intervening a posteriori on the new individuals, but rather by choosing the crossover point (once the two parents have been selected) in such a way that their descendants' average biases are as close as possible to ½.

4   Experimental Results

The results shown here refer to experiments whose details are given in Table 3. In the figures of this Section, blue indicates the standard GA, orange the blocked GA and yellow the balanced GA.

Table 3. The parameter values used for simulations

Parameter	Value
Number of generations	100
Number of networks in population	100
Number of nodes per networks	50
Number of inputs per node	2
Average bias in initial population	1/2
Number of initial conditions per network	10000
Crossover probability	0.7
Mutation probability per node	0.02
Threshold θ	0.8
Number of individuals in elite E	3

A first observation is that, as expected, the standard GA performs better than the others (indeed, it has less vincula to respect). In Fig. 2 one can see that the average fitness increases much faster than in the remaining two cases.

It can be observed (Fig. 4) that the good performance of the standard GA is bound to a significant decrease of the Derrida parameter, which indicates that the ordered regime prevails.

---

[2] The position of these mutations within the string coding the individuals is randomly chosen, whereas their direction ($0 \rightarrow 1$ or $1 \rightarrow 0$) is predisposed to reach the desired bias.

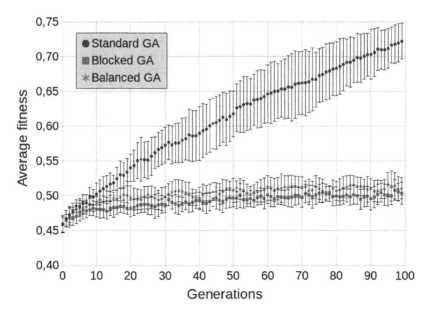

Fig. 2. Average fitness (with standard error) vs. time (generations) for the various GAs that have been considered

However, these observations concern the behaviour of the whole population, or rather of its average properties. If however we concentrate on the best individual of the blocked and balanced GAs, we see that they also achieve a high fitness (Fig. 3), without losing their dynamical properties, i.e. their criticality (Fig. 4). This is the most significant result of this work: it was not at all obvious a priori that it might be achieved.

It is important to check whether the good results shown above are just the outcome of some peculiar random properties of RBNs. So one can consider a very large number of purely randomly generated networks, and can look at the frequency of occurrence of high grey levels in their attractors. In Fig. 5 one sees the distribution of the fitness of 10000 "individuals" generated at random, with 2 connections per node and bias ½. It is worth to observe that no network in this set has achieved a fitness value greater than 0.7 – while all the three GAs have achieved much higher fitness.

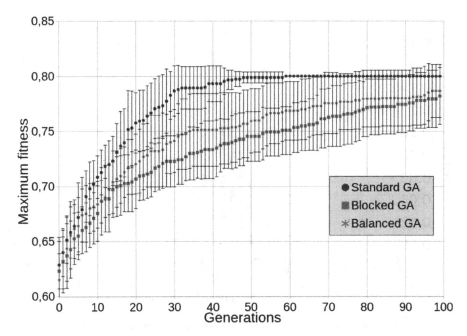

Fig. 3. Maximum fitness (with standard error – 15 complete searches performed for each GA kinds) vs. time (generations) for the various GAs that have been considered

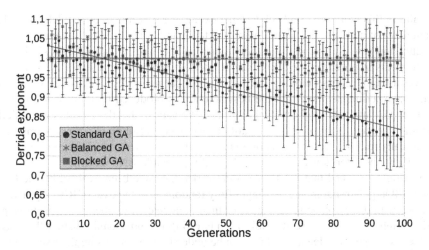

Fig. 4. Average value of the Derrida exponent vs. time (generations) for the various GAs that have been considered

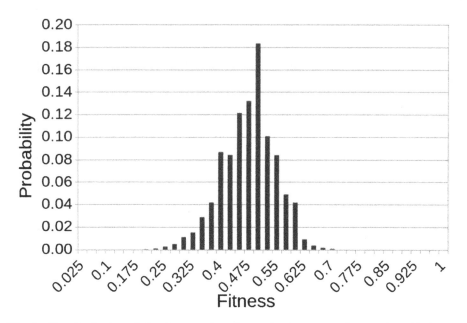

Fig. 5. The distribution of the fitness values for randomly generated networks with $k_{in}= 2$, $p = 0.5$.

5 Conclusions

The aim of this work was to check to what extent it is possible to evolve RBNs so that the number of active nodes along their attractors attain a target value (averaged across the attractors), while maintaining their dynamical regime set on criticality. The two requirements imposed on the RBNs might interfere and a priori it is not clear whether an evolutionary process moving only across critical networks can reach the goal. In fact, our experiments show that the best individuals produced by the "criticality constrained" GA attain the highest level of fitness. We believe that this result is particularly important because it proofs that criticality constrained evolution is not in contrast with biologically realistic requirements on the attractors of the network. This contribution is indeed a further step towards more biologically plausible BNs models.

It should be noted that the Boolean networks that have been evolved by the GAs, while still largely random, are no longer fully random as in the case of RBNs generated ex-novo with the corresponding values of their parameters (number of connections per node, number of nodes). So it would be interesting to understand whether they have evolved some peculiar features which can be understood by analysing their structure or the properties of their attractors.

In this respect, it is interesting to observe that in a recent paper (Daniels et al. 2018) the authors have analysed the properties of 67 published Boolean genetic networks which have been proposed as models of specific genetic circuits on the basis of available biological data. These networks show a tendency to be critical, although purely random networks with the same parameters would rather be in different regimes.

Among the possible explanations, the authors cite the presence in the biologically motivated networks of a high fraction of canalizing functions.

This does not seem to be the case in our evolved critical networks, on the basis of preliminary data, not shown here. So achieving a good understanding of the properties of evolved critical networks is a challenging task which deserves further investigation.

References

Aldana, M.: Boolean dynamics of networks with scale-free topology. Phys. D **185**(1), 45–66 (2003)

Aldana, M., Coppersmith, S., Kadanoff, L.P.: Boolean dynamics with random couplings. In: Kaplan, E., Marsden, J., Sreenivasan, K.R. (eds.) Perspectives and Problems in Nonlinear Science, pp. 23–89. Springer, New York (2003). https://doi.org/10.1007/978-0-387-21789-5_2

Aldana, M., Balleza, E., Kauffman, S.A., Resendiz, O.: Robustness and evolvability in genetic regulatory networks. J. Theor. Biol. **245**, 433–448 (2007)

Bastolla, U., Parisi, G.: The modular structure of Kauffman networks. Phys. D **115**(3–4), 219–233 (1998a)

Bastolla, U., Parisi, G.: Relevant elements, magnetization and dynamical properties in Kauffman networks: a numerical study. Phys. D **115**(3–4), 203–218 (1998b)

Benedettini, S., Villani, M., Roli, A., Serra, R., Manfroni, M., Gagliardi, A., Pinciroli, C., Birattari, M.: Dynamical regimes and learning properties of evolved Boolean networks. Neurocomputing **99**, 111–123 (2013)

Bornholdt, S.: Boolean network models of cellular regulation: prospects and limitations. J. R. Soc. Interface **5**, S85–S94 (2008)

Braccini, M., Roli, A., Villani, M., Serra, R.: Automatic design of Boolean networks for cell differentiation. In: Rossi, F., Piotto, S., Concilio, S. (eds.) WIVACE 2016. CCIS, vol. 708, pp. 91–102. Springer, Cham (2017). https://doi.org/10.1007/978-3-319-57711-1_8

Cheng, X., Sun, M., Socolar, J.: Autonomous Boolean modelling of developmental gene regulatory networks. J. R. Soc. Interface **10**, 1–12 (2012)

Daniels, B.C., et al.: Criticality distinguishes the ensemble of biological regulatory networks. Phys. Rev. Lett. **121**, 138102 (2018)

Damiani, C., Kauffman, Stuart A., Serra, R., Villani, M., Colacci, A.: Information transfer among coupled random Boolean networks. In: Bandini, S., Manzoni, S., Umeo, H., Vizzari, G. (eds.) ACRI 2010. LNCS, vol. 6350, pp. 1–11. Springer, Heidelberg (2010). https://doi.org/10.1007/978-3-642-15979-4_1

Damiani, C., Serra, R., Villani, M., Kauffman, S.A., Colacci, A.: Cell-cell interaction and diversity of emergent behaviours. IET Syst. Biol. **5**(2), 137–144 (2011)

Derrida, B., Pomeau, Y.: Random networks of automata: a simple annealed approximation. Europhys. Lett. **1**(2), 45–49 (1986)

Di Stefano, M.L., Villani, M., La Rocca, L., Kauffman, S.A., Serra, R.: Dynamically critical systems and power-law distributions: avalanches revisited. In: Rossi, F., Mavelli, F., Stano, P., Caivano, D. (eds.) WIVACE 2015. CCIS, vol. 587, pp. 29–39. Springer, Cham (2016). https://doi.org/10.1007/978-3-319-32695-5_3

Drossel, B.: Random boolean networks. In: Schuster, H.G. (ed.) Reviews of Nonlinear Dynamics and Complexity, vol. 1. Wiley, New York (2008)

Gershenson, C.: Classification of random Boolean networks. In: Standish, R.K., Bedau, M.A., Abbass, H.A. (eds.) Artificial Life VIII: Proceedings of the Eight International Conference on Artificial Life, Sydney, Australia, pp. 1–8. MIT Press (2002)

Gershenson, C.: Guiding the self-organization of random Boolean networks. Theory Biosci. **131**, 181–191 (2012)

Graudenzi, A., Serra, R., Villani, M., Damiani, C., Colacci, A., Kauffman, S.A.: Dynamical properties of a Boolean model of gene regulatory network with memory. J. Comput. Biol. **18**, 1291–1305 (2011a)

Graudenzi, A., Serra, R., Villani, M., Colacci, A., Kauffman, S.A.: Robustness analysis of a Boolean model of gene regulatory network with memory. J. Comput. Biol. **18**(4), 559–577 (2011b)

Harris, S.E., Sawhill, B.K., Wuensche, A., Kauffman, S.A.: A model of transcriptional regulatory networks based on biases in the observed regulation rules. Complexity **7**, 23–40 (2002)

Holland, J.H.: Adaptation in Natural and Artificial Systems: An Introductory Analysis with Applications to Biology, Control, and Artificial Intelligence. U Michigan Press, Oxford (1975)

Kauffman, S.A.: The Origins of Order. Oxford University Press, Oxford (1993)

Kauffman, S.A.: At Home in the Universe. Oxford University Press, Oxford (1995)

Kauffman, S.A., Peterson, C., Samuelsson, B., Troein, C.: Random Boolean networks models and the yeast transcriptional networks. PNAS **100**, 14796–14799 (2003)

Mihaljev, T., Drossel, B.: Evolution of a population of random Boolean networks. Eur. Phys. J. B **67**, 259 (2009)

Moreira, A., Amaral, L.: Canalizing Kauffman networks: nonergodicity and its effect on their critical behavior. Phys. Rev. Lett. **94**(21), 218702 (2005)

Raeymaekers, L.: Dynamics of Boolean networks controlled by biologically meaningful functions. J. Theor. Biol. **218**(3), 331–341 (2002)

Ramo, P., Kesseli, J., Yli-Harja, O.: Perturbation avalanches and criticality in gene regulatory networks. J. Theor. Biol. **242**(1), 164–170 (2006)

Roli, A., Benedettini, S., Birattari, M., et al.: Robustness, evolvability and complexity in Boolean network robots. In: Proceedings of ECCS 2011—European Conference on Complex Systems (2011a)

Roli, A., Benedettini, S., Serra, R., Villani, M.: Analysis of attractor distances in random Boolean networks. In: Apolloni, B., Bassis, S., Esposito, A., Morabito, C. (eds.) Proceedings of WIRN2010, the 20th Italian Workshop on Neural Nets IOS Press, Amsterdam (2011b)

Roli, A., Villani, M., Serra, R., Benedettini, S., Pinciroli, C., Birattari, M.: Dynamical properties of artificially evolved Boolean network robots. In: Gavanelli, M., Lamma, E., Riguzzi, F. (eds.) AI*IA 2015. LNCS (LNAI), vol. 9336, pp. 45–57. Springer, Cham (2015). https://doi.org/10.1007/978-3-319-24309-2_4

Roli, A., Villani, M., Filisetti, A., Serra, R.: Dynamical criticality: overview and open questions. J. Syst. Sci. Complex **31**, 647–663 (2018)

Sapienza, D., Villani, M., Serra, R.: Dynamical properties of a gene-protein model. In: Pelillo, M., Poli, I., Roli, A., Serra, R., Slanzi, D., Villani, M. (eds.) WIVACE 2017. CCIS, vol. 830, pp. 142–152. Springer, Cham (2018). https://doi.org/10.1007/978-3-319-78658-2_11

Serra, R., Villani, M., Salvemini, A.: Continuous genetic networks. Parallel Comput. **27**, 663–683 (2001)

Serra, R., Villani, M.: Perturbing the regular topology of cellular automata: implications for the dynamics. In: Bandini, S., Chopard, B., Tomassini, M. (eds.) ACRI 2002. LNCS, vol. 2493, pp. 168–177. Springer, Heidelberg (2002). https://doi.org/10.1007/3-540-45830-1_16

Serra, R., Villani, M., Semeria, A.: Genetic network models and statistical properties of gene expression data in knock-out experiments. J. Theor. Biol. **227**, 149–157 (2004a)

Serra, R., Villani, M., Agostini, L.: On the dynamics of Boolean networks with scale-free outgoing connections. Phys. A **339**, 665–673 (2004b)

Serra, R., Villani, M., Damiani, C., Graudenzi, A., Colacci, A., Kauffman, S.A.: Interacting random boolean networks. In: Jost, J., Helbing, D. (eds.) Proceedings of ECCS 2007: European Conference on Complex Systems (2007a)

Serra, R., Villani, M., Graudenzi, A., Kauffman, S.A.: Why a simple model of genetic regulatory networks describes the distribution of avalanches in gene expression data. J. Theor. Biol. **246** (3), 449–460 (2007b)

Serra, R., Villani, M., Graudenzi, A., Colacci, A., Kauffman, S.A.: The simulation of gene knock-out in scale-free random Boolean models of genetic networks. Netw. Heterog. Media **2** (3), 333–343 (2008)

Serra, R., Villani, M., Barbieri, A., Kauffman, S., Colacci, A.: On the dynamics of random Boolean networks subject to noise: attractors, ergodic sets and cell types. J. Theor. Biol. **265** (2), 185–193 (2010)

Shmulevich, I., Dougherty, E., Kim, S., Zhang, W.: Probabilistic Boolean networks: a rule-based uncertainty model for gene regulatory networks. Bioinformatics **18**(2), 261–274 (2002)

Shmulevich, I., Kauffman, S.A., Aldana, M.: Eukaryotic cells are dynamically ordered or critical but not chaotic. PNAS **102**(38), 13439–13444 (2005)

Szejka, A., Drossel, B.: Evolution of canalizing Boolean networks Eur. Phys. J. B **56**, 373–380 (2007)

Villani, M., Barbieri, A., Serra, R.: A dynamical model of genetic networks for cell differentiation. PLoS ONE **6**(3), e17703 (2011)

Villani, M., Campioli, D., Damiani, C., Roli, A., Filisetti, A., Serra, R.: Dynamical regimes in non-ergodic random Boolean networks. Nat. Comput. **16**(2), 353–363 (2017)

Villani, M., La Rocca, L., Kauffman, S.A., Serra, R.: Dynamical criticality in gene regulatory networks. Complexity, **2018**, 5980636 (2018)

Self-loops Favour Diversification and Asymmetric Transitions Between Attractors in Boolean Network Models

Michele Braccini$^{(\boxtimes)}$ ⓘ, Sara Montagna ⓘ, and Andrea Roli ⓘ

Department of Computer Science and Engineering,
Alma Mater Studiorum, Università di Bologna,
Campus of Cesena, via dell'Università 50, 47522 Cesena, Italy
{m.braccini,sara.montagna,andrea.roli}@unibo.it

Abstract. The process of cell differentiation manifests properties such as non-uniform robustness and asymmetric transitions among cell types. In this paper we adopt Boolean networks to model cellular differentiation, where attractors (or set of attractors) in the network landscape epitomise cell types. Since changes in network topology and functions strongly impact attractor landscape characteristics, in this paper we study how self-loops influence diversified robustness and asymmetry of transitions. The purpose of this study is to identify the best configuration for a network owning these properties. Our results show that a moderate amount of self-loops make random Boolean networks more suitable to reproduce differentiation phenomena. This is a further evidence that self-loops play an important role in genetic regulatory networks.

1 Introduction

Boolean network (BN) models have been recently shown to provide a suitable generic model for cell differentiation [3,6,16]. The main assumption in this modelling perspective is that attractors, or sets of attractors, represent cell types. In multicellular systems differentiation is characterised by differential expression of genes, meaning that each cell type expresses only a subset of genes called *markers*. In the same way, at each attractor of the BN corresponds the dynamic activation of only a subset of nodes. Accordingly, transitions between attractors epitomise cell differentiation stages that bring changes in the pattern of active/inactive genes. During the process of cell differentiation, cell responds differently to external cues, such as epigenetic modifications. By that we mean robustness of cell states being not the same during the whole process of differentiation. Zhou et al. [17] calls this property of gene regulatory network as *relative stability*. In this view, for a network to be a suitable model for cell differentiation, one would require to have attractors characterised by different degrees of robustness, such that some of them are more responsive to external stimuli and perturbations, while others are rather insensitive to external perturbations and so more stable. This property can be expressed as *diversification in attractor robustness*. In addition, as pointed out by Zhou et al. [17] in a recent work

© Springer Nature Switzerland AG 2019
S. Cagnoni et al. (Eds.): WIVACE 2018, CCIS 900, pp. 30–41, 2019.
https://doi.org/10.1007/978-3-030-21733-4_3

on Boolean models for pancreas cell differentiation, a further requirement of the model is to be characterised by *asymmetric transition probabilities between attractors*. This further property accounts for a preferential directionality of the differentiation process, that anyway does not exclude reversibility. These two dynamical properties are the combined result of topological and functional settings of the network model instance. It is therefore important to identify specific settings that favour the arising of such properties. In this work we tackle this issue addressing the question as to whether self-loops in Boolean network models may positively contribute to attaining dynamics with diversified attractor robustness and asymmetric transitions. Results show that, *ceteris paribus*, networks in which few nodes have self-loop are more likely to exhibit the properties mentioned above.

This paper is organised as follows. In Sect. 2 we detail the model we use and we summarise previous work. We then illustrate the experimental setting and results in Sect. 3, and we conclude with Sect. 4 with an outline of future work.

2   Boolean Network Model for Cell Differentiation

In this work we deal with Boolean network models for cell differentiation, i.e. the process by which the development of specialised cell types takes place, starting from a single cell (the zygote), or the process by which fully differentiated cells are continuously renewed from adult stem cells. The development of different cell types is the result of highly complex dynamics between intracellular, intercellular, and external signals [4]. Intracellular interactions are captured in gene regulatory networks (GRNs): complex networks that regulate the gene expression. Not all genes of the genome are active simultaneously but only a subset needed to fulfill functions specific of each cell type. Thus, a particular pattern of gene expression represents a cell type.

A Boolean network is a discrete-time discrete-state dynamical system whose state is a N-tuple in $\{0,1\}^N$, $(x_1, \ldots, x_N)$. The state is updated according to the composition of N Boolean functions $f_i(x_{i_1}, \ldots, x_{i_{K_i}})$, where K_i is the number of inputs of node i, which is associated to Boolean variable x_i. Each function f_i governs the update of variable x_i and depends upon the values of variables $x_{i_1}, \ldots, x_{i_{K_i}}$. BNs have been introduced by Kauffman [8] as GRN models and proved able to capture important phenomena in biology [12]. A prominent BN model is that of Random BNs (RBNs), which are initialised completely random both in the topology and in the functions, by setting the probability to assign the value 1 at each entry of each function by means of the bias parameter p and the number of incoming inputs for every node according to the k parameter. In this work we will refer to the synchronous and deterministic BN update, whereby nodes update their state in parallel and Boolean functions are deterministic. Under this update scheme, each network state has only one successor and the steady states of the system are cyclic attractors, possibly of period one (fixed points).

Recently, a dynamical systems view of cell differentiation has been proposed [3,5,6]. In a nutshell, the state of a cell is represented by an attractor—or a set of attractors [14, 16]—in the state space of a dynamical system and the transitions between cell states correspond to transitions between attractors. Transitions between attractors are the result of noise or specific external perturbations. This model makes it possible to capture some fundamental phenomena in cell differentiation [10]. Attractors in BNs are unstable with respect to perturbations (i.e. temporary node value flips), therefore after a node flip the trajectory either returns to the same attractor or it reaches another one. Attractor transition probabilities can be computed on the basis of the perturbation mechanism adopted. In this work we suppose that only one node at a time can be perturbed and that only states belonging to an attractor can be subject of such perturbation. In practice, we apply a logic negation to each node of each state of each attractor in turn and we check in which attractor the dynamics relaxes. This hypothesis is based on the assumption that perturbations are non frequent and so the probability of affecting more than one node at a time is negligible, and the same holds for perturbations occurring during transients, which usually occupy a tiny fraction of time with respect to attractors along BN trajectory. As shown in [2], these hypotheses are quite loose and results obtained in this setting are comparable to stochastic simulation of perturbed BNs. Under these assumptions, the probability of a transition between attractor A and attractor B can be computed in principle by taking the frequency of transitions between A and B among all the possible node flips along attractor A. When networks are large, we often resort to sampling instead of enumerating all the possibilities. The probability transition matrix is usually named *Attractor Transition Matrix* (ATM). The diagonal of the ATM account for the robustness of attractors, as diagonal values represent the probability of returning to the same attractor after one flip. Moreover, in general, transition probabilities are not symmetric, i.e. $p(A \rightarrow B) \neq p(B \rightarrow A)$. We observe that the diagonal values in the ATM maybe correlated with the attractor basins, but it is important to note that a high value in the ATM diagonal does not necessarily correspond to an attractor with a large basin of attraction, because the values in the ATM are computed by considering single perturbations occurring along the attractor states, while the attractor basin is defined in terms of a fraction of the entire state space.

2.1 Diversification and Asymmetry

A BN suitable to represent a differentiation process should exhibit different degrees of robustness, in the same way as cells at different differentiation stages are more or less sensitive to external perturbations. This property can be evaluated by quantifying the different values along the ATM diagonal and their range. Furthermore, in a recent work [17], Zhou and collaborators add another important requirement: the dynamics among attractors should be asymmetric, i.e. $p(A \rightarrow B)$ and $p(B \rightarrow A)$ should be different enough to observe a significant degree of irreversibility. This property can be evaluated by quantifying the distribution of values along the ATM rows.

To quantitatively evaluate these two properties, we defined two functions. They are not meant to be a formal definition for the properties themselves, but in our view they provide a good quantitative approximation of their quality and make it possible to compare different network configurations. Given the ATM, whose values are denoted by $T_{i,j}$—where i is the index of rows, and j the index for columns—we order rows so that values on the main diagonal are in ascending order. The matrix is by definition square of size m, where m is the number of attractors. In the following, with ATM, we will refer to this sorted matrix.

Diversification in attractor robustness is estimated on the basis of the following function:

$$f_1 = \sum_{i=2}^{m} (T_{i,i} - T_{i-1,i-1}) = T_{m,m} - T_{1,1} \tag{1}$$

This function estimates the range of attractor robustness. We observe that $0 \leq f_1 \leq 1$, but in general—and mainly in random models—it decreases with m as the more are the options to escape from an attractor, the lower the probability of returning to it after a perturbation.

Asymmetry in transition probabilities is defined in terms of the sum of transition probabilities in the triangle above (Q_a) and below (Q_b) the main diagonal:

$$f_2 = Q_a - Q_b = \sum_{i=1,j=i+1}^{m-1} T_{i,j} - \sum_{i=2,j=i-1}^{m} T_{i,j} \tag{2}$$

The intuition behind this definition is that high values of f_2 characterise asymmetric transitions between attractors. Moreover, as the transition matrix is sorted by main diagonal values, the function estimates the extent to which transitions from less robust to more robust attractors are favoured. In principle, f_2 may range in $[-m + 1, m - 1]$ but the actual distribution of values strongly depends upon the models used.

In general, we may assume that the higher f_1 and f_2 computed on an ATM of a Boolean network the higher the potential of that network to model a differentiation process.

2.2 Self-loops

Since network topology and functions impact the BN attractors landscape [1], in a previous work [11] we studied the impact of self-loops. A self-loop in graph theory is defined as an arc that connects a vertex to itself, and in the context of BNs this implies that the state of a node with a self-loop at time t depends also on the state of the very same node at time $t - 1$. There, we have shown that a major effect of incrementally adding self-loops in RBNs is that *(i)* the number of attractors increases (in some cases exponentially) and *(ii)* the probability of returning to the same attractor after a perturbation decreases with the fraction of nodes with self-loops. In fact, this last effect might be detrimental to cell dynamic if generalised to all attractors. Therefore, as self-loops have been observed in genetic networks reconstructed from real data, this effect should be limited to few attractors and anyway be compensated by other positive effects, maybe concerning cell differentiation itself. In this work we investigate the impact of self-loops on the properties mentioned above, with a twofold aim: identify possible

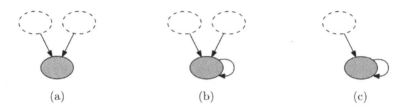

Fig. 1. a: Generic node generated following the original RBN model with $k = 2$, self-loops are not allowed. b: **AUGM-*** cases, self-loop added starting from (a). c: **CONST-*** cases, incoming link removed and self-loop added starting from (a). Outcoming arcs are not drawn since both the RBN model and our models do not impose constraints on them.

structural network characteristics that favour their use as differentiation models and find support to the appearance of self-dependencies in biological genes.

3   Experimental Results

We initially sampled RBNs with $n = 15$, $k = 2$ and $p = 0.5$—following the long standing hypothesis according to which real GRNs operate in a critical regime (or ordered but not chaotic) [15]— subsequently modified with self-loops according to the following four different schemas:[1]

CONST-OR: removed an incoming link and replaced the input with a self-loop, and changed the node boolean function into an OR between the node value and the previous function;

AUGM-OR: added a self-loop and changed the node boolean function into an OR between the node value and the previous function;

CONST-RND: removed an incoming link and replaced the input with a self-loop, without changing the node boolean function;

AUGM-RND: added a self-loop and extended the truth table randomly (with the same bias used for generating the original RBN).

In all the listed cases, the choice of the incoming link to be substituted and the node to which to add the self-loop was performed in a random fashion, choosing with uniform probability among the nodes. For computational reasons, we limited both the maximal number of nodes with self-loops and of nodes in the BNs so as to make feasible the exhaustive exploration of BNs' state space, as well as the perturbations for generating the ATM. Statistics on larger BNs, requiring a sampling of the possible initial states and perturbations, are subject of future work. See Fig. 1 for a graphical representation of these configurations. Note that in our models there is actually no semantics associated to 0 and 1. However, since for the sake of simplicity we chose a specific canalising function, the OR function, this implies that if 1 is associated with the active state of the node, OR acts as a canalising activating function—and, clearly, OR with self-loops means self-activation. As

---

[1] As done in [11].

originally introduced by Kauffman [8], a canalising function is a Boolean function in which there exists an input value that fully determines the output value, regardless the values of other inputs. To be coherent in the discussion of the results, we stick to this choice and hereafter we designate 1 as the active state. Anyway, the fact that we observe a specific effect of OR functions just means that this effect can be achieved by any canalising function of this kind. Moreover, as we have shown in [11], the effect is produced by the combination of self-loops and OR functions together, rather than being the consequence of an increased fraction of OR functions alone. As f_1 and f_2 depend on the number of attractors and in an ongoing work we have observed that the distribution of the number of attractors is not uniform among RBNs of a given size, in light of this we have sampled the BNs space until the desired fixed number of nets had reached and then the statistics we computed are based on the same number of nets (30) per number of attractors, from 1 to 20—hence, statistics are computed over 600 networks. Indeed, we believe that the advantage of self-loops should be observed *ceteris paribus*, i.e. evolutionarily speaking, once the network has reached its minimal configuration in terms of attractors. In addition, when BNs are used for modelling real cells, the first step is usually to configure a network with a given number of attractors (cell types), as done for example in [17]. Results are shown by means of boxplots, so as to have a visual reckon of the distribution, and a plot with maximum, mean and median (the minimum value is omitted as it is the same for all the statistics for each function). On the x-axis we find the number of self-loops and on the y-axis either f_1 or f_2. Generic statistics on attractors are omitted because not relevant for this contribution; however, the interested reader can find such statistics in our previous work [11]. An in-depth analysis of attractors number distribution in this class of BNs is subject of ongoing work.

Results concerning robustness diversification (measured by means of f_1) are summarised in Figs. 2, 3, 4 and 5. We first note that, in all the cases, mean and

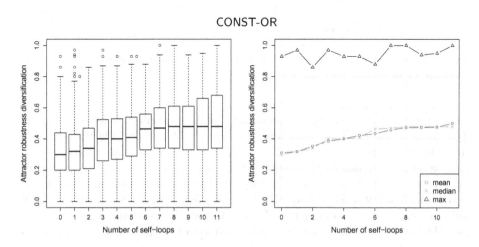

Fig. 2. Boxplot (left) and main statistics of f_1 (right), in the case with $k = 2$ and self-loops combined in OR.

AUGM-OR

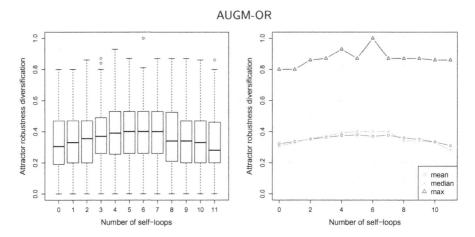

Fig. 3. Boxplot (left) and main statistics of f_1 (right), in the case with self-loops added to the nodes in OR.

CONST-RND

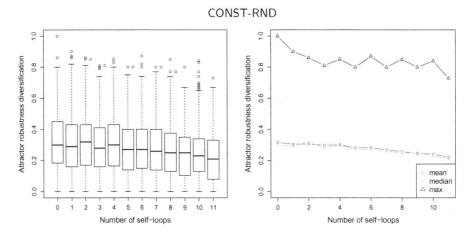

Fig. 4. Boxplot (left) and main statistics of f_1 (right), in the case with $k = 2$ and self-loops combined as a random function.

median are almost overlapping, meaning that the distribution is symmetrical. Moreover, as the maximum (shown also in the right plots for clarity) is always much higher than the mean and follows approximately the same shape, we can conclude that the distribution is quite wide—a property that favours evolutionary processes. We observe that in those cases in which self-loops play a self-activating function (OR cases), the diversification steadily increases (CONST-OR) or reaches a maximum at a moderate amount of nodes with self-loops (AUGM-OR). We observe that, when the self-loop may play any functional role

AUGM-RND

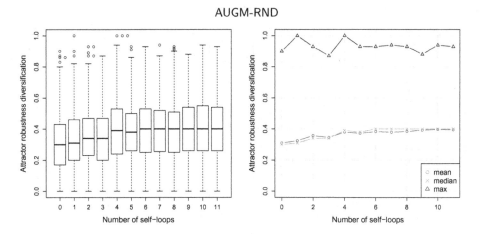

Fig. 5. Boxplot (left) and main statistics of f_1 (right), in the case with self-loops added to the nodes in a random function.

CONST-OR

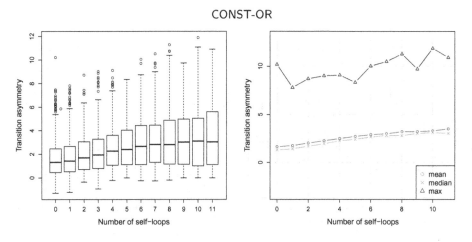

Fig. 6. Boxplot (left) and main statistics of f_2 (right), in the case with $k = 2$ and self-loops combined in OR.

– i.e. when it is combined in a random function – this effect is limited, if not negative.

Results concerning the asymmetry of transitions between attractors are summarised in Figs. 6, 7, 8 and 9. Results are analogous to the previous case: when self-loops play a self-activating function (OR cases), the asymmetry increases steadily (CONST-OR) or up to a point after which it starts to decrease (AUGM-OR). Conversely, when the self-loop is associated to a random function, the average impact on asymmetry is negligible.

AUGM-OR

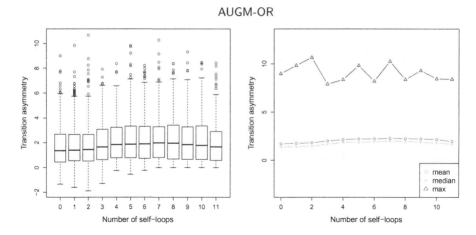

Fig. 7. Boxplot (left) and main statistics of f_2 (right), in the case with self-loops added to the nodes in OR.

CONST-RND

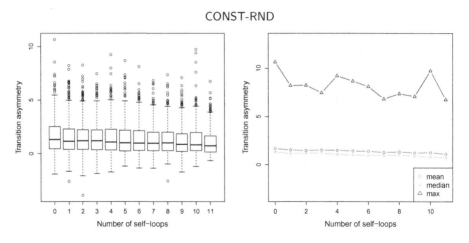

Fig. 8. Boxplot (left) and main statistics of f_2 (right), in the case with $k = 2$ and self-loops combined as a random function.

Summarising, these results support the conjecture that, in BN models, a small fraction of node with self-loops associated to a canalising function may favour both robustness diversification and asymmetry in transition probabilities. This result observed in a computational model is indeed complemented by experimental evidence in real cells where self-activation/inhibition schemes are found in a limited, but not negligible, number of genes [13].

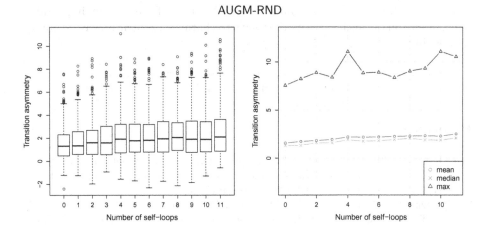

Fig. 9. Boxplot (left) and main statistics of f_2 (right), in the case with self-loops added to the nodes in a random function.

4   Conclusion and Future Work

According to the ensemble approach [9], it is important to identify structural and functional properties of genetic regulatory network models that make them more suitable for reproducing typical cell dynamics. In this perspective, we have investigated the effect of self-loops on RBNs addressing the question as to whether they may provide a positive contribution to modelling cell differentiation. Attractors in BNs epitomise cell types and transitions between attractors occur when attractor states are perturbed, either by specific signals or perturbations. We have defined two functions as proxies for measuring two prominent properties acknowledged to play an important role in BN models for differentiation: diversification in attractor robustness and attractor transition asymmetry. Results show that a small fraction of canalising self-loops (approximately between 0.25 and 0.3) favours higher values of these functions. This result sheds light on the positive role of self-loops in BNs for modelling cell dynamics. Moreover, by the outcome of this study we contribute answering the question raised in [11] concerning the existence of a specific fraction of self-loops enabling an optimal balance between robustness and flexibility. In addition, this investigation may provide insights on the evolutionary processes that biological cells have undergone. This contribution is just another step in the direction of detecting structural and functional characteristics (*bricks*) in GRN models that make them suitable for modelling cell differentiation processes. Further goals in our research agenda involve the identification of other bricks to be used as elementary building blocks in the problem of designing GRNs for biological as well as artificial purposes. Moreover, since our measures are based on a particular procedure to assess the attractors' robustness recapitulated by the ATM, is of paramount importance the comparison of this last with other ways to characterise their relative stability, as done in [7].

Acknowledgements. We thank the anonymous referees for useful comments and suggestions. Andrea Roli is a member of the INdAM Research group GNCS.

References

1. Ahnert, S., Fink, T.: Form and function in gene regulatory networks: the structure of network motifs determines fundamental properties of their dynamical state space. J. R. Soc. Interface **13**(120), 278–289 (2016)
2. Braccini, M., Roli, A., Villani, M., Serra, R.: A comparison between threshold ergodic sets and stochastic simulation of boolean networks for modelling cell differentiation. In: Pelillo, M., Poli, I., Roli, A., Serra, R., Slanzi, D., Villani, M. (eds.) WIVACE 2017. CCIS, vol. 830, pp. 116–128. Springer, Cham (2018). https://doi.org/10.1007/978-3-319-78658-2_9
3. Furusawa, C., Kaneko, K.: A dynamical-systems view of stem cell biology. Science **338**, 215–217 (2012)
4. Huang, S.: The molecular and mathematical basis of Waddington's epigenetic landscape: a framework for post-Darwinian biology? Bioessays **34**(2), 149–157 (2012)
5. Huang, S., Eichler, G., Bar-Yam, Y., Ingber, D.: Cell fates as high-dimensional attractor states of a complex gene regulatory network. Phys. Rev. Lett. **94**, 128701:1–128701:4 (2005)
6. Huang, S., Ernberg, I., Kauffman, S.: Cancer attractors: a systems view of tumors from a gene network dynamics and developmental perspective. In: Seminars in Cell & Developmental Biology, vol. 20, no. 7, pp. 869–876 (2009). Structure and Function of the Golgi Apparatus and Systems Approaches to Cell and Developmental Biology
7. Joo, J.I., Zhou, J.X., Huang, S., Cho, K.H.: Determining relative dynamic stability of cell states using boolean network model. Sci. Rep. **8**(1), 12077 (2018)
8. Kauffman, S.: The Origins of Order: Self-Organization and Selection in Evolution. Oxford University Press, Oxford (1993)
9. Kauffman, S.: A proposal for using the ensemble approach to understand genetic regulatory networks. J. Theor. Biol. **230**, 581–590 (2004)
10. Mojtahedi, M., et al.: Cell fate decision as high-dimensional critical state transition. PLOS Biol. **14**(12), e2000640:1–e2000640:28 (2016)
11. Montagna, S., Braccini, M., Roli, A.: The impact of self-loops in random boolean network dynamics: a simulation analysis. In: Pelillo, M., Poli, I., Roli, A., Serra, R., Slanzi, D., Villani, M. (eds.) WIVACE 2017. CCIS, vol. 830, pp. 104–115. Springer, Cham (2018). https://doi.org/10.1007/978-3-319-78658-2_8
12. Nykter, M., et al.: Gene expression dynamics in the macrophage exhibit criticality. Proc. Nat. Acad. Sci. **105**(6), 1897–1900 (2008)
13. Raj, A., Rifkin, S., Andersen, E., Van Oudenaarden, A.: Variability in gene expression underlies incomplete penetrance. Nature **463**(7283), 913–918 (2010)
14. Serra, R., Villani, M., Barbieri, A., Kauffman, S., Colacci, A.: On the dynamics of random boolean networks subject to noise: attractors, ergodic sets and cell types. J. Theor. Biol. **265**(2), 185–193 (2010)

15. Shmulevich, I., Kauffman, S.A., Aldana, M.: Eukaryotic cells are dynamically ordered or critical but not chaotic. Proc. Nat. Acad. Sci. U.S.A. **102**(38), 13439–13444 (2005)
16. Villani, M., Barbieri, A., Serra, R.: A dynamical model of genetic networks for cell differentiation. PloS One **6**(3), e17703 (2011)
17. Zhou, J., Samal, A., Fouquier d'Hérouël, A., Price, N., Huang, S.: Relative stability of network states in boolean network models of gene regulation in development. Biosystems **142–143**, 15–24 (2016)

Economic, Societal and Technological Applications

Evolution of Workers' Behaviour in Dual Labor Markets

Shira Fano[1]([✉])([iD]) and Debora Slanzi[2,3]([iD])

[1] Department of Economics and Statistics, University Federico II of Naples,
Via Cintia - Monte Sant'Angelo, 80126 Naples, Italy
shira.fano@unina.it
[2] Department of Management, Ca' Foscari University of Venice,
Cannaregio 873, 30121 Venice, Italy
debora.slanzi@unive.it
[3] European Centre for Living Technology,
Dorsoduro 3911, Calle Crosera, 30123 Venice, Italy

Abstract. The simultaneous increase in the use of temporary contracts and the productivity slowdown recently experienced in some OECD countries, fostered a growing interest in analysing the link between these phenomena.

In this paper we study the effect of the use of temporary contracts on workers' incentives and in particular we focus on effort decisions of temporary workers. We implement an agent-based model where workers interact in the labor market and compete for permanent contracts. Workers choose how much effort to exert in production and, using reinforcement learning, they update their strategies on the basis of past experience.

The main result is that optimal effort strategies depend on the share of available permanent contracts. When the share is low, workers do not bet on their conversion and supply low effort. As the share increases workers exert higher effort but, when it is too high, they have the incentive to shirk since they are confident of being confirmed. Therefore, the relationship between the share of permanent contracts and workers' effort, and consequently labor productivity, has an inverted-U-shape.

Keywords: Agent-based model · Temporary contracts · Effort · Reinforcement learning

1 Introduction

Most of the reforms that have recently been implemented in European labor markets contribute to create what in the literature is called a *dual labor market*, featuring the coexistence of two types of contracts: permanent and temporary contracts; [3]. The motivation of this work builds on the observation of two empirical facts: on one hand, an increase in the use of temporary contracts and, on the other, a slowdown in labor productivity in some OECD countries; see [5].

© Springer Nature Switzerland AG 2019
S. Cagnoni et al. (Eds.): WIVACE 2018, CCIS 900, pp. 45–56, 2019.
https://doi.org/10.1007/978-3-030-21733-4_4

In Italy, for example, the sharp increase in the share of temporary contracts is due to a number of reforms that increased the possibility of using this type of agreements; see [5]. Since then, temporary contracts are typically used for many different reasons: screening purposes, temporarily fill-in for staff who are absent or on leave, or to accommodate fluctuations in demand; in many cases employers also save in labor costs and social security benefits.

The aim of this paper is to study the link between the use of temporary employment and labor productivity. The channel we will investigate is that temporary contracts have an effect on workers' incentives, and in particular on their willingness to exert high effort and, consequently, this may have an effect on firms' labor productivity. We implement an agent-based model where workers and firms interact in a dual labor market.[1] In the model, temporary workers compete for a limited number of permanent contracts and they face the following *trade-off*: exerting high effort is costly but it increases the chances of obtaining a permanent contract. In this environment, workers choose how much effort to exert in the production process and update their strategies on the basis of past experience; agents use a form of individual reinforcement learning as a learning algorithm, see [15].

This paper is related to different strands of literature: empirical papers studying the effect of temporary employment on productivity, [4, 11]; studies of workers' behaviour and incentives under different contracts and agent-based models of the labor market; [8]. The work of Guadalupe [9] is the first paper that looks at behavioural responses of temporary contracts showing they cause significantly higher accident rates; our focus is instead on workers' effort. Few empirical papers have documented the effect of temporary employment on workers' effort decisions; this is mainly related to the difficulty of finding good proxies of effort. Among others, three examples using respectively Swiss, Italian and Spanish data are respectively [7], [10] and [6]. In the first paper, effort is proxied by unpaid overtime work and absences; the authors show evidence that temporary workers provide higher effort than permanent employees. The second paper looks at the effect of a change in the employment protection legislation regime on absenteeism, used to proxy effort. The main finding is that the number of days of absence per week increases significantly once employment protection is granted at the end of a three-month probation period, therefore, highly protected contracts may induce lower effort. Finally, [6] analyses the effect of having a large gap in firing costs between permanent and temporary workers on total factor productivity at the firm level. The authors show that firms' temporary-to-permanent conversion rates and consequently temporary workers' effort decrease when the gap increases. Differently from the previous contributions, using an agent-based model we take into account the additional competition channel faced by temporary workers competing for permanent positions in the same firms. Leading labor economists such as [8] suggest the use of these techniques to study the interaction between workers and firms in the labor market, with the aim of replicating

---

[1] For an introduction to complexity and agent-based models see [12] and [1].

stylized facts and analysing the effects of specific policies (e.g. training policies, unemployment benefits etc...).

For a recent review on agent-based models applied to labor markets see [14]; early examples are [2] and [16]. The rest of the paper is organized as follows: Sect. 2 describes the characteristics of the model, Sect. 3 presents the computational results and Sect. 4 summarized and concludes the paper.

2   The Model

In the labor market there are N_W workers and N_F firms with $N_W \gg N_F$. Each worker is endowed with one unit of labor which is the only factor of production in the economy; firms supply an homogeneous good. Initially, workers are randomly assigned to firms, all firms employ the same number of workers and all vacancies are filled, therefore, labor force participation is constant. Moreover, u workers are not allocated to any firm and start the period as unemployed. We simply assume that the production function of firm j, Y_j, is defined as the sum of effort provided by the firms' employees:

$$Y_j = \sum_{i=1}^{q_j} e_{ij} \tag{2.1}$$

where q_j is the number of workers employed in firm j and e_{ij} is effort exerted by worker i when matched with firm j.

Two types of contracts characterize the labor market: temporary and permanent contracts; what makes the two contracts different is their duration. Workers with permanent contracts remain matched with the same firm, unless the firm is hit by an exogenous shock that destroys all permanent contracts in the firm. Workers with temporary contracts are employed for a maximum amount of time d; during this period they remain temporary or can become permanent. After d rounds their contract ends and, if their contract has not been converted into permanent, they separate from the firm and become unemployed.

The problem faced by temporary workers is deciding how much effort they should exert in the production process. The strategy S_i of a temporary worker is defined by a discretized set of effort choices $e_{ijk} \in \{1, 2, \ldots, 10\}$ with associated probabilities p_{ijk} such that $\sum_{k=1}^{10} p_{ijk} = 1$ and $p_{ijk} \geq 0$ for all workers. Initially, workers do not know how much effort they should exert in the production process, therefore, all strategies are chosen with equal probability. We simulate the model under two different scenarios. In the first, we assume that workers stick to the strategy S_i also when their temporary contract is upgraded to permanent. In the second, instead, we assume that when workers are converted into permanent they do not sample an effort value from their distribution and, instead, exert a fixed level of effort e^*, exogenously determined. The intuition is that when converted into permanent workers might decide to change their strategy and, for example, lower their effort. Unemployed workers exert 0 effort. All workers are initially employed with temporary contracts. Once workers are allocated to firms, they sample an effort value from their distribution and production occurs.

Each firm can employ only a given fraction P of workers with permanent contracts, for example due to institutional regulations or financial constraints. If in a firm the current fraction of permanent contracts is smaller than P, the conversion process takes place. We assume that firms can observe the level of effort exerted by workers with temporary contracts. Firms therefore rank temporary workers by decreasing level of effort and the top ranked temporary workers become permanent, until the share P is reached, while the others remain temporary; ties are broken randomly.

We assume the utility of a worker with a permanent contract is greater than the utility of a worker employed with a temporary contract. Therefore, workers within each firm compete for permanent contracts. Temporary workers face the following trade-off. Exerting high effort is a costly investment, but it increases the probability that their contract is converted into permanent. Workers suffer a loss of value that is strictly positive and increasing in effort, $c(e_{ijk}) = \alpha e_{ijk}^{\beta}$ with $\alpha > 0$ and $\beta \geq 1$. All workers simultaneously make their effort decisions, without knowledge on the level of effort exerted by the other workers in the firm. After the conversion process takes place, workers learn their new status, permanent if their contract has been upgraded and temporary if not. The payoff of worker i is defined as:

$$\pi_i(S_i, S_{-i}) = \begin{cases} w - \alpha e_{ijk}^{\beta} + x_T \text{ if temporary} \\ w - \alpha e_{ijk}^{\beta} + x_P \text{ if permanent} \end{cases} \qquad (2.2)$$

were we assume that all employed workers receive the same exogenous wage w.[2] $X \in \{x_T, x_P\}$ is a non-monetary benefit that is different according to the type of contract and takes two values: x_P and x_T, respectively for permanent and temporary workers, with $x_P > x_T$.[3]

In the initial stage workers choose the level of effort to exert from the set of feasible strategies with equal probability. Workers keep track of payoffs obtained with the different strategies and, as time passes, they realized that some strategies work better than others. Workers learn how much effort they should exert in the production process only when they are temporary and they are in a firm that can convert some temporary workers into permanent, to reach the share P, so after the job destruction of permanent contracts occurs. We model this as a process of individual reinforcement learning; average payoffs drive the learning process. Worker i will choose effort e_{ijk} with probability:

$$p(e_{ijk}) = \frac{exp^{\lambda \cdot \text{payoffAve}(i, e_{ijk})}}{\sum\limits_{k=1}^{10} exp^{\lambda \cdot \text{payoffAve}(i, e_{ijk})}} \qquad (2.3)$$

---

[2] In the formula $\pi_i(S_i, S_{-i})$ is the payoff of worker i using strategy S_i, when all other temporary workers are exerting strategy S_{-i}.

[3] Written in this way, the payoff is simple to interpret, but w, x_T and x_P are constant parameters therefore we could simplify the expression using just two different constants, one for each type of contract.

where $\lambda > 0$ determines the speed of the learning process and payoffAve(i, e_{ijk}) are average payoffs of worker i, when he played strategy e_{ijk}. In this learning process strategies that lead to relatively higher payoffs will be played with higher probability in the next rounds.[4]

Every d rounds temporary contracts end and workers separate from firms. Workers that were previously unemployed become temporary and the temporary workers that became unemployed are either randomly matched to a new firm (or the same one by chance) or remain unemployed.

Moreover, in a randomly determined order, in each round one firm is hit by a job destruction shock and permanent workers separate from firms. Temporary and permanent workers that separated from firms are randomly reallocated to firms in the next round; in each round, the number of employed workers remains constant, as firms fill all their vacancies, but workers reallocate across the three states: temporary, permanent or unemployed. We call period a sequence of rounds, such that each firm has updated once the share of its permanent workers. A new period begins, with an updated allocation of workers, contracts and strategies. After enough stages, workers learn the optimal level of effort they should exert to maximize their expected payoffs.

3   Computational Results

In this section, we discuss the results of the model for a representative set of parameters. In Table 1 the description of the parameters used in the simulation is presented. We consider an economy with $N_W = 300$ workers; 10 workers are allocated to each firm, hence, there are $N_F = 30$ firms in the labor market. We assume that in a given simulation all firms can employ the same number of workers with permanent contracts. Therefore, we average across firms simply to net out sampling variation. We assume all workers earn an exogenous wage and normalize it to $w = 1$; the non-monetary benefit temporary workers get if they are (not) converted into permanent is set to 0 (-1). We observe interactions among workers in the labor market for 500 periods. In the model the workers move across different states and they can be permanent or temporary at different times. Nevertheless, we will focus on the second group and in particular on strategies learnt by temporary workers when they are in firms that can upgrade some contracts into permanent. We start by looking at average payoffs earned by temporary workers during the reinforcement learning process and show that the algorithm converges to a steady state which is an approximation of an equilibrium. Then, we describe the strategies evolved by temporary workers at the end of the simulation.

3.1   Payoffs

As the learning process takes place temporary workers update their strategies and increase the probability of playing effort choices that lead to higher payoffs.

---

[4] Equation (2.3) is known as Gibbs-Boltzmann probability measure, used for example in [13].

Table 1. Description and value of the parameters used for the simulations.

Parameter	Description	Value
N_W	Number of workers	300
N_F	Number of firms	30
q_j	Number of workers per firm	10
u	Number of unemployed (among N_W)	10
d	Temporary contract maximum duration	10
γ	Job destruction of permanent contracts	$1/N_F$
λ	Learning parameter	10
P	Share of permanent contracts	$\{0.1, 0.2,..., 1\}$
t	Periods	500
w	Wage	1
α	Cost of 1 unit of effort	$U \sim [0.05, 0.15]$
β	Convex cost parameter	1
x_T	Non-monetary benefit if temporary	-1
x_P	Non-monetary benefit if permanent	0

We conduct a complete run of the model ($t = 500$ periods) for each of the possible values of the share of permanent contracts. Figure 1 depicts the time series of average payoffs earned by temporary workers, when they are in firms that can convert workers into permanent, as the learning process takes place.

In each data-point all firms updated once their share of permanent contracts to reach the desired share P, therefore, each point is the average payoff of $N_W = 300$ workers. Each time series corresponds to a simulation for a different share of permanent contracts and moving from bottom to top $P = \{0.1, 0.2, ..., 1\}$. As expected, the higher is the share of available permanent contracts P the larger are average payoffs earned by workers. Nevertheless, in the different simulations workers have different learning patterns. For low values of P, say up to $P = 0.6$, payoffs initially decrease and then increase before converging; for higher values of P instead payoffs follow an opposite pattern, first increasing than decreasing and for $P = $ payoffs increase over time. Moreover, the speed of convergence differs across simulations. For low values of the share of permanent contracts, say up to $P = 0.7$, the learning process is fast and approximately 10 to 15 updates are sufficient to reach convergence. Instead, for higher values of P the learning process is faster in the initial stages but converges slowly in a high number of iterations.

3.2   Strategies

Figure 2 depicts strategies learnt by workers at the end of a simulation; each barplot corresponds to a different value of the share of permanent contracts

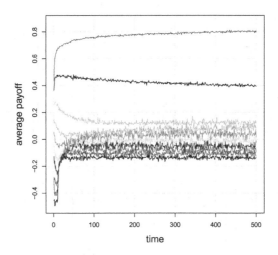

Fig. 1. Time series of average payoffs for different values of the share of permanent contracts, from bottom to top $P = \{0.1, 0.2, ..., 1\}$.

$P = \{0.1, 0.2, ..., 1\}$. At the end of the learning process workers evolve strategies that are very similar, but not identical both because of sampling variation and because workers have different effort costs, sampled from a uniform distribution. Therefore, we compute and plot workers' strategies averaging across all workers in the model, at the end of a simulation. The support of effort values is represented on the x-axis and the probability of choosing each strategy on the y-axis. Some patterns clearly emerge. As shown by the plots, workers' optimal strategy changes as a function of the share of available permanent contracts and, in general, workers learn to play mixed strategies. For example, when $P = 0.1$ workers obtain higher payoffs exerting minimum effort and therefore play effort equal to 1 with higher probability. In this case, only one worker out of ten is promoted to a permanent position, therefore, workers realize that it is not worth it to bear high effort costs. Nevertheless, when workers exert maximum effort chances are high that they are chosen for promotion, therefore, on average the strategy $e_{ijk} = 10$ is chosen with 11 percent of probability.

Moving from the case $P = 0.1$ to $P = 0.2$ the probability of playing $e_{ijk} = 1$ decreases from 0.51 to 0.45 and the probability of playing $e_{ijk} = 10$ increases from 0.11 to 0.2. As the share of available permanent contracts increases workers realize that their chances of being promoted increase, therefore, they optimally decrease the probability of exerting minimum effort and increase the probability of exerting maximum effort. This is true up to the case $P = 0.5$ but, as the share of available permanent contracts further increases, something changes. Workers decrease their effort and, as P increases, the distribution shifts to the left; when $P = 1$ workers choose to exert the minimum effort level with probability 0.64.

Why is there a tipping point after which temporary workers decrease their effort? The intuition is the following. Within each firm, temporary workers

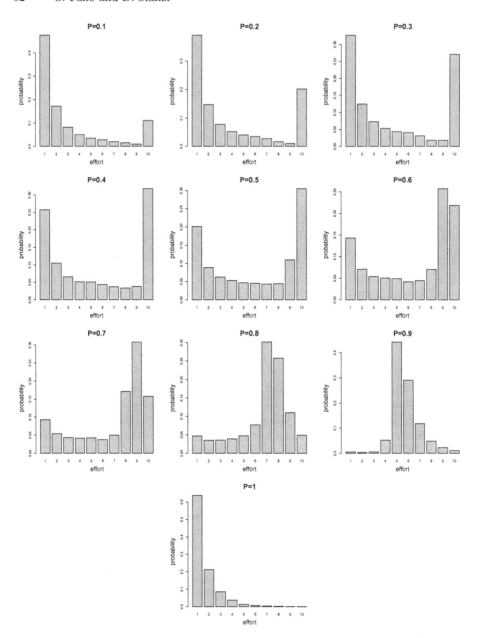

Fig. 2. Workers' average strategy at the end of a simulation for all possible values of the share of permanent contracts in $P \in \{0.1, 0.2, ..., 1\}$, on the x-axis effort values are in $e_{ijk} \in \{1, 2, ..., 10\}$.

compete among each other to get permanent contracts and, when only few workers can be converted into permanent, competition induces workers to increase their effort, as the number of available promotions increases. However, when the share of permanent contracts increases above $P = 0.5$, the pressure to compete for permanent contracts decreases as workers realize that, even exerting low effort, their contract will anyway be upgraded into permanent with high probability. In other words, temporary workers have an incentive to shirk as there is no need for them to work hard and compete for permanent contracts.

3.3   Effort and Productivity

The share of available permanent contracts induces different incentives on workers' willingness to exert low/high effort and as a consequence shapes workers' strategies. We take an aggregate approach and look at the effect of the trade-off faced by temporary workers on average effort and consequently on firm productivity. Figure 3 shows the expected value of effort exerted by all temporary workers in the model at the end of a simulation.

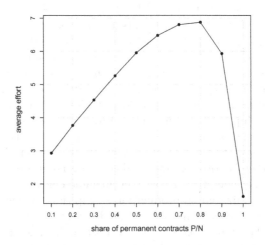

Fig. 3. Workers' average effort for each value of the share of permanent contracts $P \in \{0.1, 0.2, ..., 1\}$.

The graph summarizes results for 10 different runs of the model, one for each of the possible values of the share of permanent contracts $P = \{0.1, 0.2, ..., 1\}$. Each data-point is the expected value of effort from a different simulation and it is computed using the average strategies plotted in the previous figure. The main message is that the relationship between the share of permanent contracts and average effort has an inverted-U-shape. As the number of available contract upgrades increases, workers learn to exert higher effort, as this increases their chances to get a permanent contract, but, if the share of permanent contracts is too high average effort decreases. Temporary workers do not feel the pressure to compete for promotions as, with high probability, they will anyway get a permanent contract and therefore they decrease their effort. If temporary workers do not change their effort strategies when they become permanent, from firms' point of view it is optimal to convert 80% of temporary workers into permanent as at this point effort is maximized. In this case average effort is 6.87 out of 10, instead, the lowest levels of effort correspond to the cases in which all workers are temporary and all workers are permanent, average effort is respectively 2.93 and 1.62. Recall that in this labor market production of firms is defined as the sum of effort exerted by employed workers. Figure 4 *left* and *right* shows the relationship between the share of available permanent contracts and labor productivity at the firm level, computed as the sum of effort over the number of workers, within each firm. The only difference in the two plots is the assumption on workers' behaviour when their contract is converted into permanent. In the simulations corresponding to the *left* plot we assume permanent workers stick to the strategy they learnt when they were temporary and competing for promotion, and simply sample an effort value from their distribution also when they are permanent. On the *right* instead we assume that when workers are converted into permanent they switch to a fixed level of effort that is set to the minimum level $e^* = 1$. Each data-point represents labor productivity of one of the 30 firms in the labor market; the red line joins the average labor productivity for all values of the parameter P. The results of the first assumption on permanent workers' behaviour (Fig. 3, *left*) show that there is a considerable amount of noise and different firms have different productivity values, even when they have the same share of permanent workers. Nevertheless, when considering average values the relationship between the share of available permanent contracts and labor productivity shows the same pattern as Fig. 3 on workers' effort. In fact, in the model productivity is a consequence of effort decisions. Therefore if firms could observe workers' effort decisions and the conversion process was not costly, firms would optimally set the share of permanent contracts to 80%, inducing high effort, to maximize labor productivity. Empirical evidence instead shows that yearly transition probabilities from fixed-term to permanent contracts are relatively small, they never exceed 50% and are as low as 12–13% in Portugal and Spain. In light of the model, this low temporary-to-permanent conversion probability may be one of the factors causing low productivity values recently observed in some OECD countries, as firms are not providing temporary workers the "right" incentives to exert high effort.

Figure 4 *right* summarizes the outcome of the model when we assume that workers that become permanent switch to the minimum level of effort $e^* = 1$. Under this assumption, the model suggests that firms should convert 40% of temporary workers into permanent to maximize labor productivity. At this point average labor productivity is 3.6. Note that the scale on the y-axis on the two plots is different and, as expected, higher levels of labor productivity can be reached in the scenario plotted on the *left*. The black lines are average labor productivity plus/minus one standard deviation. Note that, as expected, when the share of permanent contracts increases above 50%, the standard deviation monotonically decreases as more workers are exerting the minimum effort level.

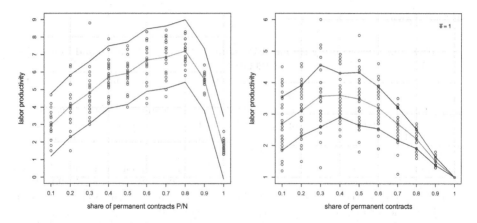

Fig. 4. Share of permanent contracts and labor productivity under two different assumptions on permanent workers' behaviour. The black lines in the *right* plot are average labor productivity plus/minus one standard deviation.

4 Concluding Remarks

This paper is a contribution to the recent and growing literature trying to assess the effect of temporary employment on labor market outcomes. We focus on behavioural aspects of this phenomenon and, in particular, the goal of this paper is to assess weather, and under which conditions, temporary employment induces an increase in workers' willingness to exert high effort. We implement an agent-based model where workers and firms interact in a dual labor market, with temporary and permanent contracts. The main result is that temporary workers' optimal effort depends on the share of available permanent contracts; the relationship between the share of permanent contracts and effort, has an inverted-U-shape. Our results should be taken as suggestive rather than con-clusive: the model is very simple and therefore could be improved in several ways. For example, in this simulation firms cannot choose or adjust the share of permanent contracts, as it is an exogenous parameter, but it could instead be a firms' choice variable to maximizes profits, taking into account workers' effort responses. Moreover, effort is assumed to be observable but a more realis-tic scenario would be to observe a noisy measure of it. For OECD countries the transition probability that a temporary contract is converted into permanent is relatively small, never larger than 50% and as low as 12%–13% in Portugal and France. Therefore, the model suggests that converting too few contracts into permanent may be providing workers incentives to exert low effort and, conse-quently, this may be one of causes of low productivity values, recently experiences in some European countries.

References

1. Batten, D.F.: Discovering Artificial Economics. How Agents Learn and Economies Evolve. Westview Press, Boulder (2000)
2. Bergmann, B.R.: Micro-to-macro simulation: a primer with a labor market example. J. Econ. Perspect. **4**(1), 99–116 (1990)
3. Boeri, T.: Institutional reforms and dualism in European labor markets. In: Handbook of Labor Economics, vol. 4, Part B, pp. 1173–1236 (2011)
4. Boeri, T., Garibaldi, P.: Two tier reforms of employment protection: a honeymoon effect? Econ. J. **117**(521), F357–F385 (2007)
5. Cappellari, L., Dell'Aringa, C., Leonardi, M.: Temporary employment, job flows and productivity: a tale of two reforms. Econ. J. **122**(562), F188–F215 (2012)
6. Dolado, J.J., Ortigueira, S., Stucchi, R.: Does dual employment protection affect TFP? Evidence from Spanish manufacturing firms (2012)
7. Engellandt, A., Riphahn, R.T.: Temporary contracts and employee effort. Labour Econ. **12**(3), 281–299 (2005)
8. Freeman, R.B.: War of the models: which labour market institutions for the 21st century? Labour Econ. **5**(1), 1–24 (1998)
9. Guadalupe, M.: The hidden costs of fixed term contracts: the impact on work accidents. Labour Econ. **10**(3), 339–357 (2003)
10. Ichino, A., Riphahn, R.T.: The effect of employment protection on worker effort: absenteeism during and after probation. J. Eur. Econ. Assoc. **3**(1), 120–143 (2005)
11. Lotti, F., Viviano, E.: Why Hiring Temporary Workers. Banca d'Italia, Rome (2012)
12. Miller, J.H., Page, S.E., LeBaron, B.: Complex adaptive systems: an introduction to computational models of social life. J. Econ. Lit. **46**(2), 427–428 (2008)
13. Neugart, M.: Labor market policy evaluation with ACE. J. Econ. Behav. Organ. **67**(2), 418–430 (2008)
14. Neugart, M., Richiardi, M.: Agent-based models of the labor market. LABORatorio R. Revelli working papers series, 125 (2012)
15. Roth, A.E., Erev, I.: Learning in extensive-form games: experimental data and simple dynamic models in the intermediate term. Games Econ. Behav. **8**(1), 164–212 (1995)
16. Tesfatsion, L.: Introduction to the special issue on agent-based computational economics. J. Econ. Dyn. Control **25**(3), 281–293 (2001)

Evolution of Generosity and Its Infrastructure in Self-organizing Cooperative Societies

Elpida Tzafestas[1,2(✉)]

[1] Laboratory of Cognitive Science, Department of History and Philosophy of Science, University of Athens, University Campus, Ano Ilisia 15771, Greece
etzafestas@phs.uoa.gr
[2] Chair of Automatic Control Engineering,
Electrical and Computer Engrg. Department, Technische Universität München,
Theresienstr. 90, 80333 Munich, Germany

Abstract. We are studying a society of evolving cooperative agents that show a continuous tit-for-tat like behavior in an adequately modified Iterated Prisoner's Dilemma game. Each agent evaluates the action of its opponent with the help of a threshold as cooperative or defective and responds differently to the two cases. The evolutionary mechanism consists in copying the behavior of more successful agents met at random in the society. First, we study various evolutionary schemes and we show that copying of the evaluation threshold does not offer any evolutionary advantage, while copying of the visible actions leads consistently to higher fitness. In all cases, higher fitness has to be attributed, somewhat counter-intuitively, to the tendency of society to be dominated by extremely generous agents rather than by rationally reciprocal agents, as one might expect from the experimental setup. Moreover, for generosity to become prominent and visible, the society needs to start from initially rational settings rather than random or more natural ones. These findings are consistent across many interaction configurations. A final test on whether such initial proto-rationality may be selected by evolution and/or co-evolve with evolution of generosity shows that rationality in reciprocity has to pre-exist as infrastructure for this particular social context and therefore must be selected beforehand or in parallel for some other reason.

Keywords: Cooperation · Self-organization · Social learning · TFT · Pavlov · Generosity · Rationality · Reciprocity

1 Introduction

A major issue on the intersection of artificial life and theoretical biology is cooperative behavior between selfish agents. The cooperation problem states that each agent has a strong personal incentive to defect, while the joint best behavior would be to cooperate. This problem is traditionally modeled as a special two-party game, the Iterated Prisoner's Dilemma (IPD). At each cycle of a long interaction process, the agents play the Prisoner's Dilemma. Each of the two may either cooperate (C) or defect (D) and is assigned a payoff defined by the following table.

© Springer Nature Switzerland AG 2019
S. Cagnoni et al. (Eds.): WIVACE 2018, CCIS 900, pp. 57–71, 2019.
https://doi.org/10.1007/978-3-030-21733-4_5

Agent	Opponent	Payoff
C	C	3 (=Reward)
C	D	0 (=Sucker)
D	C	5 (=Temptation)
D	D	1 (=Punishment)

Usual experiments with IPD strategies are either tournaments or evolutionary experiments. In tournaments, each agent plays against all others and scores are summed in the end. In evolutionary experiments, populations of IPD agents play in tournaments and successive generations retain the best agents of the previous generation in proportions analogous to their score sums.

The first notable behavior for the IPD designed and studied by Axelrod [1, 2] is the Tit For Tat behavior (TFT, in short):

> *Start by cooperating,*
> *From there on return the opponent's previous move*

This behavior has achieved the highest scores in early tournaments and has been found to be fairly stable in evolutionary settings. TFT demonstrates three important properties, shared by most high scoring behaviors in IPD experiments.

- It is good (it starts by cooperating)
- It is retaliating (it returns the opponent's defection)
- It is forgiving (it forgets the past if the defecting opponent cooperates again)

Further agent strategies include stochastic ones [8], the Pavlov strategy [9] that cooperates when it has played the same move as its opponent, the Gradual strategy [3], recent ZD strategies [11] and others. In a rather thorough report [6] have systematically investigated IPD strategies with memory depth 1 and 2 and have come up with general conclusions and directives about what constitutes a successful IPD strategy. More theoretically, the issue of cooperation as studied through the IPD and other similar games has been revolving around the issues of direct reciprocity [15], kin selection, indirect reciprocity or punishment, group selection and how such mechanisms can evolve [4, 7].

In this paper we are interested in studying whether direct reciprocity can evolve from a minimal behavioral configuration that allows self-organization and social learning. Thus, we use a parametric TFT agent model that allows adaptation and learning of its continuous parameters and that can therefore lead to social self-organization.

2   Reference Model

We are studying a society of interacting adaptive agents in a modified continuous prisoner's dilemma context. In this setting, an agent is represented by a triplet (C, D, T) where $0 \leq C, D, T \leq 1$. These parameters are used to assess the opponent's move and respond to it, as follows:

IF (opponent output ≥ T)
THEN the opponent is considered **cooperative**,
in which case the agent responds with C
ELSE the opponent is considered **defective**
in which case the agent responds with D

So, this is a tit-for-tat-like agent model that we expect to react to cooperation with cooperation and to defection with defection. The objective is to study a society of heterogeneous such agents that adapt socially and to see what behaviors emerge. More specifically we are interested in understanding whether a common tit-for-tat norm emerges and what are the resulting values for C, D and T of the agents. Note here that the C and D parameters comprise the **execution or action part** of the agent that is directly visible and observable from the outside, i.e. by the other agents, and that constitutes the interaction medium between agents. The T parameter expresses the **assessment or evaluation part** of the agent and can be thought of as the personality or **emotional** component of the agent, since the evaluation of the same external signal may be very different across agents.

As a first reference experiment, we run societies of heterogeneous agents without any adaptation and record the final average scores per agent. We initialize all agents in society in one of three possible ways:

- A "**default**" mode: C random in (0.1, 1), D random in (0, C) and T random in (0, 1)
- A "**rational**" mode: C random in (0, 1), D random in (0, C) and T random in (D, C), and
- A **fully random** mode: C, D and T random in (0, 1) and uncorrelated

The different ways of initialization serve to identify whether different initial conditions for the society have an impact on the social trajectory taken later. The "rational" mode is actually a behaviorally consistent mode and expresses reciprocity, which is the only "rational" behavior in the usual IPD game, i.e. the behavior that can and should be displayed by each and every participant for the best social outcome (full cooperation) to emerge. Reciprocity means that if an opponent is considered cooperative by an agent, because its action exceeds T, it makes sense to respond cooperatively by the same standards, that is to respond with a value which also exceeds T, and accordingly for the D case. Rationality also functions as a self-evaluation metric: an agent should perceive as cooperative its cooperation move, and as defective its defection move. Although this view is by no means a full-fledged view of rationality for which open philosophical debates exist, it is a starting point for its study and follows the often-cited coherence criterion of rationality [10].

Unless otherwise stated, all results are taken by averaging 50 simulations of 50 agents that play with every other agent 100 rounds of the modified IPD for each one of 50 generations (or 2 generations in the absence of social adaptation). For ease of reference and consistency across the otherwise heterogeneous agents, the final external score for each round is taken with the usual IPD score matrix presented earlier, whereas in reality each agent responds differently to its opponents according to its C,D and T values.

	Score
Fully random	225
Default	201
Rational	237

As these results show, the default behavior of the population is clearly not cooperative and suboptimal, since the average scores are far from the theoretical cooperation score of 300 (=100 cycles x reward 3 per cycle). This is hardly surprising, since the agents both evaluate their opponents in a personalized manner (their thresholds T's differ) and act in a personalized manner too (their C's and D's also differ). Our study attempts to shed light on what happens when mechanisms of social adaptation and evolution are in place. Does the population become more cooperative, and if so, how and why?

3 Social Evolution

We have therefore designed social evolution experiments, where each generation round works as above and the passage from generation to generation happens as follows. Every agent A selects randomly another agent B in the population and compares their scores. If B's score in the previous round has been higher than A's, then A copies or imitates the behavior of B. We have investigated three different imitation modes or algorithms:

- A "**CD only**" mode: agent A copies agent B's C and D values, that is agent A imitates agent B's execution part
- A "**T only**" mode: agent A copies agent B's T value, that is agent A imitates agent B's evaluation part, and
- A "**CD and T**" mode: agent A copies agent B's C, D and T values, that is agent A imitates agent B's both evaluation and execution parts
- We also experiment with a uniform mix of algorithms, where about 1/3 of agents use each of the previous three modes

In all cases, there is a mutation probability (set to 5% in all our subsequent experiments), that an agent will adopt new random values for C, D, and T, according to the current initialization scheme of the population (default, rational or fully random, as presented in the previous section).

We immediately observe that the CD-only and, to a lesser degree, the CD-and-T modes incur improvements for the average population in terms of average score, but that this is not the case for the T-only mode, as Fig. 1 shows.

By closely inspecting the internals of the agents in the population, we observe that the relation between C,D and T values of an agent in the socially successful cases have on average evolved toward the "generosity" region, where $D \geq T$ (see Fig. 2). We thus run the experiments and record the proportions of "rational" and "generous" agents, that are the agents for which the relation $C > T > D$ or $C > D > T$ holds, respectively. For reference, we compare with the corresponding measures of the previous no evolution experiments, where the proportions of rational and generous agents did not change throughout the experiment since there was no adaptation (except for the small mutation).

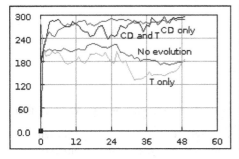
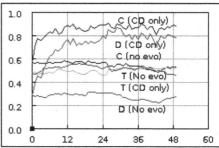

Fig. 1. (x-axis: time, y-axis: average score) Comparison between four experiments starting with the exact same population of "default" (C, D, T) agents and running for 50 generations: (a) without social evolution, (b) with CD only evolution, (c) with T only evolution, and (d) with CD and T evolution. The CD-only population achieves consistently the highest scores, with CD and T following with comparable but unstable scores, whereas the no evolution and the T-only case are remarkably lower. Notice that because of the mutation present in the system, the scores in the no evolution case also fluctuate from generation to generation, but the trends do not change.

Fig. 2. (x-axis: time, y-axis: average C,D,T) Evolution of average C, D and T in the population in the first and second of the experiments of Fig. 1. The CD-only population has on average very high C that is higher than average D, which is itself very high and higher than average T. The average T is about 0.5 in both populations, as expected since it is randomly drawn and does not change as a result of direct selection.

We obtain the following results:

FULLY RANDOM	**Score**	**Rational**	**Generous**
No evolution	225	18%	15%
CD only	**291**	12%	**64%**
T only	134	6%	6%
CD and T	248	15%	38%
Mix models	235	9%	27%

(continued)

(*continued*)

DEFAULT	Score	Rational	Generous
No evolution	201	28%	28%
CD only	**291**	31%	**60%**
T only	173	20%	19%
CD and T	287	49%	45%
Mix models	235	25%	39%

RATIONAL	Score	Rational	Generous
No evolution	237	100%	0%
CD only	**299**	34%	**66%**
T only	153	28%	8%
CD and T	299	44%	56%
Mix models	259	31%	48%

In all three cases (default, rational or fully random initialization), we observe that:

- CD-only achieves the highest average scores with CD and T closely following
- T-only achieves unacceptable average scores (even lower than the no-evolution case)
- For the evolutionarily most successful social case (CD-only) the proportion of generous agents is extremely high (over 60% even when the agents are born rational), while for the next best case (CD and T) the proportion of generous agents is still very high, significantly higher than the no-evolution case, and
- The unacceptable T-only case shows very low generosity levels compared to the no evolution case

These results can be conceptually summarized as follows:

- Imitation of the evaluation (or emotional) part of another agent is suboptimal. What works is imitation of another agent's execution part. Simply put, it does not pay to try to copy a more successful agent's **personal/emotional understanding** of a situation. What does possibly pay is to copy the agent's **actions**. There is an additional argument why this result seems reasonable: it is hard to deduce the other agent's threshold value T, while its actions C and D are directly observable (but even if T were visible, imitating it would not work).
- Social score rise goes hand in hand with generosity rise. Thus the schemes that do not allow individual generosity to flourish, do not allow the society to thrive either. This is a stronger result than some of the views in Okasha and Binmore [12] that claim that sometimes irrational responses can nevertheless function well socially, and
- For generosity to rise, the agents should be born what we called "rational" or natural punishers. And when they do (as well as, sometimes, when they don't), most of the agents end up "generous"

From the above, it is deduced that social evolution favors "CD only" imitation and rationality at birth. Before proceeding to examine whether these meta-behaviors could evolve, we run experiments at modified social settings to verify that our findings so far hold in a broader self-organizational perspective.

4 Networks

First, we run experiments with populations that do not run in tournaments (everyone with everyone else), but in networks, that is each agent is connected to a number of other agents with which it interacts and can socially imitate in every cycle. We have experimented with random networks where every agent is randomly connected to K other agents (K = 10, 20) and with small world networks where every agent is connected to its 6 closest neighbours and there are overall K random connections between non-neighbours in the network (K = 30, 50, 70).

We report below the results for the case of a random network with K=10, but the results are analogous in all the other networks studied. The basic findings of the fully connected society still hold: "CD only" and to a lesser degree "CD and T" are the best social imitation models, "T only" is suboptimal and high scores are correlated with high generosity.

FULLY RANDOM	Score	Rational	Generous
No evolution	223	17%	15%
CD only	**286**	13%	**51%**
T only	145	8%	3%
CD and T	241	21%	31%
Mix models	238	10%	27%
DEFAULT	Score	Rational	Generous
No evolution	199	28%	28%
CD only	**287**	33%	**55%**
T only	173	25%	17%
CD and T	278	51%	38%
Mix models	243	30%	39%
RATIONAL	Score	Rational	Generous
No evolution	239	100%	0%
CD only	**300**	41%	**56%**
T only	168	37%	8%
CD and T	297	56%	43%
Mix models	262	30%	48%

5 Other Interaction Schemes

Next, we run experiments with populations that run in networks as above, but either social imitation is possible outside of the network as well (panmictic imitation) or the network is reinitialized at each step. We have experimented with random and small world networks as in the previous section.

We report below the results for the case of a small world network with K = 30 and "panmictic" social imitation, but the results are analogous in all the other networks studied. The basic findings of the fully connected society still hold: "CD only" and to a lesser degree "CD and T" are the best social imitation models, "T only" is suboptimal and high scores are correlated with high generosity.

FULLY RANDOM	Score	Rational	Generous
No evolution	223	17%	15%
CD only	**292**	17%	**68%**
T only	133	6%	3%
CD and T	264	22%	35%
Mix models	230	16%	16%
DEFAULT	Score	Rational	Generous
No evolution	198	28%	28%
CD only	**293**	20%	**74%**
T only	171	23%	17%
CD and T	290	39%	56%
Mix models	221	26%	26%
RATIONAL	Score	Rational	Generous
No evolution	238	100%	0%
CD only	**297**	20%	**79%**
T only	152	32%	7%
CD and T	294	100%	0%
Mix models	241	59%	14%

We also report next the results for the case of a small world network with K = 30 and random encounters at each step, i.e. reinitialization of the network at each step. The results are analogous in all the other networks studied. The basic findings of the fully connected society once more hold: "CD only" and to a lesser degree "CD and T" are the best social imitation models, "T only" is suboptimal and high scores are correlated with high generosity.

FULLY RANDOM	Score	Rational	Generous
No evolution	225	17%	16%
CD only	**292**	19%	**69%**
T only	133	5%	3%
CD and T	260	33%	27%
Mix models	230	18%	16%
DEFAULT	Score	Rational	Generous
No evolution	206	26%	25%
CD only	**290**	25%	**70%**
T only	161	21%	15%
CD and T	282	35%	56%
Mix models	218	26%	26%

(*continued*)

(continued)

RATIONAL	Score	Rational	Generous
No evolution	236	81%	4%
CD only	**297**	15%	**85%**
T only	144	31%	5%
CD and T	293	100%	0%
Mix models	240	60%	13%

6   Pavlov-like Agents

We have also investigated the case of Pavlov-like rather than TFT-like agents that are based on the so-called Pavlov model of Nowak and Sigmund [9], are represented by a vector of five parameters (CC, CD, DC, DD, T) and function as follows:

> **IF (opponent output ≥ T)**
> **THEN** the opponent is considered **cooperative (Coop)**,
> **ELSE** the opponent is considered **defective (Def)**
>
> **IF (self output ≥ T)**
> **THEN** self is considered **cooperative (Coop)**,
> **ELSE** self is considered **defective (Def)**
>
> **IF (self is Coop) AND (opponent is Coop)**
> the agent responds with CC
> **IF (self is Def) AND (opponent is Def)**
> the agent responds with DD
> **IF (self is Coop) AND (opponent is Def)**
> the agent responds with CD
> **IF (self is Def) AND (opponent is Coop)**
> the agent responds with DC

Nowak and Sigmund [9] have concluded that an agent has to respond cooperatively to the CC and DD cases (the pair stands for the last moves of self and opponent) and defectively in the CD and DC cases. Thus, the rationality or behavioral consistency criterion in this case is whether CC, DD > CD, DC. The generosity criterion is whether DD>CC, which is an unusual relation between CC and DD from an everyday behavioral perspective. In this case, CD imitation is translated as copying of all four action values of the agents, namely CC, CD, DC and DD. The results are as follows:

FULLY RANDOM	Score	DD > CC	CC > T
No evolution	260	49%	51%
CD only	259	77%	28%
T only	236	51%	48%
CD and T	**278**	**73%**	37%
Mix models	256	55%	46%
DEFAULT	Score	DD > CC	CC > T
No evolution	267	50%	56%
CD only	271	79%	39%
T only	257	48%	68%
CD and T	**280**	**64%**	54%
Mix models	266	57%	54%
RATIONAL	Score	DD > CC	CC > T
No evolution	273	48%	100%
CD only	293	42%	45%
T only	254	50%	75%
CD and T	**296**	**53%**	100%
Mix models	265	54%	72%

These are analogous to the results with the TFT-like model, with social success going hand in hand with rise of generosity, failure of the T-only imitation mode and CD-only, CD-and-T the successful imitation models. However, in this case the CD-and-T model is slightly superior than the CD-only model, and this ought to be attributed to the different function of T in this case, compared to the TFT model: here the question is whether two agents are on the same side of T or not and not on whether a particular opponent action is above or below T.

7 Perturbations

In an additional attempt to become sure about the direction of social evolution, we have performed perturbation experiments with regular TFT-like agents, where after populations have stabilized (after 50 generations) we inject 5 fully random agents and let the new population run again for another 50 generations and re-stabilize. We take the same measures as before, but this time we take them twice, in the end of the two phases, that is just before perturbation and after re-stabilization. As the results of the following table show, after perturbation and re-stabilization we obtain slightly higher scores and higher generosity levels than before perturbation, except for the case of initially rational agents where scores are already too high and generosity levels rather stable. Notice that all numbers are slightly lower than in the reference table of Sect. 3, because we have used an 80% probability of social imitation so as to slow down evolution and be able to better observe its trend.

FULLY RANDOM	Score	Rational	Generous
CD only	**274**	20%	**42%**
	284	22%	**48%**
T only	167	12%	6%
	157	10%	4%
CD and T	233	18%	27%
	238	20%	29%
Mix models	237	14%	25%
	236	12%	24%
DEFAULT	Score	Rational	Generous
CD only	**280**	40%	**44%**
	287	38%	**48%**
T only	193	30%	21%
	184	28%	18%
CD and T	268	45%	37%
	283	50%	40%
Mix models	240	33%	32%
	240	29%	35%
RATIONAL	Score	Rational	Generous
CD only	**296**	54%	**42%**
	295	4%	**46%**
T only	179	42%	11%
	183	38%	13%
CD and T	295	71%	27%
	289	63%	30%
Mix models	261	45%	36%
	265	37%	**43%**

We interpret these results as showing that the rise of generosity is an adaptive change in the long-term and as such it is favored by population level perturbations. Therefore, the trend of evolution is toward generosity rise when selection acts on social score. This trend may not be visible if the system is too slow for any reason (speed can be modeled via a lower imitation probability, as above), but the only thing that evolution can discover is generosity.

8   Imitation Gene

We have seen so far that a population with the possibility to self-organize through social imitation becomes on average more cooperative and achieves higher social fitness levels when imitation concerns the CD part or the whole of behavior, and not the assessment or T part alone.

We now proceed to investigate whether an imitation "gene" with alleles for each of the imitation modes (CD only, T only, CD and T) would work in the same social context and whether it would allow the functional values of the imitation mode to be selected.

We run our experiments as before, but now on completion of each evolutionary round, an agent imitates another randomly selected agent if the latter is more successful and also copies its imitation mode. As the results below show, in all cases the populations achieve higher scores than without evolution, but a little lower than without an imitation gene (with a fixed, non evolvable imitation mode), generosity rises and the T-only allele practically disappears (the whole population consists almost exclusively of CD-only and CD-and-T agents). The populations with rational initialization show a rather particular evolution, with rational agents prevailing in the end. Overall, we may say that an imitation gene, if it emerges, may indeed lead to selection of the appropriate imitation mode(s), as was predicted by our earlier analysis.

FULLY RANDOM	Score	Rational/Generous	CD only/CD and T
No evolution	235	9%, 27%	33%, 33%
Evolution	252	20%, 44%	34%, 50%
DEFAULT	Score	Rational/Generous	CD only/CD and T
No evolution	235	25%, 39%	33%, 33%
Evolution	283	27%, 64%	56%, 36%
RATIONAL	Score	Rational/Generous	CD only/CD and T
No evolution	259	31%, 48%	33%, 33%
Evolution	290	69%, 29%	34%, 62%

9 Initialization Gene

We finally examine in the same way the case of an initialization "gene" with alleles for each of the initialization modes (default, rational, fully random). We add a fourth initialization mode, the "natural" initialization where with 60% probability an agent is initialized as rational, otherwise as fully random. This last mode captures the evident observation of everyday life that the majority of a population conforms to a rational norm but there exist significant diversions of all kinds.

We run our experiments as before, but now on completion of each evolutionary round, an agent imitates another randomly selected agent if the latter is more successful and also copies its initialization mode. As the results below show, in all cases the presence of an initialization gene mix in the population combined with the appropriate imitation mode (CD only or CD and T) leads to fairly high scores that cannot really be further improved by selection on the initialization gene, although a slight trend toward higher percentages of the rational and the natural gene is to be observed. The T-only case is suboptimal as in all the previous cases and the final generosity of the population has a slightly downward trend, still remaining very high, however. These results suggest that the "rational" initialization gene would not be selected once the imitation gene were already in place and would not be selected in the absence of imitation because then the scores are consistently too low and do not allow evolution. But, as the last table below shows, there is a possibility that rational initialization can be promoted by evolution if the imitation and the initialization genes co-evolve, which is implemented as agents copying after a round a more successful agent's imitation gene or its initialization gene with equal probabilities. Thus, it seems that evolutionary selection can account for the preservation and promotion of rationality, as is defined in our experimental context, but cannot account for its appearance - this very issue is sometimes discussed in the biological literature [5].

CD ONLY	Score	Rational/Generous	Rat. gene/Nat. gene/ Def. gene
No evolution	292	18%, 76%	25%, 25%, 25%
Evolution	293	20%, 74%	26%, 30%, 26%
T ONLY	Score	Rational/Generous	Rat. gene/Nat. gene/ Def. gene
No evolution	180	26%, 21%	25%, 25%, 25%
Evolution	165	19%, 7%	4%, 26%, 4%
CD AND T	Score	Rational/Generous	Rat. gene/Nat. gene/ Def. gene
No evolution	289	65%, 30%	25%, 25%, 25%
Evolution	291	71%, 23%	34%, 30%, 10%
Imi OR Init gene	Score	Rational/Generous/ CD/CD & T	Rat. gene/Nat. gene/ Def. gene
No evolution	242	23%, 46%, 33%, 33%	25%, 25%, 25%
Evolution	290	60%, 33%, 17%, 83%	29%, 31%, 16%

10 Discussion

We have studied a population of self-organizing agents that play complete tournaments of an IPD game and whose behavior is defined by a number of continuous parameters that are allowed to evolve socially with the aid of an appropriate imitation mechanism. The behavioral space is meant to include the usual reciprocal tit-for-tat-like behavior that we would expect to evolve in principle. Social evolution can take many forms. We have shown that imitation of the evaluation or emotional component is suboptimal and would be wiped out by evolution, while the functional imitation mechanism is the one that takes into account only the actions of agents, that is the visible part of their behavior. It is no surprise then that mechanisms that can lead to higher individual performance by remaining invisible to the outside are so efficient weapons for the agents (these are mechanisms such are ruse, manipulation etc.).

Now, rather astonishingly, the expected reciprocal behavior does not emerge from social evolution as defined. What emerges evolutionarily instead is a highly generous population profile, where agents prefer to be significantly forgiving and generous toward defective partners. Apparently, this profile is both socially optimal and easy to discover, although it remains locally vulnerable to free riders, as is well known from the general literature. These results are also obtained in many different interaction setups, and most notably in network instead of tournament interactions and in a different behavioral space where we would expect a Pavlov-like behavior to emerge. In all cases, the resulting social profile is highly generous.

These conclusions have been found to depend also rather crucially on the parameter initialization for agent behaviors: when agents are born rational, the society can evolve to become cooperative in which case the agents become generous. We have further conducted social meta-evolution studies to confirm that the right social imitation mechanism and the right behavioral initialization mechanism would evolve, were they able to be represented genetically. There the results are mixed: the social imitation mechanism can prevail evolutionarily, provided that appropriate alleles can appear and be acted upon by the actual evolutionary process, whereas the behavioral initialization mechanism (the "rational" gene) has only a limited contribution to final fitness and is thus hard to discover evolutionarily in this context.

Our understanding of the last results is that rationality in behavioral initialization is a property that has to pre-exist for successful social evolution to happen and should therefore have evolved independently and for some other reason. We believe that self-monitoring, as a precursor of general mind reading, might be a good reason to develop the kind of rational behavioral consistency necessary for evolution of more complex social behaviors and this is an avenue of research we plan to take next. This idea is inscribed in a social behavioral approach and loosely reflects the perspective of rationality as an ecological concept [14], not necessarily tied to or leading to intelligent behavior and efficiency [13].

References

1. Axelrod, R.: The Evolution of Cooperation. Basic Books, New York (1984)
2. Axelrod, R., Hamilton, W.D.: The evolution of cooperation. Science **211**, 1390–1396 (1981)
3. Beaufils, B., Delahaye, J.-P., Mathieu, P.: Our meeting with gradual: a good strategy for the iterated prisoner's dilemma. In: Proceedings of the Artificial Life V Conference, Nara, Japan (1996)
4. Gintis, H.: The Bounds of Reason: Game Theory and the Unification of the Behavioral Sciences. Princeton University Press, Princeton (2009)
5. Khalil, E.: Survival of the most foolish of fools: the limits of evolutionary selection theory. J. Bioecon. **2**, 203–220 (2000)
6. Mathieu, P., Delahaye, J.-P.: New winning strategies for the iterated Prisoner's Dilemma. J. Artif. Soc. Soc. Simul. **20**(4), 12 (2017)
7. Nowak, M.: Five rules for the evolution of cooperation. Science **314**, 1560–1563 (2006)
8. Nowak, M., Sigmund, K.: Tit for tat in heterogeneous populations. Nature **355**, 250–253 (1992)
9. Nowak, M., Sigmund, K.: A strategy of win-stay, lose-shift that outperforms tit-for-tat in the prisoner's dilemma game. Nature **364**, 56–58 (1993)
10. Polonioli, A.: Evolution, rationality and coherence criteria. Biol. Theory **9**, 309–317 (2014)

11. Press, W.H., Dyson, F.J.: Iterated prisoner's dilemma contains strategies that dominate any evolutionary opponent. Proc. Natl. Acad. Sci. **109**(26), 10409–10413 (2012)
12. Okasha, S., Binmore, K. (eds.): Evolution and Rationality: Decisions, Co-operation and Strategic Behavior. Cambridge University Press, Cambridge (2012)
13. Stanovich, K.E.: Rationality and the Reflective Mind. Oxford University Press, Oxford (2011)
14. Todd, P.M., Gigenenzer, G., ABC Research Group: Ecological Rationality Intelligence in the World, Oxford University Press, Oxford (2012)
15. Trivers, R.: The evolution of reciprocal altruism. Q. Rev. Biol. **46**(4), 35–57 (1971)

Unveiling Latent Relations in the Photonics Techno-Economic Complex System

Sofia Samoili[1,2](✉) ⓘ, Riccardo Righi[1,2] ⓘ, Montserrat Lopez-Cobo[1,2] ⓘ,
Melisande Cardona[1,2] ⓘ, and Giuditta De Prato[1,2] ⓘ

[1] European Commission, Joint Research Centre (JRC), Seville, Spain
{sofia.samoili,riccardo.righi,montserrat.lopez-cobo,
melisande.cardona,giuditta.de-prato}@ec.europa.eu
[2] Edificio EXPO, Calle Inca Garcilaso, 3, 41092 Seville, Spain

Abstract. The aim of this study is to capture a technology's pathway by identifying emerging subdomains in a complex system of economic processes. The objective is to uncover indirect latent relations among agents interacting in a specific techno-economic segment (TES). A methodology, including an "Extract-Transform-Load" (ETL) process preceding the two steps aimed for analysis, is developed to analyse a TES regarding R&D economic processes of the photonics technology. In the first step, economic relevant R&D activities (EU funded projects and patents) are analysed through a multilayer network (MLN) of agents, considering their interactions in three dimensions, which represent occurred and latent relationships: co-participations in economic activities, common geographical location provenance, common use of technological terms. Then communities are detected (Infomap Algorithm for MLN), and their ongoing within and between connections are studied, as potential factors that affect the entire structured technological ecosystem. In the second step, technological subdomains associated with method-oriented and application-oriented activities are identified through topic modelling. Using the MLN structure, the textual information of the corpus of documents describing the aforementioned economic R&D activities is associated to agents, and the topic model (Latent Dirichlet Allocation) uncovers additional potential semantic connections among them. Subsequently, the results of the MLN community detection and of the topic modelling based on the descriptions of economic activities are considered. Hence, the latent relations of agents are mapped.

Keywords: Agent-artefact space · Complex networks ·
Bottom-up meso-structures · Community detection · Topic modelling ·
Semantic analysis · Natural language processing

Disclaimer: The views expressed are purely those of the author and may not in any circumstances be regarded as stating an official position of the European Commission.

S. Cagnoni et al. (Eds.): WIVACE 2018, CCIS 900, pp. 72–90, 2019.
https://doi.org/10.1007/978-3-030-21733-4_6

1   Introduction

In order to follow the evolution of economic productive activities, R&D processes of economic production were investigated in the beginning of 90's [13, 15, 23], particularly by focusing in information and interactions circulation among agents (people, enterprises and institutions). While the main objective of this literature was to study the ability of expansion of national economic systems, the introduction of such approach fostered the analysis of the interactive dynamics that characterise the bottom-up development of these processes at a micro-scale [15, 28] and at a meso-scale of analysis [6, 24, 30]. Network dynamics and technology development research invoked institutional policy makers' consideration to also assess these relations.

In the prospect of comprehending interactive dynamics able to unleash the emergence of bottom-up meso-structures, the development of the techno-economic segment (hereinafter TES) analytical approach aims to analyse specific techno-economic interconnected systems and describing their dynamics [29]. Targeting also non-official heterogeneous data sources, and studying the complex underlying worldwide networks of agents, locations and technologies, TES refers to largely integrated technological (and non-technological) domains in the ICT industry that usually do not correspond to industrial or products classification. To this scope, an integrated method is developed and presented here for the R&D only part of the interconnected system, with the following stages. The flowchart of the methodological approach is presented in Fig. 1.

A. **ETL process:** "Extract-Transform-Load" (ETL) for data collection related to a specific technology, data preprocess, and keyword extraction to reduce text dimensionality
B. **Network structure:** multilayer three-level network development for unveiling latent relationships based on apparent relationships
C. **Community detection:** for analysis of strongly interacting groups of agents,
D. **Topic modelling:** for technological areas' identification, evolution, and semantic analysis.

The present first TES analysis covers the photonics industrial segment. Photonics is identified as one of the six important Key Enabling Technologies (KETs) for Europe's competitiveness [9, 34]. The technological domain of Photonics covers computational methods and applications regarding the light generation, detection and management. The methods include conversion of sunlight to electricity for renewable energy production, and the applications vary among photodiodes, LEDs, lasers and other electronic components and equipment used from a plethora of fields as ICT, life sciences, industrial manufacturing, etc. [34].

In the following sections only the stages aimed for analysis will be presented, namely stages B and C as the first analytical step, and stage D for the second step. In *Step 1* of the analysis (B and C stages), economic relevant R&D activities (EU funded projects and patents) are analysed. As the acknowledged innovation theory addresses interactions as a critical factor in the exaptation process, hence

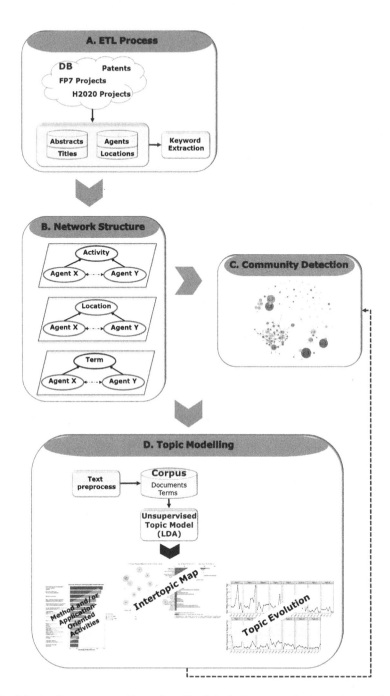

Fig. 1. Schematic representation of methodological approach to capture a technology's pathway. The dashed line illustrates the perspective semantic analysis within the resulted communities.

in the evolution of the agent-artefact space [20–22], a network of agents is created among them. The first dimension of the network represents (a) the interactions occurred among agents through co-participations in specific type of economic activities. Then, in order to address and represent latent relationships, a second dimension regarding (b) the geographical proximity and another one regarding (c) the use of similar technological elements, are added to the network. The three dimensions are selected so as to include the three aspects that in certain works on socio-economic complex systems [21,26] and on bio-chemical complex systems [3] are discussed as relevant in the process of the bottom-up meso-structures' formation. Correspondingly, these aspects are: (a) *activity/metabolism*, (b) *proximity/localization* and (c) *functional behaviour/information*[1]. In order to inquire the aforementioned dimensions and uncover key agents and activities, a multi-layer network (MLN) is formed, in which each layer represents one of the aforementioned dimensions[2]. Then, to identify groups of agents that, due to proximity in three dimensions, are more probable to interact intensively, the Infomap Algorithm for MLN is implemented [11]. Communities are so mapped, therefore indicating ongoing interactions within and, by means of the resulting overlaps, also between the detected groups.

In *Step 2* of the analysis (stage D), the captured dynamics are further studied, as they represent potential factors that affect the entire interconnected system. In order to unveil technological subdomains with method-oriented and application-oriented activities, a semantic analysis of the techno-economic research field of photonics is pursued. The textual information of the corpus of documents describing the aforementioned economic R&D activities that are identified and used in the previous step, are considered to structure the MLN. Topic modelling is implemented, so as to unveil technological subdomains associated with methods (e.g. chemistry) and implementations (e.g. photonic devices), that would subsequently reveal potential semantic connections among the agents. Topics are essentially summaries of the most pertinent themes of the large collection of documents. So they are used to communicate rapidly the subjects on which the agents are working. Agents grouped into the same topic do not necessarily collaborate. However, the fact that they are found active in the same topic indicates a potential aspirant collaborative relationship, or a competitive relationship. Both kinds of relationships foster innovation and suggest vibrant innovation processes, and hence prospective compelling technological sub-areas. A generative three-level hierarchical Bayesian model is employed to identify the topics that are generated based on the collected documents, namely the Latent Dirichlet Allocation (LDA). Therefore, the knowledge of a technological domain, which was only a property of experts, is approximated through this statistical, hence unbiased, method that extracts the documents' thematic content as top-

---

[1] In this context, the concept of "functional behaviour/information" is referred to agents' individual technological orientation.

[2] The layers of network can be considered one at a time to compute statistical indices and rankings of agents and activities/locations/technological terms. This part, at the moment, is out of the scope of the work.

ics [32]. A topic is a probability distribution of terms, which occurs from the underlying semantic structure of terms found in documents [4,25,32]. Each document is composed by one or several topics, with the latter being a combination of terms from several documents. This bag-of-words assumption is common to natural language statistical models [1,4,32]. Latent connections between agents are thence uncovered, as part of the natural language processing analysis. The implementation of the model is tested on the techno-economic research field of photonics with worldwide activities.

The methodological background of the network structure and community detection, and of the topic modelling will be further analysed in Subsects. 2.1 and 2.2 respectively. Subsequently, the results of the two-step analysis are presented in Sect. 3. With this last part it is possible to further investigate the co-appeareance of agents and activities in topological groups, and the presence similar content in topic groups. These patterns can subsequently provide indications for the evolution of the technology. In conclusion, the presented multidimensional methodology enables the interpretation of the occurred latent relationships of the agents and their interactions.

2   Methodological Background

2.1   *Step 1*: Multilayer Network Structure and Community Detection

The set of considered economic agents is structured based on two of the worldwide most important activities of developments in productive processes. The first type of considered activities are participations in European Projects (FP7 and H2020), while the second is patent applications. The first embodies the concept of R&D processes, i.e. qualitatively new economic processes of production. The second type addresses differently R&D processes, since the included actions fix technological combinations that may not be yet formally established. After considering these two activities, the focus is set to those involved in the field of photonics. In this way, the set of agents that develop activities regarding the evolution of photonic-related technologies, is identified. Following the aim of the present study, the introduced approach focuses on interactions and information exchanges that form a network populated by identified agents. Economic agents are represented as nodes of the network, and a multidimensional space of relationships is modeled by placing different types of connections in different layers of the MLN. From a conceptual point of view, the following conjectures are established in order to justify the consideration of (i) co-participations in economic activities (first layer), (ii) common geographical location provenance (second layer), and (iii) common use of technological terms (third layer).

The first conjecture is made in order to capture relationships really occurred among agents. The hypothesis is that agents, by co-participating in a same activity (i.e. one project in FP7, or H2020, or Patent), exchange relevant information among them. Therefore, when co-participations occur, involved agents are considered as being connected. Since the analysis aims to capture the structure of interactions for technological development, the dimension regarding information exchange necessarily represents the starting point of this work. This is the first network layer that is defined.

The second essential considered dimension addresses geographical information, as agents can establish deep connections with the place where they locate their activities. More precisely, common socio-economic habits/traditions and economic processes' integration can emerge among agents rooted in a same geographic area. This phenomenon, which favours the flourishing of fruitful and innovative interactions, is identified in economic literature with the concept of 'industrial district' [2,7]. Therefore, connections are established when agents are located in the same region (one granularity level under the national level). The second dimension of the analysis is so justified, and the second layer of network is then structured.

The third dimension is conceptualised based on the conjecture that agents, moving towards the development of specific technological field, endorse the use of specific technology-related terms. As R&D activities are here considered, the relevant terms extracted from these activities' description[3] are used to investigate the presence of agents' convergent paths/semantic proximity in terms of their technological developments [10,12,17]. Therefore, a connection is established among all the agents using a same term (regardless the activity). This last dimension, aimed at investigating agents' qualitative orientations, is represented by the third layer of the MLN.

Agents' interactions in three different dimensions are so represented by means of a MLN with three different layers in which the agents endorse the described types of interactions. Three additional points regarding the structure of the MLN. First of all, while initially each layer is set as a bipartite network, with agents (*first-type* node) connected to other nodes (*second-type*) whose nature depends on the layer[4], then each layer is transformed in its one-mode projection based on the *first-type* of nodes, i.e. agents. Therefore, in the final MLN only 'agents-to-agents' connections are present. Secondly, all the connections are undirected and their weight is computed on the basis of the number of shared *second-type* nodes[5]. Finally, inter-layers connections are added to the connections considered until now (i.e. intra-layer connections). Therefore, the three 'state-nodes' of agent X, i.e. X_a and X_b and X_c where a and b and c indicate the layers, are always connected [11].

After having structured the MLN, the Infomap community detection algorithm for MLN is implemented [11]. This algorithm uses a two-level binary description based on Huffman coding and on MapEquation [14,18,27] and its

---

[3] Terms are extracted from EU funded projects' abstracts and from patent applications' descriptions.

[4] In the first layer, the types of nodes are "agents" and "activities"; in the second layer, "agents" and "locations"; in the third layer, 'agents' and 'technological terms'.

[5] For example, if agents X and Y (*first-type* nodes) co-participate in 3 activities (*second-type* nodes), the weight of the edge $\overline{XY}$ equals 3. In the second layer the weights are all equal as agents can have one and only one location.

implementation in socio-economic complex-networks is discussed in [26]. As this algorithm minimises the length of the description of a random flow that circulates throughout the considered network, the resulting communities can be interpreted as groups of agents with intense information exchange. Regarding the settings of its implementation, in order to balance the weights of the three layers, a principle regarding the density of the layers is here taken into account. More specifically, for each layer the ratio between (i) the density of the most dense layer and (ii) its density[6] is used as a multiplication factor for the weight of each connection belonging to that layer. In addition, Infomap algorithm is set to detect overlapping communities, i.e. agents can belong to more than one community. As a consequence, an interconnected structure of communities can emerge.

2.2   *Step 2*: Topic Modelling

An emerging technology may trigger interactions across several technological fields and geographical locations. Moreover, agents' spatial and economic process-related relations convey heterogeneous characteristics to the agents, which may be direct or indirect. The transversal distribution of direct or latent interactions, jointly with the heterogeneous profiles of agents, raises the issue of how to effectively detect the complex network of a technology, the technological subdomains, and most importantly the evolution of an emerging technology.

The convergence to a common use of a set of terms in order to communicate, creates a thematic group or topic. The agents using this topic adopt a common language to communicate and exchange information [10,17], and this creates topic relations. Thence, the topic relations can be directly apparent, when the agents collaborate to an activity and use a common set of terms to communicate, or else a topic.

The topological relations in conjunction to the topic relations of a complex network's structure, is a subject that has not been thoroughly studied. Relevant literature presents various methods and reports reasonable performance [12,35]. This final part of the suggested approach aims to associate and interpret all the aforementioned information, so as to render comprehensive information on innovative technological pathways that will allow policy makers and R&D managers to make timely and effective decisions. In order to capture the pathway of the technology, its subdomains should be identified, to assess their persistence, disappearance or emergence through interdisciplinary activities. To this end, the thematic content of the research and patenting activities that represent the interconnected system's development is considered through topic modelling.

The technology's subdomains are approached as topics, based on a number of documents that represent the activities performed by a technology. This conjecture is drawn from the idea that every collected activity, hence document, has one or multiple thematic subjects. To have an overview of the most salient thematic

---

[6] In an undirected graph the density is defined as the number of connections divided by $N \cdot \frac{N-1}{2}$, where N is the number of nodes.

subjects of all the documents, these subjects should be grouped and provide the most pertinent topics of the entire collection of documents. Previously, in order to define the topics of the corpus that the documents form for technology mining, so with real-world corpora, expert assessment was invoked, which moreover requires a further refinement of the analysis [8]. To avoid this subjective approach, a generative hierarchical Bayesian mixed-membership model for discrete data is employed, to identify the topics that are generated based on the collected documents, namely the Latent Dirichlet Allocation (LDA) [5,19]. The assertion is that based on the co-occurrence of terms - the probability distribution of terms - in a document, one or multiple topics are formed. The LDA model, as a mixed-membership model, returns the most probable topics from each document, and then from the entire corpus. So each document may be consisted of a mixture of topics, as the model allows to a document to belong to several topics simultaneously, which happens also in real-world. Respectively, a topic is a mixture of terms from several documents [4,25,32]. Accordingly, the hypotheses that are made are the following:

- A technology is approximated by a number of collected activities, which is assumed to be representative of the complex network of this technology.
- Each detected activity (patent, project) is represented by a document.
- Each document is represented by a set of terms (or else words, hereinafter interchangeably used).
- A mixture of terms creates a topic, regardless the document to which it belongs.
- A term may be assigned to one or more topics. This non-exclusive assignment of a term to a topic is sustained by the observation that in a natural language words do not belong to one topic only.
- The order of terms in a document and the order of documents in a corpus are disregarded (exchangeability assumption) [1,5,32]. So each document may be a mixture of topics, which are mixtures of words (bag-of-word-assumption) [5,32].
- Each topic represents a combination of subdomains or one subdomain of the technology.

Probabilistic Generative Model Notation. To formalise the aforementioned, let the basic unit be a term, or word w, which is an element of dictionary, namely unique words, $W = \{w_1, ..., w_V\}$. A document, which is a sequence of words, is denoted by $d = \{d_1, d_2, ..., d_N\}$. A corpus, which is a set of documents, is denoted by $D = \{d_1^1, d_2^2, ..., d_N^M\}$. The generative process for each document in a corpus provided by the LDA model, is outlined in the seminal article of Blei et al. [5].

Since a topic model assumes a latent structure to approach the entirety of set of words as a computable distribution over K topics, to identify the topic distribution of the corpus and the words assigned to each topic, the learning process of the LDA is then implemented. More specifically, for a topic index k, the goal is to compute the word-topic distribution $P(w|k)$, namely the most important words w of a topic k, and the topic-document distribution $P(k|d)$, namely the prevailing topics of a document, so as to eventually converge to a robust set of topics in the corpus and compute the $P(k|w)$. Analytically, $P(w|k)$ is the probability of a word w_i assigned to a topic $k_i = j$, represented by a set of multinomial distributions ϕ over the W dictionary of words, so that $P(w_i|k_i = j) = \phi_w^j$. Accordingly, $P(k)$ is the probability distribution of topics within a document d, represented by a set of multinomial distributions θ over the K topics, so that a w in d is assigned to topic $k_i = j$, based on $P(k = j) = \theta_j^d$.

However, to define in a corpus the probabilities of word instances per topic, and the set of topics, involves enumerating a very large discrete state space and compute a probability distribution ($P(k|w)$) on that space, which requires the computation of $P(w|k)$, through ϕ and θ. So ϕ and θ will be estimated through LDA and prior probability distributions, or else priors. Let α and β be the parameters of the priors, called hyperparameters, each of them having a single value. The Dirichlet priors are conjugate priors to the multinomial distribution. Namely, as the prior distributions of the multinomial parameters are Dirichlet, respectively Dirichlet will be the posterior distributions $\phi \sim Dirichlet(\alpha)$ and $\theta \sim Dirichlet(\beta)$, which renders possible the computation of the joint distribution $P(w, k) = P(w|k) \cdot P(k)$ through integration of ϕ and θ separately. The integration of ϕ results to the computation of $P(w|k)$, and of θ to the $P(k)$.

The evaluation of the posterior distribution $P(k|w) = \frac{P(w,k)}{\sum_k P(w,k)}$ has to be indirectly computed, as the denominator creates a state space too large to enumerate, through sampling from the target distribution with Markov Chain Monte Carlo (MCMC) [16,32]. The target distribution is approximated by a Markov chain, and then samples are selected from this chain through Gibbs sampling, which does not require tuning. All the conditional distributions of the target distribution are sampled and a sequence of observations used to approximate the latent variables of the LDA is returned. So finally, for each sample among the set of samples from the predicted $P(k|w)$ posterior distribution of words as mixtures of topics, the ϕ and θ can be estimated [16].

Topic Distances and Visualisation. Interdisciplinarity and relevance of the ensued technology-related topics is subsequently pursued, based on inter-topic distances. The hypothesis is that if two topics appear close in distance and their topic content is not thematically relevant, this points to a potential emergence of a new subdomain from the activities of these subdomains in a subsequent time period. The relevance of the topics is computed through a weight parameter, the topic prevalence with Principal Components Analysis (PCA), and the inter-topic distances with Jensen-Shannon divergence. The interdisciplinarity aspect points to potential generation of new subdomains in a subsequent time period, based on the common use of terms from co-participation to activities subdomains that were assigned together to a topic.

Let the *relevance metric* be the relevance of a term w to topic k given a weight parameter λ. This weight parameter determines the weight given to the probability of a term under a topic relative to its lift, on a log scale. It is computed as the ratio of a term's probability within a topic to its marginal probability within the corpus. A lift of $\lambda = 1$ results in a ranking of terms according to their topic-specific probability, and lift of $\lambda = 0$ to a ranking solely according to their lift. The lift parameter decreases the appearance of globally (in the corpus) frequent terms in high ranking places. However, rare terms that occur to very few or a single topic could appear in high rankings, decreasing the interpretability of a topic if the term is very rare [31,33].

3   Results and Discussion

Communities. The identification of cohesive groups of agents, namely communities, may assist in recognising recursive elements regarding agents' interactions and to shape and design policy interventions targeted to specific interest groups. The resulting communities are formed by agents more likely to share information in any of the three considered dimensions: activity, location and technology. After the analysis of Infomap output, communities $c.1$ and $c.2$ have been removed from the analysis as they were grouping together all the players participating in EU projects $(c.1)$, and all the patenting players $(c.2)$. Some descriptive statistics regarding the detected communities are presented in the Appendix A. Through the identity of the agents in each community, the community's profile is explored. In addition, the information regarding the structure of communities, i.e. how communities generate a structured network by having agents in common, is considered. Figure 2 immediately reveals which communities are the most connected and with which ones they share agents. Further analysis would entail the identification of the technological subdomains in which the communities are involved.

The community detection analysis in the multilayer network of R&D in photonics reveals the presence of over one hundred communities. Many communities are isolated, as their agents are not involved in other communities. This is the case of a large set of very small communities made of agents that patented alone, or that participated in few EU projects with low number of participants. When the communities' structure is observed from a country perspective, some elements emerge. While Japanese agents are mainly grouped just in community $c.3$, Chinese agents populate four large communities, namely $c.4$, $c.5$, $c.7$ and $c.10$. Two of them $(c.5$ and $c.7)$ are connected (as they have agents in common), while the remaining ones are independent. The connection involving $c.5$ and $c.7$ reveals the presence of collaborations or technological convergence between the agents of these two communities. On the opposite, $c.4$ and $c.10$ do not have relevant convergences with other large communities and they have only smaller neighbouring communities. Therefore, the two countries with the highest propensity to develop patents show two community structures that are very different from each other. The intertwined single structure made of multiple communities observed in Fig. 2 is mainly populated by European agents. The communities reveal the presence of supra national patterns involving in different ways the countries of the Union. Some of these communities are mainly dominated by agents in a single country, e.g. $c.6$ (almost all in France), $c.13$ (the majority in United Kingdom), $c.22$ and $c.24$ (the majority of agents in Germany). Then,

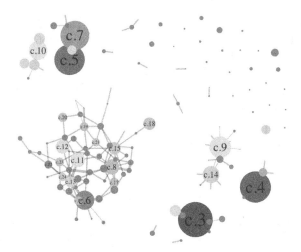

Fig. 2. Structure of Photonics communities of agents detected by Infomap algorithm, in a Fruchterman-Reingold force-based layout. The largest components and some isolated communities are here presented. Each node represents a group of agents, i.e. a community. The size of the nodes is proportional to the number of agents belonging to the communities. The labels indicate the 24 most relevant communities (by amount of Infomap flow). Communities *c.1* and *c.2* have been removed from the analysis as they were grouping together all the players participating in EU projects (*c.1*), and all the patenting players (*c.2*). The width of the links is proportional the number of agents simultaneously belonging to the two communities involved.

there are many heterogeneous communities composed by agents from different countries. Some of them are mainly made of agents from two countries, like *c.8*, which includes nine agents from Germany and seven from Italy, *c.17*, which includes six agents from Germany and six from Italy, and *c.12*, which includes seven agents from United Kingdom and six from Italy. Some communities present a larger mix, as they include agents from many different countries. This is the case of *c.11*, a medium size community whose 21 agents participated in 14 FP7 projects, 5 H2020 projects and in 1 patent.

Topic Identification. Another potential grouping of agents is examined assuming that as the technological subdomains do not operate exclusively one from another, considering that they may exchange applications and methods, they present relationships that may create thematic topics. These topics ensuing from interdisciplinary combinations of the subdomains of the technology's system, are targeted to be identified with the topic modelling. Some of the subdomains that are found within one or more topics are for instance: fiber optics and waveguides, photonic devices, optical materials, light pulses, etc (see Fig. 3 and Appendix B). The potential overlap of topics sharing subdomains is studied with the thematic distance between the topics. This analysis provides insights about plausible emergence of new specialised topics, or about possible combinations of several topics into a single one due to the application of common methods.

Fifteen topics are identified in the photonics technological landscape over the period 2008 to 2016. The topics are mapped in an interactive representation based on their thematic distance. A snapshot of this map is presented in Fig. 4. To inquire each topic's prevalence over the corpus of the technology's activities, all the resulting topics are ranked in descending order based on their occurrence frequency (Fig. 3). Moreover, the topics are classified according to the kind of use these topics are more associated with. The activities that characterise each topic are classified as follows: (i) only application-oriented, (ii) only research method-oriented, or (iii) both. A more detailed presentation of the contents of each topic per (i), (ii) or (iii) is provided in Appendix B. The colours of the bars are used to highlight this classification. The most frequently occurring topic is the multidisciplinary topic 2, which contains three interdisciplinary subdomains: fiber optics and waveguides, general optics, and lasers. All detected subdomains demonstrate activities in applications. It is followed by the topic 3 related to the subdomains of photonic devices (applications-oriented subdomain), and of physical foundations (methods-oriented subdomain). This reveals that the basic physical methods are intensively investigated for the development of photonic devices. The third most frequently occurring subdomain is regarding optical materials, such as display devices and LEDs, and it is identified only in topic 6. Subdomains regarding applications occur more frequently than subdomains regarding methodological aspects in the photonics interconnected system. This implies that the most significant evolution is expected mainly by the interactions within the subdomains regarding applied research. Furthermore, the detected combinations of subdomains within each topic indicate the potential upcoming paths of development for the considered technology.

Topic Distances. In Fig. 4, the topics resulted from the topic model are illustrated after a PCA analysis, in order to identify which topics, over the entire period 2008–2016 in the photonics R&D activities, are closer to each other. In case that the observed topics appear thematically very close to each other, e.g. the topic consisted of subdomains regarding photonic devices employing physical foundations methods (topic 3) and the topic on optical materials (topic 6), or in case that the topic appears to extensively thematically overlap with another, e.g. the topics of photonic devices applications employing methods from chemistry and biology (topic 13), of lasers for optical sensing employing methods from biology (topic 14) and of fiber optics and waveguides applications employing methods from quantum optics and physical foundations (topic 9), it is likely that their evolution will be intertwined. Namely, when topics are close in thematic distance, eventually they will either merge into a new single multidisciplinary topic including stronger relations between their corresponding subdomains, or they will diverge and create more specialised and independent topics, where their subdomains will not demonstrate interdisciplinary relations. In the first case, the destination becomes common, and in the second the origin remains common.

The terms of each topic are displayed on the side of the map, offering a comparative ranking of the most relevant terms within the topic and across all the topics. Hence, the terms that describe the subdomain that appear in the topic more pertinently are depicted by red bars Fig. 4, and the most relevant terms of the topic in the entire photonics domain, namely the terms that are relevant for

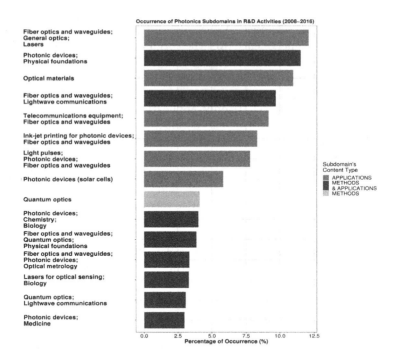

Fig. 3. Occurrence of photonics topics in R&D activities per type of topic, 2008–2016.

other topics too, are depicted by blue bars. The illustration is given here for the highest ranked topic (topic 2), but the observations are made for all.

There, it is possible to identify which topics, over the entire period 2008–2016 in the photonics R&D activities, are closer to each other. In case that the observed topics appear thematically very close to each other, e.g. the topic consisted of subdomains regarding photonic devices employing physical foundations methods (topic 3) and the topic on optical materials (topic 6), or in case that the topic appears to extensively thematically overlap with another, e.g. the topics of photonic devices applications employing methods from chemistry and biology (topic 13), of lasers for optical sensing employing methods from biology (topic 14) and of fiber optics and waveguides applications employing methods from quantum optics and physical foundations (topic 9), it is likely that their evolution will be intertwined. Namely, when topics are close in thematic distance, eventually they will either merge into a new single multidisciplinary topic including stronger relations between their corresponding subdomains, or they will diverge and create more specialised and independent topics, where their subdomains will not demonstrate interdisciplinary relations. In the first case, the destination becomes common, and in the second the origin remains common.

The terms of each topic are displayed on the side of the map, offering a comparative ranking of the most relevant terms within the topic and across all the topics. Hence, the terms that describe the subdomain that appear in the topic more pertinently are depicted by red bars 4, and the most relevant terms of the

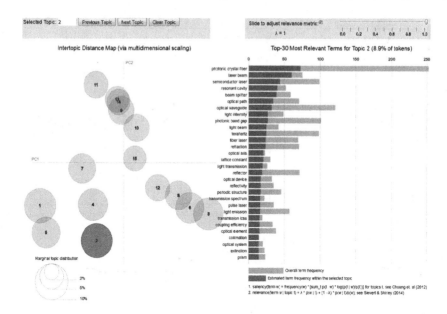

Fig. 4. Inter-topic distance map for R&D activities in photonics, 2008–2016 (left). Top-30 most relevant terms in topic 2 (right). Red bars indicate frequency of occurrence of a term within the topic, and blue bars frequency of occurrence of the term across all topics of the corpus. Note: For the visualisation the *LDAvis R package* is used. (Color figure online)

topic in the entire photonics domain, namely the terms that are relevant for other topics too, are depicted by blue bars. The illustration is given here for the highest ranked topic (topic 2), but the observations are made for all.

Topic Dynamics. To delineate the performance of the observed technological topics, the popularity of each topic, namely the topic's probability of occurrence based on the technology-related collected documents, is analysed on a yearly basis over the time period from 2008 to 2016 (Fig. 5). However, given the short time period between its establishment and the end of the considered study period, definitive conclusions are not to be deduced. Moreover, it is noted that the number of collected activities during the last three years of the study period present a downward trend (ranging from 1.6 to 2.7 times less activities between 2014 and 2016, in comparison to the average number of activities between 2008 and 2013), due to delays in the registration of the patenting activities.

The popularity of the multidisciplinary topic with subdomains regarding applications of fiber optics and waveguides, general optics and lasers (topic 2) is among the highest in the photonics interconnected system. This is corroborated by the high occurrence of the topic, as mentioned in the previous indicator. Moreover, a 15% mean increase in occurrence is shown during the period 2014–2016 in comparison to 2008–2013. A similar interpretation can be proposed also considering the high occurring topic of optical materials applications (topic 6): its

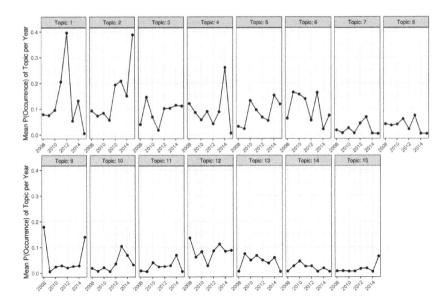

Fig. 5. Topic evolution based on topic-document probability in Photonics R&D activities, 2008–2016.

mean occurrence increases of 4.8% during the period 2014–2016, after a drop in 2013. Also the topic of photonic devices and of methods of physical foundations occurred rather highly (topic 3, 11% mean occurrence during 2008–2016). In particular, stabilisation is observed after a period of fluctuation and final increase in 2012. The mean low popularity of the technological topic on quantum optics (topic 11, 3% mean occurrence during 2008–2016), after a marginal increasing peak in 2014, confirms the topic's lower ranking in terms of occurrence that is found in the intertopic map. This variation is marginal and may conceal any trend due to the aforementioned issues of delay in registration and uptake of decisions.

4   Conclusions and Perspectives

The heterogeneity and spatial dimensions of agents and activities within emerging technologies, as well as the complex interactions that develop due to these factors, and the lack of correspondence to standard classifications (industrial or products), demand a methodology that identifies characteristics of the technology and the evolution of their relationships. The presented methodology through community detection and semantic analyses successfully detects not only the established R&D applications of the photonics technology based on collaborations of agents, but most importantly the latent relations of agents that appear in homogeneous groups due to spatial or thematic interactions. The analysis of these dynamic groups' attributes offers valuable insights, which were not acknowledged without the proposed method. The identified technological pathway and subdomains in conjunction with the yielded observations, provide valuable suggestions for the development of timely and reliable policies.

The perspectives of this ongoing study comprise automatic detection of the corpus to improve topics' robustness, and semantic analysis within the resulted communities. In particular, the presence of multiple topics within the same community, or the presence of the same specific topic in distant and not else related communities, will be examined. Lastly, the TES methodology will be implemented for the entire complex network of the technology, so as to cover both R&D and non-R&D activities.

A   Appendix: Detected Communities

In the following table, some descriptive statistics of the main detected communities are provided.

Descriptive statistics regarding detected communities.
For each community, four statistics are here reported:
- number of players
- number of players by region (in parenthesis the country)
- number of players by institutional type
- number of activities by type

Community: c.3
N. of Players: 65; N. of Players by Region: Tokyo (JPN) 65; N. of Players by Instit. Type: companies 56, gov. non-profit 4, universities 5; N. of Activities by Type: FP7 1, patent 313.

Community: c.4
N. of Players: 53; N. of Players by Region Jiangsu (CHN) 53; N. of Players by Instit. Type: companies 27, gov. non-profit 27 public research institutes 4, universities 20; N. of Activities by Type: patent 193.

Community: c.5
N. of Players: 49; N. of Players by Region: Beijing (CHN) 49; N. of Players by Instit. Type: companies 18, companies gov. non-profit 2, gov. non-profit 3, public research institutes 11, universities 14, unknown 1; N. of Activities by Type: patent 290.

Community: c.6
N. of Players: 48; N. of Players by Region: Île de France (FRA) 47, Prov. Vlaams-Brabant (BEL) 1; N. of Players by Instit. Type: companies 33, gov. non-profit 4, public research institutes 7, universities 4; N. of Activities by Type: FP7 86, H2020 20, patent 32.

Community: c.7
N. of Players: 43; N. of Players by Region: Guangdong (CHN) 43; N. of Players by Instit. Type: companies 29, gov. non-profit 3, public research institutes 1, universities 10; N. of Activities by Type: patent 161.

Community: c.8
N. of Players: 24; N. of Players by Region: Aquitaine (FRA) 1, Dresden (DEU) 1, Hannover (DEU) 2, Hovedstaden (DNK) 1, Liguria (ITA) 2, Lombardia (ITA) 2, Piemonte (ITA) 2, Prov. Hainaut (BEL) 1, Provence-Alpes-Côte d'Azur (FRA) 1, Région de Bruxelles-Capitale/Brussels Hoofdstedelijk Gewest (BEL) 1, Stuttgart (DEU) 2, Thüringen (DEU) 1, Toscana (ITA) 1, Zahodna Slovenija (SVN) 2, Zürich (CHE) 1; N. of Players by Instit. Type: companies 16, gov. non-profit 1, public research institutes 2, universities 5; N. of Activities by Type: FP7 15, H2020 4.

Community: c.9
N. of Players: 40; N. of Players by Region: Daejeon (KOR) 1, Gyeonggi-do (KOR) 1, Seoul (KOR) 38; N. of Players by Instit. Type: companies 25, gov. non-profit 2, universities 13; N. of Activities by Type: FP7 1, patent 125.

Community: c.10
N. of Players: 31; N. of Players by Region: Shanghai (CHN) 31; N. of Players by Instit. Type: companies 14, gov. non-profit 2, public research institutes 5, universities 10; N. of Activities by Type: FP7 1, patent 120.

Community: c.11
N. of Players: 21; N. of Players by Region: Braunschweig (DEU) 1, Cataluña (ESP) 1, Centre (FRA) 1, Devon (GBR) 1, Dorset and Somerset (GBR) 1, Emilia-Romagna (ITA) 1, Gloucestershire, Wiltshire and Bristol/Bath area (GBR) 1, Lazio (ITA) 1, Münster (DEU) 1, País Vasco (ESP) 1, Poitou-Charentes (FRA) 1, Praha (CZE) 2, Prov. Vlaams-Brabant (BEL) 1, Stockholm (SWE) 1, Thüringen (DEU) 1, West Midlands (GBR) 1, Wielkopolskie (POL) 3, Wien (AUT) 1; N. of Players by Instit. Type: companies 12, public research institutes 2, universities 6, unknown 1; N. of Activities by Type: FP7 14, H2020 5, patent 1.

Community: c.12
N. of Players: 22; N. of Players by Region: Attiki (GRC) 1, Campania (ITA) 3, Cataluña (ESP) 3, Hovedstaden (DNK) 1, Inner London - West (GBR) 7, Kentriki Makedonia (GRC) 1, Lazio (ITA) 1, Lombardia (ITA) 2, Région de Bruxelles-Capitale/Brussels Hoofdstedelijk Gewest (BEL) 1, Syddanmark (DNK) 2; N. of Players by Instit. Type: companies 12, companies gov. non-profit 2, public research institutes 2, universities 6; N. of Activities by Type: FP7 21, H2020 9.

Community: c.13
N. of Players: 18; N. of Players by Region: Área Metropolitana de Lisboa (PRT) 1, Braunschweig (DEU) 1, Devon (GBR) 4, Dorset and Somerset (GBR) 1, Hamburg (DEU) 1, Hampshire and Isle of Wight (GBR) 1, Île de France (FRA) 2, Lazio (ITA) 1, Norte (PRT) 1, Oberbayern (DEU) 1, Severovýchod (CZE) 1; N. of Players by Instit. Type: companies 14 public research institutes 1, universities 3; N. of Activities by Type: FP7 15, H2020 4, patent 2.

Community: c.14
N. of Players: 30; N. of Players by Region: Gyeonggi-do (KOR) 30; N. of Players by Instit. Type: companies 23, gov. non-profit 1, universities 5, unknown 1; N. of Activities by Type: patent 115.

Community: c.15
N. of Players: 22; N. of Players by Region: Ar Riyad (SAU) 1, Área Metropolitana de Lisboa (PRT) 1, Bucureşti - Ilfov (ROU) 1, Comunidad de Madrid (ESP) 1, HaMerkaz (ISR) 12, Jerusalem (ISR) 2, Kentriki Makedonia (GRC) 1, Outer London - West and North West (GBR) 1, Prov. Liège (BEL) 1, Tel Aviv (ISR) 1; N. of Players by Instit. Type: companies 19, public research institutes 1, universities 2; N. of Activities by Type: FP7 12, H2020 2, patent 3.

Community: c.16
N. of Players: 13; N. of Players by Region: Bratislavský kraj (SVK) 2, Devon (GBR) 1, Gloucestershire, Wiltshire and Bristol/Bath area (GBR) 1, Hampshire and Isle of Wight (GBR) 1, Homyeľ (BLR) 1, Île de France (FRA) 1, Neuchâtel (CHE) 1, Łódzkie (POL) 1, Noord-Brabant (NLD) 2, Prov. Oost-Vlaanderen (BEL) 1; N. of Players by Instit. Type: companies 10, universities 3; N. of Activities by Type: FP7 4, H2020 2.

Community: c.17
N. of Players: 16; N. of Players by Region: Ankara (TUR) 1, Arnsberg (DEU) 5, Calabria (ITA) 2, Comunidad de Madrid (ESP) 1, Friuli-Venezia Giulia (ITA) 3, Hamburg (DEU) 1, Liguria (ITA) 1, Noord-Brabant (NLD) 1, South Western Scotland (GBR) 1; N. of Players by Instit. Type: companies 7, public research institutes 3, universities 6; N. of Activities by Type: FP7 16, H2020 3, patent 1.

Community: c.18
N. of Players: 22; N. of Players by Region: California (USA) 22, N. of Players by Instit. Type: companies 20, universities 2; N. of Activities by Type: FP7 1, patent 95.

Community: c.19
N. of Players: 14; N. of Players by Region: Ankara (TUR) 1, Área Metropolitana de Lisboa (PRT) 1, Bretagne (FRA) 1, Cataluña (ESP) 1, Düsseldorf (DEU) 1, Gloucestershire, Wiltshire and Bristol/Bath area (GBR) 1, Köln (DEU) 1, Latvija (LVA) 2, Région de Bruxelles-Capitale/Brussels Hoofdstedelijk Gewest (BEL) 1, Tel Aviv (ISR) 1, Toscana (ITA) 1, Mazowieckie (POL) 1, Wien (AUT) 1; N. of Players by Instit. Type: companies 10, companies gov. non-profit 1, public research institutes 2; N. of Activities by Type: FP7 2, H2020 2.

Community: c.20
N. of Players: 15; N. of Players by Region: Andalucía (ESP) 4, Attiki (GRC) 1, Cataluña (ESP) 1, Gelderland (NLD) 5, Languedoc-Roussillon (FRA) 3, Overijssel (NLD) 3; N. of Players by Instit. Type: companies 8, public research institutes 1, universities 6; N. of Activities by Type: FP7 8, H2020 5.

Community: c.21
N. of Players: 13; N. of Players by Region: Área Metropolitana de Lisboa (PRT) 1, Bretagne (FRA) 5, Comunidad de Madrid (ESP) 1, Düsseldorf (DEU) 1, Franche-Comté (FRA) 1, País Vasco (ESP) 2, Prov. Vlaams-Brabant (BEL) 1, Tel Aviv (ISR) 1; N. of Players by Instit. Type: companies 10, public research institutes 1, universities 2; N. of Activities by Type: FP7 4, H2020 2, patent 1.

Community: c.22
N. of Players: 21; N. of Players by Region: Oberbayern (DEU) 22, Sachsen-Anhalt (DEU) 1; N. of Players by Instit. Type: companies 13, gov. non-profit 4, public research institutes 1, universities 3; N. of Activities by Type: FP7 52, H2020 9, patent 13.

Community: c.23
N. of Players: 14; N. of Players by Region: Bucureşti - Ilfov (ROU) 1, City of St. Petersburg (RUS) 4, Etelä-Suomi (FIN) 2, Hampshire and Isle of Wight (GBR) 1, Lazio (ITA) 1, Moskva (RUS) 1, Schleswig-Holstein (DEU) 1, Sør-Trøndelag (NOR) 2, Utrecht (NLD) 1; N. of Players by Instit. Type: companies 9, gov. non-profit 1, public research institutes 2, universities 2; N. of Activities by Type: FP7 5, H2020 1, patent 3.

Community: c.24
N. of Players: 14; N. of Players by Region: Berlin (DEU) 3, Dorset and Somerset (GBR) 1, Mecklenburg-Vorpommern (DEU) 1,Oberbayern (DEU) 1, Salzburg (AUT) 1, Severovýchod (CZE) 2, Stockholm (SWE) 1, Unterfranken (DEU) 4; N. of Players by Instit. Type: companies 8, public research institutes 1, universities 5; N. of Activities by Type: FP7 7, H2020 4.

Note: The first two communities, namely "c.1" and "c.2", have been removed from the analysis, as they were basically grouping together all the players participating in EU project (the 1st community), and all the patenting players (the 2nd community).

B   Appendix: Association of Subdomains and Method- or Application-Oriented Activities of the Photonics Market Found Based on R&D Activities (2008–2016)

In the following table, the description of topics and the contained subdomains is presented.

Topic index	Topic's Content (identified subdomains per topic)		Topic's top keywords
	Applications	Methods	
2	Fiber optics and waveguides; General optics; Lasers	-	photonic crystal fiber; laser beam; semiconductor laser; resonant cavity; beam splitter
3	Photonic devices	Physical foundations	etching; light emitting diode (LED); nitride; buffer; compound semiconductor
6	Optical materials		display device; liquid crystal; resin; light emitting diode (LED)
4	Fiber optics and waveguides	Lightwave communications	multiplexing; integrated circuit; optical waveguide; optical signal coupler
1	Telecommunications equipment; Fiber optics and waveguides	-	microwave antenna; optical signal; coupler; frequency band
12	Ink-jet printing for photonic devices; Fiber optics and waveguides	-	microsphere; polystyrene; photonic band gap; curing; ink
5	Light pulses; Photonic devices; Fiber optics and waveguides	-	photonic crystal fiber; coupler; fusion; broadband; bragg grating
8	Photonic devices (solar cells)	-	etching; lithography; crystalline silicon; electron beam; solar energy
11	-	Quantum optics	information processing; data storage; quantum communication; quantum cryptography
13	Photonic devices	Chemistry; Biology	optoelectronic; biotechnology; imager; terahertz; instrumentation
9	Fiber optics and waveguides	Quantum optics; Physical foundations	optoelectronic; nanophotonic; nanotechnology; compatibility; readout
10	Fiber optics and waveguides; Photonic devices	Optical metrology	microfluidic; biosensor; metrology; contamination; fluidic
14	Lasers for optical sensing	Biology	scalability; cascade; immunity; photodiode; lidar
7	Quantum optics	Lightwave communications	broadband; transceiver; signal processing; power consumption; heterogeneous integration; digital signal processing
15	Photonic devices	Medicine	power consumption; transmitter; nitride; foundry; integrated circuit; biopsy

References

1. Aldous, D.J.: Exchangeability and related topics. In: Hennequin, P.L. (ed.) École d'Été de Probabilités de Saint-Flour XIII—1983. LNM, vol. 1117, pp. 1–198. Springer, Heidelberg (1985). https://doi.org/10.1007/BFb0099421
2. Becattini, G.: The Marshallian industrial. In: Industrial districts, vol. 37 (1990)
3. Bedau, M.A., Packard, N.H., Rasmussen, S.: Protocells: Bridging Nonliving and Living Matter. MIT Press, Cambridge (2009)
4. Blei, D.M., Lafferty, J.D.: Topic models. In: Text Mining: Classification, Clustering, and Applications, vol. 10, no. 71, p. 34 (2009)
5. Blei, D.M., Ng, A.Y., Jordan, M.I.: Latent Dirichlet allocation. J. Mach. Learn. Res. **3**(Jan), 993–1022 (2003)
6. Breschi, S., Malerba, F.: Sectoral innovation systems: technological regimes, schumpeterian dynamics, and spatial boundaries. In: Systems of Innovation: Technologies, Institutions and Organizations, pp. 130–156 (1997)

7. Brusco, S.: The idea of the industrial district: its genesis. In: Industrial Districts and Inter-firm Co-operation in Italy, pp. 10–19 (1990)
8. Chuang, J., Manning, C.D., Heer, J.: Termite: visualization techniques for assessing textual topic models. In: Proceedings of the International Working Conference on Advanced Visual Interfaces, pp. 74–77. ACM (2012)
9. Commission of the European Communities: COM(2009) 512. Preparing for our Future: Developing a Common Strategy for Key Enabling Technologies in the EU. Communication from the Commission to the European Parliament, the Council, the European Economic and Social Committee and the Committee of the Regions, September 2009
10. Cronen, V., Pearce, B.: Communication, Action and Meaning: The Creation of Social Realities (1980)
11. De Domenico, M., Lancichinetti, A., Arenas, A., Rosvall, M.: Identifying modular flows on multilayer networks reveals highly overlapping organization in interconnected systems. Phys. Rev. X **5**(1), 011027 (2015)
12. Ding, Y.: Community detection: topological vs. topical. J. Informetr. **5**(4), 498–514 (2011)
13. Dosi, G., Freeman, C., Nelson, R., Silverberg, G., Soete, L., et al.: Technical Change and Economic Theory, vol. 988. Pinter, London (1988)
14. Fortunato, S., Hric, D.: Community detection in networks: a user guide. Phys. Rep. **659**, 1–44 (2016)
15. Freeman, C.: Networks of innovators: a synthesis of research issues. Res. Policy **20**(5), 499–514 (1991)
16. Griffiths, T.L., Steyvers, M.: Finding scientific topics. Proc. Natl. Acad. Sci. **101**(suppl 1), 5228–5235 (2004)
17. Hacklin, F.: Management of Convergence in Innovation: Strategies and Capabilities for Value Creation Beyond Blurring Industry Boundaries. Springer, Heidelberg (2007). https://doi.org/10.1007/978-3-7908-1990-8
18. Huffman, D.A.: A method for the construction of minimum-redundancy codes. Proc. IRE **40**(9), 1098–1101 (1952)
19. Jurafsky, D., Martin, J.H.: Speech and Language Processing (2014)
20. Lane, D., Maxfield, R., et al.: Foresight, Complexity, and Strategy. Santa Fe Institute New Mexico, Santa Fe (1997)
21. Lane, D.A.: Complexity and innovation dynamics. Handbook on The Economic Complexity of Technological Change, vol. 63 (2011)
22. Lane, D.A., Maxfield, R.R.: Ontological uncertainty and innovation. J. Evol. Econ. **15**(1), 3–50 (2005)
23. Lundvall, B.A., Dosi, G., Freeman, C.: Innovation as an interactive process: from user-producer interaction to the national system of innovation, **1988**, 349–369 (1988)
24. Malerba, F., Orsenigo, L.: Technological regimes and sectoral patterns of innovative activities. Ind. Corp. Change **6**(1), 83–118 (1997)
25. Papadimitriou, C.H., Raghavan, P., Tamaki, H., Vempala, S.: Latent semantic indexing: a probabilistic analysis. J. Comput. Syst. Sci. **61**(2), 217–235 (2000)
26. Righi, R.: A methodological approach to investigate interactive dynamics in innovative socio-economic complex systems. Statistica Applicata - Ital. J. Appl. Stat. **30**(1), 113–142 (2018)
27. Rosvall, M., Bergstrom, C.T.: Maps of random walks on complex networks reveal community structure. Proc. Natl. Acad. Sci. **105**(4), 1118–1123 (2008)
28. Russo, M., Hughes, T.: Complementary innovations and generative relationships: an ethnographic study. Econ. Innov. New Technol. **9**(6), 517–558 (2000)

29. Samoili, S., Righi, R., Lopez-Cobo, M., De Prato, G.: Modelling emerging topics in a techno-economic segment (TES) network. In: XII Workshop on Artificial Life and Evolutionary Computation (2017)
30. Saxenian, A.: Regional networks: industrial adaptation in silicon valley and route, vol. 128 (1994)
31. Sievert, C., Shirley, K.: LDAvis: a method for visualizing and interpreting topics. In: Proceedings of the Workshop on Interactive Language Learning, Visualization, and Interfaces. pp. 63–70 (2014)
32. Steyvers, M., Griffiths, T.: Probabilistic topic models. In: Handbook of Latent Semantic Analysis, vol. 427, no. 7, pp. 424–440 (2007)
33. Taddy, M.: On estimation and selection for topic models. In: Artificial Intelligence and Statistics, pp. 1184–1193 (2012)
34. Van de Velde, E.I.C., et al.: Feasibility study for an EU monitoring mechanism on key enabling technologies (2012)
35. Zhou, D., Manavoglu, E., Li, J., Giles, C.L., Zha, H.: Probabilistic models for discovering e-communities. In: Proceedings of the 15th International Conference on World Wide Web, pp. 173–182. ACM (2006)

Combining Machine Learning and Agent Based Modeling for Gold Price Prediction

Filippo Neri[✉] [ID]

Department of Electrical Engineering and Information Technologies,
University of Naples, Naples, Italy
filippo.neri.email@gmail.com

Abstract. A computational approach combining machine learning (simulated annealing) and agent based simulation is shown to approximate financial time series. The agent based model allows to simulate the market conditions that produced the financial time series and simulated annealing optimize the parameters for the agent based model. The originality of our approach stays in the combination of financial market simulation with meta-learning of its parameters. The original contribution of the paper stays in discussing how the methodology can be applied under several meta-learning conditions and its experimentation on the real world SPDR Gold Trust (GLD) timeseries.

Keywords: Agent based modeling · Simulated annealing · Financial markets · Prediction of the SPDR Gold Trust GLD time series

1 Introduction

Financial markets and financial time series have raise the curiosity of scientists since a long time. It is then not a surprise to discover that scientists of many areas like Economics, Statistics, and Computer Science have studied how to model financial time series and possibly how to predict them. Given the great variety of Artificial Intelligence techniques that have been applied in several context [15,22], one has to wonder if such techniques could be leveraged to model complex systems like financial markets or economic interactions. In particular, computer scientists have developed Agent Based Modeling (ABM) and Agent-based Computational Economics (ACE) to try and model financial time series. Researchers in ABM field focus their study on systems, without any domain restrictions, by developing computational models of a system's elementary components and of their relative interactions [2,6], while researchers in ACE focus their investigation in studying economic processes modeled as societies of interacting agents [8,13,15–17,26,28]. However, considering that financial markets remain substantially unpredictable, research contributions on their behavior are actively sought for.

The originality of our approach, that we discuss here, stays in the combination of financial market simulation and meta-learning of its parameters and the

© Springer Nature Switzerland AG 2019
S. Cagnoni et al. (Eds.): WIVACE 2018, CCIS 900, pp. 91–100, 2019.
https://doi.org/10.1007/978-3-030-21733-4_7

original contribution of this paper stays in discussing how the methodology can be applied under several meta-learning conditions and its experimentation on the real world SPDR Gold Trust (GLD) timeseries.

Existing research on modeling financial markets in the artificial intelligence community usually falls into one of the following approaches:

a) evaluating or learning trading strategies for some given financial instruments (commodities, bonds, shares, derivatives, etc.) [5, 9, 25];

b) developing artificial markets, whose internal dynamics can be controlled, in order to study which "features" of the markets are responsible for the formation of notable phenomena (price bubble, for instance) that are observable in real markets [1, 27];

c) and modeling the time series of the values/prices for some financial assets [12, 14].

The citations above for the three categories were made with the only intent to provide some examples of the listed research approaches and without any claim to be exhaustive. Our research when classified according to the above categories would belong to the third one. Other research directions related to our work are that of meta-learning and hyper-heuristics [3] and in the future we will also investigate how to exploit results from the hyper parameter optimization field [4, 22]. For instance according to the meta heuristic field of research our study could be classified as belonging to the family of hyper-heuristics concerned with adaptive parameter control.

As already said here we will show how a Learning Financial Agent Based Simulator (L-FABS) [18–21] can approximate the SPDR Gold Trust time series over an extended period of time and under various experimental settings.

The rest of the paper is organized as follows: in Sect. 2 we show how simulated annealing can be applied to realise meta learning in an agent based market. In Sect. 3, the experimental session is discussed and in Sect. 4 we compare our methodology to that used by other researchers.

2   Meta Learning in the L-FABS Simulator

In this section, we describe how a meta learning capability can be realized in the Learning Financial Agent Based Simulation (L-FABS for short) [21] so that it may find the best model for a given time serie. The reader is invited to refer to [19, 21] for a detailed description of the system. Learning in L-FABS consists of finding the vector of the parameters that control the simulation and the agents behavior in the market. In particular, the learning task consists of finding the vector of risk/reward propensity rates for the agents-investors plus any additional parameter object of experimentation, in order to approximate the given time series with a minimum error. Any machine learning technique able to optimize a vector of values while minimizing a given error function could be selected. Examples of suitable machine learning algorithms include among the others: genetic algorithms [7], decision trees [23], neural networks [24], simulated annealing [11]. We selected simulated annealing because of its simplicity and popularity and because thanks to our previous research experience in evolutionary computation we are well aware that evolutionary learning can produce very good results in a short amount of time.

As error function to be minimized, we selected one that could evaluate how well two time series are similar: the Mean Average Percentage Error (MAPE) is a suitable choice. The MAPE is commonly used in Statistics when two data samplings have to be compared in term of a non dimensional measure such as an percentage of the absolute difference between the data as is defined as:

$$MAPE(X,Y) = \frac{1}{N} \sum_{i=1}^{N} \left| \frac{x_i - y_i}{x_i} \right|$$

Given two time series X and Y, the lower the MAPE value, the closer the two are.

We also selected the classic simulated annealing algorithm as in [11]. Simulated annealing is a searching algorithm that iteratively search for the minimum of a given function E (Energy or Error function) by generating at each step random candidate points for the minimum in the proximity of the current candidate minimum point which represents the "center" of the exploration. At the end of each step, the Simulated Annealing may move the "center" of its exploration at a newly generated point with a given probability. In our L-FABS, the function E is the MAPE and its domain elements are the vectors of parameters governing the simulation behavior.

3 Empirical Evaluation of L-FABS

The experiments reported in this section have been done on the learning set/test set containing the following data:
Learning set: SPDR Gold Trust (GLD ticker) close value data from 31 October 2012 till 31 December 2015 and
Test set: SPDR Gold Trust close value data from 1 January 2016 up to 31 October 2017. The dataset has been freely acquired from the finance section of yahoo.com.

Two main groups of results are reported: in one L-FABS estimates the next value of the time serie (the next trading day closing value), in the other L-FABS estimates the seven days ahead value of the time serie. The seven days ahead prediction has been selected as it is the most far ahead prediction made by other learning systems and thus could serve as an interesting comparison data.

Before explaining the obtained results, the function used to estimate the market mood, the Sentiment, has to be defined. Our approach does not impose any restriction on how complex is the function to estimate the market mood. For our experiments, we implemented the Sentiment function as follows to keep it as simple and as general as possible:

function Sentiment(time, mavgDays)
    begin=time-1
    end=time-mavgDays
    if (MAVG(PredictedData, begin, end) <
      MAVG(RealData, begin, end))
      then return(α)
      else return(β)

The variables RealData and PredictedData give access to the time series of the real and predicted values. α and β will assume the constant values of 0.95 (a bullish mood) and 0.25 (bearish mood) in some experimental settings when no learning is active while will be determined by simulated annealing in those settings where learning is active. As usual the Moving AVeraGe function (MAVG) is defined as:

$$\text{MAVG(index,t,n)} = \frac{\sum_{k=0}^{n-1} index(t-k)}{n}.$$

In our experiments the Sentiment function can be only called as either Sentiment (time, 1), case identified in the following with S1, or as Sentiment (time,5), case identified with S5. In case S1, only the previous day values of the two time series are used, while in case S5, the averages of the latest previous five days in the two time series are used to estimate the market mood.

In the Tables 1 and 2 we report the experimental results averaged over 10 runs in terms of the forecast errors measured by MAPE on the test set. In Table 1 L-FABS uses 200 rounds of simulated annealing and in Table 2 L-FABS uses 400 rounds of simulated annealing. The columns in the tables stand for: "values for α and β" reports the values for the α and β parameters to be used in the Sentiment function as described above; "Sentiment" indicates if the Sentiment value is calculated with modality S1 or S5; "Day to predict" indicates the number of days ahead for which a prediction of the time serie is made; and, finally, the measured errors on the test set are reported in terms of the MAPE value on the test set.

As can be noted each table is divided in two parts: the first four rows are experiments where no learning is allowed (simulation annealing is disabled) thus constant values for α and β are used. Instead, in the last four rows of each table, learning is allowed and thus the values for α and β are learned by means of simulated annealing.

This means that the first four rows in each table, in an ideal world, would report the exactly the same MAPE values as they both refer to the same experimental setting. In practice as the experiments without learning have been rerun while constructing both table, the slightly different MAPE values in the two table represent two different statistically valid samples extracted from the same population. And while the population mean is unchanged across experiments, the MAPE values are just estimated of the real population mean and thus the estimated mean values slightly differ across samples as Statistics tells that it would happen.

The second part (latest four rows) of the tables instead report results from two completely different set of experiments where meta-learning of the agent based market simulator is performed via simulated annealing. In the first table, 200 rounds of simulated annealing are allowed while in the second 400 rounds are used.

Also please note that when meta-learning is allowed the α and β values are not reported in the table because it would not make sense to average across 10 runs the α and β values and report such figures. Just to satisfy any potential curiosity, here is a sample of actually learned α and β values, presented as pairs of values, in some of the experiments: $< 0.72, 0.18 >$, $< 0.93, 0.01 >$, and $< 0.98, 0.02 >$. For the inquisitive mind, it is not required that $\alpha + \beta = 1$; they are not probabilities.

Table 1. Experimental results on dataset GLD without simulated annealing or using 200 rounds of simulated annealing.

α and β	Sentiment	Day to predict	MAPE %
0.95, 0.25	S1	1	5.14 ± 0.06
0.95, 0.25	S5	1	5.45 ± 0.02
0.95, 0.25	S1	7	3.47 ± 0.10
0.95, 0.25	S5	7	3.92 ± 0.1
Learned values	S1	1	0.73 ± 0.02
Learned values	S5	1	0.73 ± 0.03
Learned values	S1	7	2.04 ± 0.04
Learned values	S5	7	2.02 ± 0.03

From the obtained results, the most evident result is that using meta-learning (implemented with simulated annealing in our case) makes a significant difference in reducing the MAPE values across experiments. When meta learning is not used, it is easier to predict 7 days ahead close values than 1 day ahead values. This finding appears to be at first counterintuitive, but it is due to the fact that the GLD time series, for the period under study, has the characteristic to regress to its moving average after being subjected to wild swings in the short term. When meta learning is used, the results show that the prediction of the next day close for the GLD time series tends to be easier or more accurate than the prediction of the seven days ahead values. Thus it appears that meta-learning has been able to overcome the noise introduced by short term wild swings in the time series. Overall the MAPE values when meta learning is used or when meta learning is not used are clearly better in a statistically significant way. With respect to the GLD timeseries for the period under study, it also emerges that using only the previous day close for estimating the market mood, Sentiment

Table 2. Experimental results on dataset GLD without simulated annealing or using 400 rounds of simulated annealing.

α and β	Sentiment	Day to predict	MAPE %
0.95, 0.25	S1	1	5.03 ± 0.02
0.95, 0.25	S5	1	5.37 ± 0.02
0.95, 0.25	S1	7	3.43 ± 0.11
0.95, 0.25	S5	7	3.74 ± 0.02
Learned values	S1	1	0.71 ± 0.02
Learned values	S5	1	0.74 ± 0.02
Learned values	S1	7	2.06 ± 0.04
Learned values	S5	7	2.07 ± 0.03

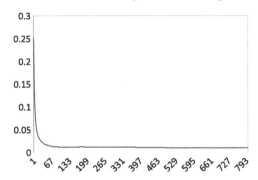

Fig. 1. Convergence curve of the learning algorithm in L-FABS reporting the MAPE error, as measured on the learning set, for the best model found during a generic run of the system.

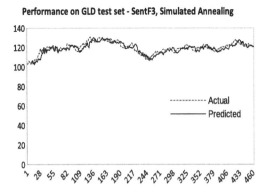

Fig. 2. An example of the actual and predicted GLD time series when testing L-FABS on with settings: enabled simulated annealing, S1, and day to predict 7.

S1, is as good as using the moving average of the latest five days close values, Sentiment S5 in terms of MAPE. Another interesting experimental finding is that L-FABS appears to be robust across experimental settings, in the sense that the MAPE values in different but similar experimental setups tend to stay close. Compare experiments across the Tables 1 and 2 in pair and odd rows. This is an important feature that we believe asks for further investigation.

The experiments also confirm that simulated annealing is a good function optimizer and in fact the meta leaning in L-FABS is able to find a parameter settings after about 100 cycles of simulated annealing. Figure 1 shows the curve of convergence of the MAPE error for the best parameter setting found at a given cycle.

For the sake of completeness, we also show a graph of the forecasted GLD time series, as predicted by L-FABS, and of the real GLD time serie in Fig. 2. The reported graph is an exemplar of the typical results obtained by L-FABS a given experimental settings. As it can be seen from the graph, the dashed line (actual) and the continuous line (predicted) are very close confirming the MAPE figures that have been reported in the tables.

4   Experimental Comparison of L-FABS to Other Systems

Even though the focus of the paper is not to compare L-FABS to other systems, we provide a reasoned summary of how L-FBAS compare with respect to other approaches here. In details, we compare its performances with respect to those obtained on the same dataset by alternative approaches for which enough implementation details have been given in the literature [14] so they can act as an useful benchmark. The dataset used in this experimentation contains the following data. As learning set: DJIA close value data from 3 Jan 1994 to 17 Dec 2003 and as test set: DJIA close value data from 18 Dec 2003 to 23 Oct 2006. The dataset has been freely acquired from the finance section of yahoo.com. This dataset has been select because it has been used by other authors to compare their systems. In Table 3, we compare the prediction errors, as given by the MAPE measure by using a Particle Swarm Optimization algorithm (PSO) [10] and a Multi-Layer Perceptron (MLP) [29], whose parameters have been set up as in [14], with our agent based approach L-FABS. The results for L-FABS are relative to a Sentiment determined as in case S1 and using 400 rounds of simulated annealing.

Before commenting on the error figures, we want to point out how elaborate are the input features given to PSO and MLP in the mentioned study. This means that a lot of pre-processing of the data has to be undertaken without really any justification for the specific manual pre-processing other than the posteriori observation that it enables the system to produce good results. On the contrary the input given to L-FABS is only the time series of the data for which a model has to be learned and the system itself will adjust its parameters by learning. Just as an example, any learning/prediction in PSO or MLP requires: the real value of the time serie at the current time t plus a number of financial technical indicators such as: EMA10, EMEA20, EMEA30, ADO, and some others.

As an example, EMA10 stands for the Exponential Moving Average calculated over 10 previous periods and is defined as EMA(t, j = 10) = value(t−1) × a + EMA(t−1, j−1)*(1−a) where value(t) is the value at time t of the time series under consideration and the smoothing factor a is defined as a = 2/(j + 1).

The results in Table 3, shows that the forecasting errors of L-FABS are better than those obtained by of PSO and MLP. Moreover, it is evident, as observed in the previous section, that the forecasting error increases when farther into the future the prediction is to be made. And this holds for all the systems. This observation can be interpreted as evidence that the information contained in the time series up to the current time has a decreasing usefulness in predicting future values the farther we move ahead in time. This finding also confirms what we expect to happen in real world financial markets. Otherwise, statisticians or machine learning scientists would all have become rich long time ago by trading stocks.

An additional consequence for the latest observation is that even if we use information rich input data, like those built on technical indicators that provide a way to summarize the past behavior of the time series, the predictive performances of the models would still decrease the farther into the future the time to be predicted is.

Table 3. Experimental results averaged on 10 runs for time series DJIA.

Day to predict	PSO MAPE %	MLP MAPE %	L-FABS MAPE %
1	0.65	1.06	0.57
7	1.47	5.64	1.39

5   Conclusions

We have described a meta learning methology combining agent based simulation with simulation annealing where the interacting agents simulates the investors behavior in a financial market for a specified asset. We have empirically evaluated the methodology implementing the system L-FABS and we have reported a number of experimental findings on the SPDR Gold Trust and the DJIA time series.

The main research results are: (a) financial time series are amenable to approximation obtained by combining simulated annealing and agent based simulation in a meta learning system; (b) an effective meta learning techniques for approximating financial time series can be obtained by combining two simple artificial intelligence techniques: a robust and effective evolutionary learning method together with a similarly easy to understand and define set of agents-investors; (c) the MAPE values observed in L-FABS are comparable to those obtained by other state-of-the-art modeling approaches based on neural networks and particle swarm optimization thus confirming the good quality of our system.

An additional research direction to be investigated would be to understand how the L-FABS's performances would scale when longer time series are taken into consideration. In principle the computation cost should increase linearly with the length of the time series, however it would be worth to empirically investigate the case.

References

1. Arthur, W.B., Holland, J.H., LeBaron, B., Palmer, R., Taylorm, P.: Asset pricing under endogenous expectation in an artificial stock market. In: The Economy as an Evolving Complex System II, pp. 15–44. Santa Fe Institute Studies in the Sciences of Complexity Lecture Notes (1997)
2. Bonabeau, E.: Agent-based modeling: methods and techniques for simulating human systems. Proc. Nat. Acad. Sci. **99**(3), 7280–7287 (2002)
3. Burke, E.K., Hyde, M., Kendall, G., Ochoa, G., Ozcan, E., Woodward, J.: A classification of hyper-heuristics approaches, handbook of metaheuristics. In: Gendreau, M., Potvin, J.Y. (eds.) Handbook of Metaheuristics. International Series in Operations Research and Management Science, pp. 449–468. Springer, Heidelberg (2009). https://doi.org/10.1007/978-1-4419-1665-5_15
4. Camilleri, M., Neri, F., Papoutsidakis, M.: An algorithmic approach to parameter selection in machine learning using meta-optimization techniques. WSEAS Transact. Syst. **13**(1), 203–212 (2014)
5. Creamer, G., Freund, Y.: Automated trading with boosting and expert weighting. Quant. Financ. **4**(10), 401–420 (2010)
6. Epstein, J.M., Axtell, R.: Growing Artificial Societies: Social Science from the Bottom Up. The Brookings Institution, Washington (1996)
7. Goldberg, D.: Genetic Algorithms in Search, Optimization, and Machine Learning. Addison-Wesley, Reading (1989)
8. Hoffmann, A.O.I., Delre, S.A., von Eije, J.H., Jager, W.: Artificial multi-agent stock markets: simple strategies, complex outcomes. In: Bruun, C. (ed.) Advances in Artificial Economics. Lecture Notes in Economics and Mathematical Systems, vol. 584, pp. 167–176. Springer, Heidelberg (2006). https://doi.org/10.1007/3-540-37249-0_12
9. Kendall, G., Su, Y.: A multi-agent based simulated stock market - testing on different types of stocks. In: Congress on Evolutionary Computation CEC 2003, pp. 2298–2305 (2003)
10. Kennedy, J., Eberhard, R.: Particle swarm optimization. In: International Conference on Neural Networks, pp. 1942–1948. IEEE press (1995)
11. Kirkpatrick, S., Gelatt, C.D., Vecchi, M.P.: Optimization by simulated annealing. Science **220**, 671–680 (1983)
12. Kitov, I.: Predicting ConocoPhillips and Exxon Mobil stock price. J. Appl. Res. Financ. **2**, 129–134 (2009)
13. Lebaron, B.: Agent based computational finance: suggested readings and early research. J. Econ. Dyn. Control **24**, 679–702 (1998)

14. Majhi, R., Sahoo, G., Panda, A., Choubey, A.: Prediction of S&P 500 and DJIA stock indices using particle swarm optimization techniques. In: Congress on Evolutionary Computation 2008, pp. 1276–1282. IEEE press (2008)
15. Neri, F.: PIRR: A methodology for distributed network management in mobile networks. WSEAS Transact. Inf. Sci. Appl. **5**(3), 306–311 (2008)
16. Neri, F.: Learning and predicting financial time series by combining natural computation and agent simulation. In: Chio, C., et al. (eds.) EvoApplications 2011. LNCS, vol. 6625, pp. 111–119. Springer, Heidelberg (2011). https://doi.org/10.1007/978-3-642-20520-0_12
17. Neri, F.: A comparative study of a financial agent based simulator across learning scenarios. In: Cao, L., Bazzan, A.L.C., Symeonidis, A.L., Gorodetsky, V.I., Weiss, G., Yu, P.S. (eds.) ADMI 2011. LNCS (LNAI), vol. 7103, pp. 86–97. Springer, Heidelberg (2012). https://doi.org/10.1007/978-3-642-27609-5_7
18. Neri, F.: Can agent based models capture the complexity of financial market behavior. In: 42nd Annual Meeting of the AMASES Association for Mathematics Applied to Social and Economic Sciences. University of Naples and Parthenope University Press, Napoli (2018, in press)
19. Neri, F.: Case study on modeling the silver and nasdaq financial time series with simulated annealing. In: Rocha, Á., Adeli, H., Reis, L.P., Costanzo, S. (eds.) WorldCIST'18 2018. AISC, vol. 746, pp. 755–763. Springer, Cham (2018). https://doi.org/10.1007/978-3-319-77712-2_71
20. Neri, F.: Combining machine learning and agent based modeling for gold price prediction. In: Cagnoni, S. (ed.) WIVACE 2018, Workshop on Artificial Life and Evolutionary Computation. Springer, Heidelberg (2018, in press)
21. Neri, F.: Agent-based modeling under partial and full knowledge learning settings to simulate financial markets. AI Commun. **25**(4), 295–304 (2012)
22. Papoutsidakis, M., Piromalis, D., Neri, F., Camilleri, M.: Intelligent algorithms based on data processing for modular robotic vehicles control. WSEAS Trans. Syst. **13**(1), 242–251 (2014)
23. Quinlan, J.R.: C4.5: Programs for Machine Learning. Morgan Kaufmann, Burlington (1993)
24. Rumelhart, D.E., Hinton, G.E., Williams, R.J.: Learning internal representations by error propagation. In: Parallel Distributed Processing: Explorations in the Microstructure of Cognition, Volume 1: foundations, pp. 318–362. MIT Press, Cambridge (1986)
25. Schulenburg, S., Ross, P.: An adaptive agent based economic model. In: Lanzi, P.L., Stolzmann, W., Wilson, S.W. (eds.) IWLCS 1999. LNCS (LNAI), vol. 1813, pp. 263–282. Springer, Heidelberg (2000). https://doi.org/10.1007/3-540-45027-0_14
26. Staines, A., Neri, F.: A matrix transition oriented net for modeling distributed complex computer and communication systems. WSEAS Trans. Syst. **13**(1), 12–22 (2014)
27. Takahashi, H., Terano, T.: Analyzing the influence of overconfident investors on financial markets through agent-based model. In: Yin, H., Tino, P., Corchado, E., Byrne, W., Yao, X. (eds.) IDEAL 2007. LNCS, vol. 4881, pp. 1042–1052. Springer, Heidelberg (2007). https://doi.org/10.1007/978-3-540-77226-2_104
28. Tesfatsion, L.: Agent-based computational economics: growing economies from the bottom up. Artif. Life **8**(1), 55–82 (2002)
29. Zirilli, J.: Financial Prediction Using Neural Networks. International Thompson Computer Press, London (1997)

A Bio-Inspired Approach to WiFi-Based Indoor Localization

Federico Bergenti and Stefania Monica[✉]

Dipartimento di Scienze Matematiche, Fisiche e Informatiche,
Università degli Studi di Parma, Parco Area delle Scienze 53/A, 43124 Parma, Italy
{federico.bergenti,stefania.monica}@unipr.it

Abstract. In this paper, the problem of indoor localization is investigated using a bio-inspired approach. The proposed approach relies on the use of WiFi networks, which nowadays can be considered a commodity available in all indoor environments. WiFi signals are used to obtain estimates of the distance between a smart device, whose position needs to be estimated, and the fixed access points of the network, which are assumed to be in known positions. Once a given number of range estimates from each available access point has been acquired, proper range averages are performed to feed the proposed localization algorithm. According to the proposed approach, localization is formulated in terms of an optimization problem, which is solved using an algorithm inspired from particle swarm optimization. Such an algorithm has been integrated in an add-on module of JADE, which is intended to execute on the smart device whose position needs to be estimated, and which was tested in relevant indoor scenarios. Experimental results in tested scenarios are shown in the last part of the paper in order to evaluate the performance of the proposed bio-inspired localization algorithm.

Keywords: Indoor localization · Particle swarm optimization · JADE

1 Introduction

Indoor localization is one of the features which next-generation mobile devices should provide to support location-aware applications and services inside buildings, where technologies such as the *Global Positioning System* (*GPS*), typically used outdoor, are unavailable. Although the relevance for applications and the number of smart devices have been constantly increasing, the problem of indoor localization is still an open issue, with no recognized leading solutions (e.g., [9,10]). Recent technologies, such as *Ultra Wide Band* (*UWB*), seem to guarantee good results for this problem (see, e.g., [14]), but they require a dedicated infrastructure and their cost can be high. For this reason, we studied localization approaches which rely on WiFi signaling, which, nowadays, is very common in the large majority of indoor environments where indoor localization could be relevant for applications, e.g., airports and train stations, shopping

© Springer Nature Switzerland AG 2019
S. Cagnoni et al. (Eds.): WIVACE 2018, CCIS 900, pp. 101–112, 2019.
https://doi.org/10.1007/978-3-030-21733-4_8

malls, and industrial warehouses [16]. According to studied approaches, localization is performed using proper parameters acquired from WiFi signals traveling from *Access Points* (*APs*) of the WiFi network to a smart device. In realistic localization scenarios, the positions of APs are assumed to be known while the position of the smart device, often denoted as *Target Node* (*TN*), is unknown and needs to be estimated. The proposed approach involves two steps. First, the acquisition of proper parameters from WiFi signals allows evaluating estimates of the distances between APs and the TN. Then, such range estimates are properly processed to obtain estimates of the position of the TN. As soon as range estimates from a sufficiently large number of APs have been acquired, position estimates are obtained using a proper localization algorithm.

A significant number of range-based localization algorithms have been studied in the literature (e.g., [25]) and they could all be used in studied localization scenarios. In this paper, we focus on a localization algorithm based on the use of *Particle Swarm Optimization* (*PSO*), which is the well-known optimization algorithm derived from the modeling of the movements of swarms [23]. The advantage of the proposed PSO-based localization algorithm is that it guarantees good localization performances, regardless of the topology of APs. At the opposite, the performance of the large majority of classic geometry-based algorithms, e.g., the *Circumference Intersection* (*CI*) algorithm [13] and the widely used *Two-Stage Maximum-Likelihood* (*TSML*) algorithm [11], strongly depends on the topology of the network and their performance can decrease significantly in critical scenarios. A comparison between the proposed algorithm and mentioned classic algorithms in critical scenarios, which emphasises that the proposed algorithm is more robust than classic alternatives, is discussed in [17, 20].

The proposed PSO-based algorithm has been implemented in a specific add-on module for the *Java Agent and DEvelopment framework* (*JADE*) [2], so that localization is performed by means of agent technology. JADE is a well-known and appreciated framework which has been developed for more than two decades and which has been successfully used for many applications, including mobile services and applications (e.g., [5, 22]). Over the years, various evolutions of JADE have been developed. Among them, it is worth mentioning *Workflows and Agents Development Environment* (*WADE*) [1, 3] which is an open-source platform for agent-based business process management that has been extensively in mission critical applications [6]. A more recent evolution of JADE is *Agent-based Multi-User Social Environment* (*AMUSE*) [4], which is an open-source platform for agent-based social networks [7] and online social games. AMUSE has already been used to evaluate the possibility to introduce indoor localization into mixed-reality games as cornerstone gameplay elements [8].

This paper is organized as follows. Section 2 discusses the localization problem and the use of WiFi signals to perform localization. Section 3 introduces relevant notation and describes the considered application scenario. Section 4 outlines the optimization-based algorithm proposed for localization. Section 5 presents illustrative experimental results, which are evaluated according to specific metrics. Finally, Sect. 6 concludes the paper.

2   Indoor Localization

The literature concerning localization algorithms is very broad and localization algorithms have been divided into different classes. Since, in our approach, localization is performed using WiFi signals, we focus on so called *active range-based localization methods*, which rely on the knowledge of inter-node distances between each AP and the considered TN. The adjective *active* refers to the fact that mentioned methods assume that all nodes are equipped with sensors and with an electronic device which actively communicates. Such types of localization algorithms involve two steps: *(i)* acquisition of estimates of the distances between each AP and the TN; *(ii)* processing of acquired range estimates to obtain estimates of the position of the TN. The first step involves the analysis of signals traveling between each pair of nodes. In particular, range estimates can be obtained by analyzing the *Time of Flight (ToF)* of signals or the *Received Signal Strength (RSS)* [24]. In order to estimate the distance between two nodes using ToF-based approaches, high time resolution in the processing of signals is required. For this reason, ToF-based approaches are not suitable when dealing with WiFi signals, whose time resolution is not sufficient to guarantee accurate range estimates. Instead, RSS-based approaches should be preferred. Actually, a classic equation can be used to compute an estimate of the distance between a transmitter and a receiver assuming that the energy of transmitted signals is known. Denoting as $P(\rho)$ the received power at distance ρ, such a classic equation, known as Friis transmission equation, can be expressed as

$$P(\rho) = P_0 - 10\beta \log_{10} \frac{\rho}{\rho_0} \tag{1}$$

where P_0 is the known power at reference distance ρ_0 and β is a parameter related to the details of the transmission [21]. Given $P(\rho)$, the value of distance ρ can be obtained by inverting Eq. (1).

The JADE add-on module uses the functionality of the smart device where it is installed to estimate the RSS of signals received from WiFi APs to support network scanning [18]. Measured RSS is used to estimate the distances between the TN where the module is installed and the APs of the network using (1). It is worth noting that the position of each AP is supposed to be known. In addition, any communication between the TN and each AP allows obtaining not only an estimate of the distance between them, but also other valuable information, such as the *Basic Service Set IDentification (BSSID)* of the AP. Hence, each mapped BSSID can be associated with the coordinates of the corresponding AP in order to ensure that each distance estimate can also be related to the coordinates of the corresponding AP. The possibility of associating the position of an AP with each distance estimate is essential for the proposed localization algorithm, as discussed in the following.

In order to provide agents with information on their current positions, the add-on module for JADE derives estimated distances from APs and uses them to estimate the position of the TN where it is executing. After the range estimates acquisition phase, collected estimates are used by the add-on module to feed one of the available localization algorithms, which is in charge of computing an estimate of the position of the TN. Finally, interested agents are informed of the current position of the TN, which is used as the position of the agents hosted on the smart device where the add-on module is executing. The current version of the add-on module includes a set of localization algorithms, and it is open to host other algorithms. However, in this paper, we only focus on one of them, which relies on the use of PSO to obtain effective localization [20]. Experimental results discussed in this paper show that the accuracy of the proposed localization algorithms is sufficient for envisioned uses as it can achieve an accuracy of less than 1 m using 4 APs inside a room of size 25 square meters.

3 Notation and Range Estimates Acquisition

Before discussing the considered localization scenario and the proposed algorithm, some notation needs to be introduced. The coordinates of APs are known and they are denoted as

$$\underline{s}_i = (x_i, y_i, z_i)^\mathsf{T} \tag{2}$$

where $i \in \{1, \dots, M\}$ and M denotes the number of APs which are used to perform localization. Denoting the true position of the TN as

$$\underline{u} = (\bar{x}, \bar{y}, \bar{z})^\mathsf{T} \tag{3}$$

the true distance between the TN and the i-th AP can be computed as

$$\rho_i = ||\underline{u} - \underline{s}_i||$$

where $i \in \{1, \dots, M\}$ and $||\underline{x}||$ represents the Euclidean norm of vector $\underline{x} \in \mathbb{R}^3$. Given the introduced notation, simple geometrical considerations show that the position of the TN can be obtained by intersecting the spheres centered in $\{\underline{s}_i\}_{i=1}^M$ with radii $\{r_i\}_{i=1}^M$, namely, by solving the following quadratic system of equations

$$\begin{cases} (x - x_1)^2 + (y - y_1)^2 + (z - z_1)^2 = \rho_1^2 \\ \vdots \\ (x - x_M)^2 + (y - y_M)^2 + (z - z_M)^2 = \rho_M^2. \end{cases} \tag{4}$$

Note that $M \geq 4$ APs need to be available in order to guarantee that (4) has a unique solution, i.e., that the position estimate can be evaluated unambiguously.

Since the true TN position is obviously unavailable in realistic localization scenarios, the values of true distances $\{\rho_i\}_{i=1}^M$ are also unavailable. Hence, localization can only rely on range estimates evaluated according to Eq. (1). In order to make statistical considerations on the performance of the proposed localization algorithm, in the experimental setup outlined in the following section, $L \geq 1$ position estimates are used to evaluate the performance of the proposed algorithm. We denote the estimated distance between the i-th AP and the TN at the j-th iteration of the algorithm as $\hat{\rho}_{i,j}$.

In order to reduce range errors due to acquisition noise and multi-path, we do not rely on a single estimates of the distance between each AP and the TN. Instead, $K \geq 1$ range estimates from each AP are acquired and their average is used to evaluate each single TN position estimate. In the following, K is set equal to 10, meaning that each one of the L position estimates is based on range estimates averaged over the last 10 consecutive estimates. In detail, the l-th TN position estimate is evaluated using the following averaged range estimates from the i-th AP

$$\hat{\delta}_{i,l} = \frac{1}{10} \sum_{j=l}^{l+9} \hat{\rho}_{i,j}. \tag{5}$$

A similar approach, with a different localization algorithms, has been used in [15]. Given such a notation, the position estimate in the l-th iteration, denoted as

$$\hat{\underline{u}}_l = (\hat{x}_l, \hat{y}_l, \hat{z}_l) \tag{6}$$

can be evaluated by solving the following system of equations

$$\begin{cases} (\hat{x}_l - x_1)^2 + (\hat{y}_l - y_1)^2 + (\hat{z}_l - z_1)^2 = \hat{\delta}_{1,l}^2 \\ \vdots \\ (\hat{x}_l - x_M)^2 + (\hat{y}_l - y_M)^2 + (\hat{z}_l - z_M)^2 = \hat{\delta}_{M,l}^2. \end{cases} \tag{7}$$

Note that the system of Eq. (7) is obtained from (4) by substituting true distances $\{r_i\}_{i=1}^M$ with their averaged estimated values at the l-th iteration of the algorithm $\{\hat{\delta}_{i,l}\}_{i=1}^M$.

4   A PSO-Based Localization Algorithm

Various range-based localization algorithms have been proposed in the literature (e.g., [25]) and all of them can be virtually integrated with the adopted JADE add-on module. In particular, the CI algorithm and the TSML algorithm have already been and used to derive experimental results [13]. The large majority of range-based localization algorithms require algebraic manipulations of matrices, whose coefficients depend on the topology of the nodes of the WiFi network. One of the inherent drawbacks of such algorithms is that involved matrices can become strongly ill-conditioned in some localization scenarios, e.g., if all nodes lay on the same plane [16]. To avoid dealing with this kind of issues, we propose to re-write the localization problem into a an optimization problem, and to solve the latter using a PSO-based approach. The application of PSO to localization problem has been recently introduced in [19] in the context of UWB networks, while here it is applied to common WiFi networks.

The starting point of the algorithm is the system of Eq. (7), which can be re-written in matrix notation as

$$\underline{1}\,\hat{\underline{u}}_l^\mathsf{T}\hat{\underline{u}}_l + \underline{A}\,\hat{\underline{u}}_l = \hat{\underline{k}}, \tag{8}$$

where $\underline{1}$ is the vector with M elements equal to 1, $\hat{\underline{k}}$ is a vector whose i−th element is $\hat{\delta}^2_{i,l} - ||\underline{s}_i||^2$, and $\underline{\underline{A}}$ is the following $M \times 3$ matrix

$$\underline{\underline{A}} = \begin{pmatrix} -2x_1 & -2y_1 & -2z_1 \\ -2x_2 & -2y_2 & -2z_2 \\ \vdots & \vdots & \\ -2x_M & -2y_M & -2z_M \end{pmatrix}. \tag{9}$$

The solution of the system of Eq. (8) can be obtained by re-writing it as a proper optimization problem. The solution $\hat{\underline{u}}_l$ which represents the position estimate of the TN at the l-th iteration of the algorithm, can be found by solving the following minimization problem

$$\hat{\underline{u}}_l = \underset{\underline{u}}{\mathrm{argmin}}\, F(\underline{u}) \tag{10}$$

where $F(\underline{u})$, denotes the fitness function, and it is defined as

$$F(\underline{u}) = ||\hat{\underline{k}} - (\underline{1}\,\hat{\underline{u}}_l^\mathsf{T}\hat{\underline{u}}_l + \underline{\underline{A}}\,\hat{\underline{u}}_l)||. \tag{11}$$

In the proposed localization algorithm, the PSO algorithm is used to solve the optimization problem in (10). According to the PSO algorithm, the set of potential solutions of an optimization problem can be modelled as a swarm of S particles which move in a properly defined search space following specific rules [12]. All particles in the swarm are randomly initialised in the search space and they are guided towards the optimal solution through iterations. At each iteration, each particle is associated with a position in the search space and with a velocity, which are iteratively updated in order to move all particles towards the solution of the optimization problem. When considering minimization problems, as in (10), the optimal solution is obtained by minimizing the fitness function (11).

The use of the PSO algorithm in the proposed localization algorithm can be summarized as follows. The search space, in our context, corresponds to the indoor environment where the TN and APs are situated. The initial position of the i-th particle is denoted as $\underline{x}^{(i)}(0)$ and its initial velocity is denoted as $\underline{w}^{(i)}(0)$, where $i \in \{1, \ldots, S\}$ is the index of a generic particle. Initial positions and initial velocities are randomly initialized and they are updated at each iteration $t > 0$, as discussed in [23]. In the following, the position and the velocity of the i−th particle at the t−th iteration are denoted as $\underline{x}^{(i)}(t)$ and $\underline{w}^{(i)}(t)$, respectively. In order to define the velocity of the i−th particle at the $(t+1)$−th iteration, let us first define the following quantities [12]

- $\underline{y}(t)$ denotes the best position globally reached so far;
- $\underline{y}^{(i)}(t)$ denotes the best position reached so far by the i−th particle;
- $\omega(t)$ is called inertial factor;
- c_1 denotes the cognition parameter;
- c_2 denotes the social parameter; and
- $R_1(t)$ and $R_2(t)$ denote two independent random variables uniformly distributed in $(0, 1)$.

Using the previous notation, the velocity of the i−th particle at the $(t+1)$−th iteration can be expressed as the sum of the following three addends [26]

$$\underline{w}^{(i)}(t+1) = \omega(t)\underline{w}^{(i)}(t) + c_1 R_1(t)(\underline{y}^{(i)}(t) - \underline{x}^{(i)}(t)) \\ + c_2 R_2(t)(\underline{y}(t) - \underline{x}^{(i)}(t)), \tag{12}$$

where $i \in \{1,\ldots,S\}$. The first addend in (12) is proportional to the velocity of the i−th particle at the previous iteration t according to the inertial factor $\omega(t)$. The second addend aims at moving each particle towards its best position reached so far, namely $\underline{y}^{(i)}(t)$, which can be expressed as

$$\underline{y}^{(i)}(t) = \arg\min_{\underline{z}\in X^{(i)}} F(\underline{z}), \tag{13}$$

where $X^{(i)} = \{\underline{x}^{(i)}(0),\ldots,\underline{x}^{(i)}(t)\}$. Finally, the third addend aims at moving each particle towards the best position reached so far by any particle in the swarm, namely $\underline{y}(t)$, which can be expressed as

$$\underline{y}(t) = \arg\min_{\underline{z}\in Y^{(i)}} F(\underline{z}), \tag{14}$$

where $Y^{(i)} = \{\underline{y}^{(1)}(t),\ldots,\underline{y}^{(S)}(t)\}$. The velocities computed according to (12) are then used to update the positions of the corresponding particles using the following formula

$$\underline{x}^{(i)}(t+1) = \underline{x}^{(i)}(t) + \underline{w}^{(i)}(t+1), \tag{15}$$

where $i \in \{1,\ldots,S\}$. The update rules for positions and velocities are inspired by the behaviors of birds in swarms. The PSO algorithm is iterated until a termination condition is met. In our setup, the termination condition is the reach of a given (maximum) number of iterations, which has been empirically set equal to 50. The position estimate of the TN corresponds to the position of the particle in the global best position obtained after the termination of the algorithm. Since we are dealing with a minimization problem, the global best position is the one corresponding to the lowest value of the fitness function. Illustrative experimental results about the performance of the PSO-based algorithm for localization purposes are shown in next section. They are obtained with a population size of $S = 40$ particles. The cognition and social parameters are both equal to 2 and the inertial factor is 0.1.

5   Experimental Results

The studied experimental indoor scenario is a square room whose side is 5 m long. The number of APs positioned inside the environment and used for localization is $M = 4$. Note that current implementation of the localization algorithm outlined in Sect. 4 can also support a larger number of APs, which is expected to improve accuracy. Given a proper reference system, the coordinates of APs, expressed in meters, are the following

$$\underline{s}_1 = (2.5, 0, 2.5)^{\mathsf{T}} \qquad \underline{s}_2 = (0, 2.5, 2.5)^{\mathsf{T}}$$
$$\underline{s}_3 = (2.5, 5, 2, 5)^{\mathsf{T}} \qquad \underline{s}_4 = (5, 2.5, 2.5)^{\mathsf{T}}. \tag{16}$$

Observe that the four APs are placed at the same height, thus laying on the same plane, makes classic geometric-based localization algorithms, such as the TSML algorithm and the CI algorithm, inapplicable. More precisely, matrices involved in such geometric-based localization algorithms become strongly ill-conditioned in such a scenario, leading to very inaccurate position estimates (see, e.g., [16,20]).

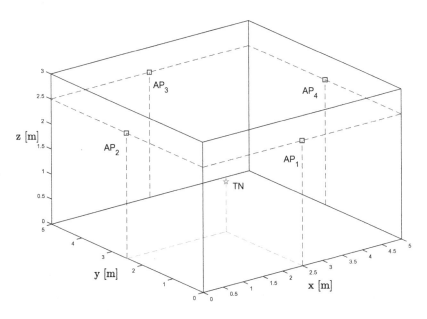

Fig. 1. The positions of the four APs (blue squares) and of the TN (red star) are shown. The walls of the room are shown as black lines. (Color figure online)

For the sake of simplicity, the performance of the proposed localization algorithm is investigated with a single TN position. However, note that the proposed algorithm could be used to simultaneously find position estimates of different smart devices, since the localization of each of them is performed by the add-on module running on the device itself. The true coordinates of the considered TN, expressed in meters, are

$$\underline{u} = (2.5, 2.5, 1)^{\mathsf{T}}. \tag{17}$$

Observe that the TN is placed in the middle of the room. The positions of the APs and of the TN are shown in Fig. 1, where the APs are marked with blue squares and the TN is marked as a red star. In this localization scenario, $L = 100$ position estimates are evaluated.

The performance of the proposed localization algorithm is evaluated in terms of proper metrics, related to distances between the true TN position and its estimates. Let us recall that, according to (3), the true TN position is denoted as $\underline{u}$ and, according to (6), its estimates at the l−th iteration is denoted as $\underline{\hat{u}}_l$. Then, the distance between the true TN position and its estimate at the l-th iteration can be computed as

$$d_l = ||\underline{\hat{u}}_l - \underline{u}|| \tag{18}$$

where $l \in \{1, \ldots, L\}$. The definition of d_l in (18) allows expressing the average distance error as

$$d_{\text{avg}} = \frac{1}{L} \sum_{l=1}^{L} d_l. \tag{19}$$

Finally, the maximum of distance errors obtained in L iterations can be computed as

$$d_{\text{max}} = \max_{l \in \{1,\ldots,L\}} d_l. \tag{20}$$

Note that in scenarios where the height of the TN can be considered approximately constant, the height of the TN is not significant to evaluate the performance of localization. In other words, errors on the estimated height of the TN can be neglected and the performance of the localization algorithm depends only on the accuracy of abscissa and ordinate of the position estimates. For this reason, another possible interesting evaluation metric is the distance between the projection of the position of the TN and the projection of its estimates on a plane parallel to the floor. This quantity can be expressed as

$$e_l = ||(\hat{x}_l, \hat{y}_l) - (x, y)||, \tag{21}$$

where $l \in \{1, \ldots, L\}$. Note that only abscissa and ordinate of the true position of the TN and of its estimates are considered in (21). As done for (18), the average value of $\{e_l\}_{l=1}^{L}$ can be computed as follows

$$e_{\text{avg}} = \frac{1}{L} \sum_{l=1}^{L} e_l, \tag{22}$$

while the maximum value of $\{e_l\}_{l=1}^{L}$ is

$$e_{\text{max}} = \max_{l \in \{1,\ldots,L\}} e_l. \tag{23}$$

Figure 2 shows the values of distance errors obtained in the localization scenario described above. In particular, the values of $\{d_l\}_{l=1}^{L}$ (magenta bars) are shown for each of the 100 performed position estimates. Observe that such results show that the proposed localization algorithm leads to sufficiently accurate position estimates for many indoor localization application, since the value of d_{max}

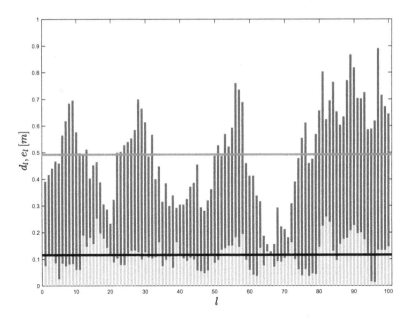

Fig. 2. The values of distance errors $\{d_l\}_{l=1}^{L}$ are shown for each iteration (magenta bars). The value of the average distance error d_{avg} is also shown (green line). Similarly, the corresponding values of $\{e_l\}_{l=1}^{L}$ are shown for each iteration (cyan bars), together with their average (black line). (Color figure online)

is lower than 0.9 m. Moreover, Fig. 2 shows that the average value of distance errors d_{avg} (green line) is nearly 0.5 m. Figure 2 also shows the values of $\{e_l\}_{l=1}^{L}$ obtained by considering only the abscissa and the ordinate of the position of the TN and of its estimates (cyan bars). As expected, such values are smaller that the corresponding values of d_l, because they are obtained by neglecting errors on the height of the position estimates of the TN. In detail, the value of e_{max} is 0.26 m, which corresponds to a third of the value of d_{max}. Consequently, also the value of e_{avg} (black line) is reduced with respect to that of d_{avg}, and it is equal to 0.11 m.

Results obtained in this illustrative scenario show that the proposed PSO-based localization algorithm has a good performance also in a scenario where other algorithms, such as the CI and the TSML algorithms, would fail, due to the fact that all APs share the same height. In addition, even if no discussion on the topic is provided in this paper, the speed of the proposed algorithm is significantly better than those of classic alternatives because of the reduced matrix computations. Results are satisfactory for many indoor applications, such as mixed-reality games in indoor environments and localization of devices in shopping malls, train stations or airports.

6   Conclusion

This paper presented a bio-inspired approach to WiFi-based localization of smart devices in indoor environments. According to the proposed algorithm, the position of a smart device in an indoor environment can be estimated using distance estimates acquired from available access points of the WiFi network. The obtained distance estimates are properly processed and they are used to feed the proposed localization algorithm, which is implemented in a specific add-on module for JADE installed on the device. According to the proposed algorithm, the localization problem is formulated in terms of a minimization problem, which is solved using the PSO algorithm. The application of the proposed algorithm is particularly well suited in some localization contexts, e.g., when all the access points of the WiFi network are placed on the same plane. Experimental results discussed in this paper were obtained in an illustrative indoor environment with this characteristic. Results show that agents can reach a localization accuracy of less than 1 m, with an average of distance errors of nearly 0.5 m. Hence, the proposed approach can be considered adequate for many application scenarios.

References

1. Banzi, M., Caire, G., Gotta, D.: WADE: a software platform to develop mission critical, applications exploiting agents and workflows. In: Proceedings of the International Joint Conference on Autonomous Agents and Multi-agent Systems (AAMAS 2008), pp. 29–36. IFAAMAS (2008)
2. Bellifemine, F., Bergenti, F., Caire, G., Poggi, A.: Jade—a Java agent development framework. In: Bordini, R.H., Dastani, M., Dix, J., El Fallah Seghrouchni, A. (eds.) Multi-Agent Programming. MSASSO, vol. 15, pp. 125–147. Springer, Boston, MA (2005). https://doi.org/10.1007/0-387-26350-0_5
3. Bergenti, F., Caire, G., Gotta, D.: Interactive workflows with WADE. In: Proceedings of the IEEE International Conference on Enabling Technologies: Infrastructures for Collaborative Enterprises (WETICE 2012), pp. 10–15. IEEE (2012)
4. Bergenti, F., Caire, G., Gotta, D.: An overview of the AMUSE social gaming platform. In: Proceedings of the Workshop From Objects to Agents (WOA 2013), CEUR Workshop Proceedings, vol. 1099. RWTH Aachen (2013)
5. Bergenti, F., Caire, G., Gotta, D.: Agents on the move: JADE for Android devices. In: Proceedings of the Workshop From Objects to Agents (WOA 2014), CEUR Workshop Proceedings, vol. 1260. RWTH Aachen (2014)
6. Bergenti, F., Caire, G., Gotta, D.: Large-scale network and service management with WANTS. In: Industrial Agents: Emerging Applications of Software Agents in Industry. pp. 231–246. Elsevier (2015)
7. Bergenti, F., Franchi, E., Poggi, A.: Agent-based social networks for enterprise collaboration. In: Proceedings of the IEEE International Conference on Enabling Technologies: Infrastructures for Collaborative Enterprises, WETICE 2011, pp. 25–28. IEEE (2011)
8. Bergenti, F., Monica, S.: Location-aware social gaming with AMUSE. In: Demazeau, Y., Ito, T., Bajo, J., Escalona, M.J. (eds.) PAAMS 2016. LNCS (LNAI), vol. 9662, pp. 36–47. Springer, Cham (2016). https://doi.org/10.1007/978-3-319-39324-7_4

9. Bulusu, N., Heidemann, J., Estrin, D.: GPS-less low cost outdoor localization for very small devices. IEEE Pers. Commun. **7**(5), 28–34 (2000)
10. Farid, Z., Nordin, R., Ismail, M.: Recent advances in wireless indoor localization techniques and system. J. Comput. Netw. Commun. **2013**, 12 (2013)
11. Ho, K.C., Lu, X., Kovavisaruch, L.: Source localization using TDOA and FDOA measurements in the presence of receiver location errors: analysis and solution. IEEE Transact. Sign. Proces. **55**(2), 684–696 (2007)
12. Kennedy, J., Eberhart, R.: Particle swarm optimization. In: Proceedings of the IEEE International Conference on Neural Networks, ICNN 1995, pp. 1942–1948. IEEE (1995)
13. Monica, S., Bergenti, F.: Location-aware JADE agents in indoor scenarios. In: Proceedings of the Workshop from Objects to Agents (WOA 2015), CEUR Workshop Proceedings, vol. 1382, pp. 103–108. RWTH Aachen (2015)
14. Monica, S., Bergenti, F.: A Comparison of accurate indoor localization of static targets via WiFi and UWB ranging. Trends in Practical Applications of Scalable Multi-Agent Systems, the PAAMS Collection. AISC, vol. 473, pp. 111–123. Springer, Cham (2016). https://doi.org/10.1007/978-3-319-40159-1_9
15. Monica, S., Bergenti, F.: An experimental evaluation of agent-based indoor localization. In: The Science and Information Computing Conference. pp. 638–646. IEEE (2017)
16. Monica, S., Bergenti, F.: Experimental Evaluation of agent-based localization of smart appliances. In: Criado Pacheco, N., Carrascosa, C., Osman, N., Julián Inglada, V. (eds.) EUMAS/AT -2016. LNCS (LNAI), vol. 10207, pp. 293–304. Springer, Cham (2017). https://doi.org/10.1007/978-3-319-59294-7_24
17. Monica, S., Bergenti, F.: Indoor localization of JADE agents without a dedicated infrastructure. In: Berndt, J.O., Petta, P., Unland, R. (eds.) MATES 2017. LNCS (LNAI), vol. 10413, pp. 256–271. Springer, Cham (2017). https://doi.org/10.1007/978-3-319-64798-2_16
18. Monica, S., Bergenti, F.: An optimization-based algorithm for indoor localization of JADE agents. In: Proceedings of Workshop From Objects to Agents (WOA 2017), CEUR Workshop Proceedings, vol. 1867, pp. 65–70. RWTH Aachen (2017)
19. Monica, S., Ferrari, G.: Swarm intelligent approaches to auto-localization of nodes in static UWB networks. Appl. Soft Comput. **25**, 426–434 (2014)
20. Monica, S., Ferrari, G.: A swarm-based approach to real-time 3D indoor localization: experimental performance analysis. Appl. Soft Comput. **43**, 489–497 (2016)
21. Patwari, N., Ash, J.N., Kyperountas, S., Hero, A.O., Moses, R.L., Correal, N.S.: Locating the nodes. IEEE Signal Process. Mag. **22**(4), 54–69 (2005)
22. Poggi, A., Bergenti, F.: Developing smart emergency applications with multi-agent systems. Int. J. E-Health Med. Commun. **1**(4), 1–13 (2010)
23. Poli, R., Kennedy, J., Blackwell, T.: Particle swarm optimization. Swarm Intell. J. **1**(1), 33–57 (2007)
24. Sahinoglu, Z., Gezici, S., Guvenc, I.: Ultra-wideband Positioning Systems: Theoretical Limits. Ranging Algorithms and Protocols. Cambridge University Press, Cambridge (2008)
25. Shen, G., Zetik, R., Thomä, R.S.: Performance comparison of TOA and TDOA based location estimation algorithms in LOS environment. In: Proceedings of the Workshop on Positioning, Navigation and Communication, WPNC 2008, pp. 71–78. IEEE (2008)
26. Shi, Y., Eberhart, R.: A modified particle swarm optimizer. In: Proceedings of the IEEE International Conference on Evolutionary Computation, ICEC 1999, pp. 69–73. IEEE (1999)

Chemical, Biological and Medical Applications

Synchronization Effects in a Metabolism-Driven Model of Multi-cellular System

Davide Maspero[1,2], Alex Graudenzi[3]✉, Satwinder Singh[3],
Dario Pescini[4], Giancarlo Mauri[3], Marco Antoniotti[3,6],
and Chiara Damiani[3,5]✉

[1] Department of Biotechnology and Biosciences,
University of Milano-Bicocca, Milan, Italy
[2] Fondazione IRCCS Istituto Nazionale dei Tumori, Milan, Italy
[3] Department of Informatics, Systems and Communication,
University of Milan-Bicocca, Milan, Italy
{alex.graudenzi,chiara.damiani}@unimib.it
[4] Department of Statistics and Quantitative Methods,
University of Milan-Bicocca, Milan, Italy
[5] SYSBIO Centre of Systems Biology, University of Milano-Bicocca, Milan, Italy
[6] NeuroMI Milan Center for Neuroscience, University of Milano-Bicocca, Milan, Italy

Abstract. Understanding the synchronization, either induced or spontaneous, of cell growth, division and proliferation in a cell culture is an important topic in molecular biology and biotechnology. Metabolic processes related to the synthesis of all the molecules needed for a new round of cell division are the basic underlying phenomena responsible for the behaviour of the population. Complex dynamics, such as population oscillations, arise when the individual members of a population divide in unison. To investigate the conditions that can determine oscillatory behaviors, we here use a multi-scale model that couples the simulation of metabolic growth, via metabolic network modelling and Flux Balance Analysis, with the simulation of population and spatial dynamics, via Cellular Potts Models. We here show that repeated oscillations in the overall number of cells spontaneously emerge, due to the synchronization of duplication events, unless cell density-dependent controls on growth are introduced.

Keywords: Multi-scale modeling · Cellular Potts Model · Flux Balance Analysis · Synchronization

1 Introduction

Synchronization phenomena are commonly observed in various natural and artificial systems and are object of investigation in a broad range of fields of science

D. Maspero, A. Graudenzi and D. Chiara—Equal contributors.

© Springer Nature Switzerland AG 2019
S. Cagnoni et al. (Eds.): WIVACE 2018, CCIS 900, pp. 115–126, 2019.
https://doi.org/10.1007/978-3-030-21733-4_9

and engineering [6,15,16]. In particular, biological systems such as single cells and multi-cellular systems with higher organization levels, such as tissues and organs, often exhibit synchronization phenomena, which are essential for their normal functioning, e.g., for coordinate motion or cell replication [20].

The cell cycle has been very well investigated over the years and many procedures have been delivered to synchronize cells in various stages of the cell cycle. It has been reported that synchronized cultures display oscillatory dynamics in the cell number [8,13,21]. In this respect, several mathematical and computational approaches to model oscillatory phenomena in cell biology have been proposed in the last years (see, e.g., [12,25]).

We here investigate the synchronization effects characterizing the dynamics of a previously introduced multi-scale model of multi-cellular systems, named FBCA (Flux Balance with Cellular Automata) [10]. The model combines a spatial/ morphological dynamical model of a general tissue, modeled via Cellular Potts Model (CPM), and a lower-level model of the metabolic activity of its constituting single cells, modeled via Flux Balance Analysis (FBA) (see Methods).

In particular, we here employ an extensive *parameter scan* strategy to identify the conditions under which the variation of the cell number displays spontaneous and repeated oscillations in time, in a model representing the morphology of a generic intestinal crypt, which is the supposed locus of colorectal cancer origination [4].

The results of the simulations point at the key role of the biomass parameter, whose accumulation drives the growth tendency and the replication pace of the cells, in the possible emergence of synchronization patterns. These results have interesting repercussions in the sphere of cancer evolution, as the characterization of complex patterns in cell population dynamics may provide new hints on the emergence of neoplastic formations.

2   Methods

FBCA, earlier introduced in [10], is here briefly described. The main idea is to represent a generic multi-cellular system (i.e. a cell culture or a tissue) via a multi-scale model that combines a representation of spatial dynamics via Cellular Potts Model (CPM) [19], and a model of cell metabolism via Flux Balance Analysis (FBA) [14] (see Fig. 1).

In CPM, biological cells are defined as sets of contiguous lattice sites over a 2D rectangular lattice L that mimics the morphology of a generic intestinal crypt [4], and cell spatial dynamics is driven by an energy minimization criterion, ruled by an Hamiltonian function $\mathcal{H}(L)$. CMP was proven to effectively reproduce complex properties of multi-cellular systems, especially with respect to cancer development [9,17,18,23]. In our case $\mathcal{H}(L)$ is composed by two terms, the first accounting for the Differential Adhesion Hypothesis (DAH) [22], the second accounting for the growth tendency of each cell, driven by biomass accumulation, which is computed via FBA.

FBA is used to compute biomass production based on the nutrient availability in the surrounding of any given cells present on the lattice, by optimizing the

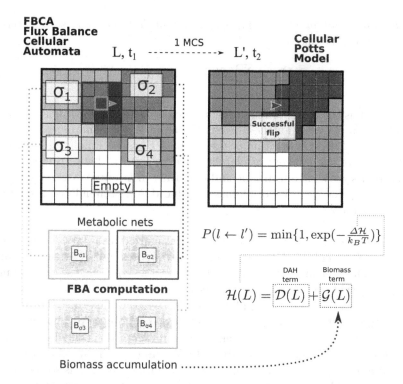

Fig. 1. FBCA model is depicted. Image modified from [10]. The morphology of a generic tissue is modeled via Cellular Potts Model, in which biological cells are represented by sets of contiguous lattice sites, which evolve via flip attempts driven by an Hamiltonian function $\mathcal{H}(L)$. $\mathcal{H}(L)$ depends on two terms, the first accounting for the Differential Adhesion Hypothesis (DAH), the second for the growth tendency of each cell due to the accumulation of biomass (see Methods). Biomass is computed via Flux Balance Analysis on cell-specific metabolic networks.

fluxes of a metabolic network associated to each cell σ. A metabolic network is defined as the set of metabolites and relative chemical reactions taking place among them in each cell.

Hamiltonian function (I): DAH term. The first term of $\mathcal{H}(L)$ is defined as follows:

$$\mathcal{D}(L) = \frac{1}{2} \sum_{\sigma_i, \sigma_j \in \mathcal{N}} J(\tau(\sigma_i), \tau(\sigma_j))(1 - \delta(\sigma_i, \sigma_j)) \tag{1}$$

where i and j are lattice sites $\in L$, σ_i is the cell id at site i, $\mathcal{N}$ is the Moore neighborhood in which j is chose, $\tau(\sigma_i)$ is the cell type of cell σ_i, δ is the Kronecker delta, $J(\tau(\sigma_i), \tau(\sigma_j))$ is the amount of energy required to maintain adjacent two cells site σ_i and σ_j. In this study we consider one cellular type and empty space, mimicking the tendency to fill the empty space if available.

Hamiltonian function (II): biomass-driven growth term. The second term of $\mathcal{H}(L)$ is defined as follows:

$$\mathcal{G}(L) = \lambda \sum_i [|\mathcal{C}(\sigma_i)| - A_{target}(\mathcal{B}_{\sigma_i})]^2 \tag{2}$$

where $|\mathcal{C}(\sigma_i)|$ is the current area of cell σ_i in lattice sites, and $\lambda > 0$ is a Lagrange multiplier that accounts for the capacity to deform a cell membrane. The volume target $A_{target}(\mathcal{B}(\sigma_i))$ is function of the biomass $\mathcal{B}(\sigma_i)$ accumulated in each cell, as a function of the nutrient availability (see below). In this setting we assume that nutrients are constant in time and uniformly distributed over the lattice. At each time step the quantity of biomass produced and accumulated is computed via FBA, as follows.

FBA computation. A metabolic network is formalized as a $M \times R$ stoichiometric matrix S, where M is the number of metabolites and R is the number of reactions, whose element $S_{m,r}$ is the stoichiometric coefficient (i.e. the number of molecules that are transformed) of metabolite m in reaction r.

Linear Programming is applied to identify the flux distribution $v = (v_1, \ldots, v_M)$ that maximizes (or minimizes) the objective function $Z = \sum_{j=1}^{M} w_j v_j$, where w_j is a coefficient that represents the contribution of flux v_j in vector v to Z, given a steady-state assumption for the abundance each metabolite, i.e., $S \times v = 0$. The Linear Programming Problem is solved to maximize, at each MCS, a pseudo-reaction that represents the conversion rate of biomass precursors into biomass, as follows:

$$\begin{array}{c} \text{maximize } b_\sigma \\ \text{subject to } Sv = 0, \ v_L \leq v \leq v_U \end{array} \tag{3}$$

where b_σ is the flux of the biomass pseudo-reactions, v_L and v_U are, respectively, the vector with minimum and maximum reaction fluxes allowed.

Extra-cellular fluxes are constrained according to the availability of nutrients in the cell's area. In detail, we constraint the intake of a given metabolite to be lower than the sum of its concentration in each of the site occupied by cell. The concentration of metabolite in each site is assumed constant in time and space.

The biomass flux obtained as per Eq. 3 is added to the $\mathcal{B}(\sigma_i)$ previously accumulated as detailed in Sect. 2.1 experimental settings. As specified above, the biomass accumulated in each cell $\mathcal{B}(\sigma_i)$ is converted into A_{target} with a conversion factor $\mathcal{F}$: $A_{target} = \mathcal{B}(\sigma_i) \cdot \mathcal{F}$. Finally, we define the *cell density* as $\rho(\sigma_i) = \frac{\mathcal{B}(\sigma_i)}{|\mathcal{C}(\sigma_i)|}$.

Dynamics. The simulation is performed via a discrete-time stochastic process (time unit: *Monte-Carlo Step-* MCS) in which $l \cdot k$ (where l is the number of lattice sites and k is an arbitrary value usually set equal to 4) lattice *transformations* are attempted. In each transformation attempt, a lattice site $l_i \in \sigma_i$ is randomly chosen over the lattice, and a second lattice site belonging to another cell $l_j \in$

σ_j is randomly chosen in its Moore neighborhood $\mathcal{N}(l_i)$. A variation of $\Delta\mathcal{H}$ is computed in case l_i switches from cell σ_i to cell σ_j: such flip attempt is maintained if $\Delta\mathcal{H} < 0$, otherwise is accepted with a probability given by a Boltzmann distribution:

$$P(l_j \leftarrow l_i) = \min\{1, e^{\left(\frac{-\Delta\mathcal{H}}{k_bT}\right)}\} \tag{4}$$

The minimization of the overall energy drives the evolution of the system, whereas k_bT allows for stochastic fluctuations.

Mitosis. We define A_{base} as the reference area of a given cell before it starts to growth. Each cell grows until it reaches $A_{mitosis}$, which is defined equal to $2 \cdot (A_{base})$ for every cell. Then it produces a daughter cell by splitting its space $|\mathcal{C}(\sigma_i)|$ along a randomly chosen horizontal or vertical direction. Daughter cells will have area (approximately) equal to $0.5 \cdot (A_{mitosis})$ and will inherit the cell properties of the parent.

2.1   Experimental Settings

In this work, we present the results of extensive simulations in different experimental settings, to investigate cell population dynamics in a space-limited environments. As metabolic network, as in [10], we used a model of human central carbon metabolism (including 270 reactions) [2,5,11]. The FBCA parameter values, as well, are the same as in [10] unless otherwise stated.

Space Shape and Cell Death. In this study we want to simulate two different space configuration:

1. To mimic a intestinal crypt, as in [9], the space is modeled as a lower-side opened cylinder formed by a single-layer cells rolled out onto a rectangular lattice with periodic boundary conditions. When cells reach the lower bound are removed from the system.
2. Cells evolve in a full closed cylinder, to increase the competition for limited space.

Furthermore, to simulate the death by mechanical compression, cells are removed when $|\mathcal{C}(\sigma_i)| < 0.5 \cdot (A_{base})$.

Initial Volume Distribution. In the simulation settings of our previous work [10] all cells were initialized with identical $|C(\sigma_i)|$. In this work, at time $MCS = 0$, the lattice is populated with cells, which are assigned a random $|C(\sigma_i)|$ and a corresponding initial biomass that ensures $\rho(\sigma_i) = \frac{1}{F}$. For the sake of simplicity, we consider that each cell at $MCS = 0$ has a rectangular shape. To investigate how the initial volumes distribution affects the simulation dynamics, we tested three different settings, with different levels of granularity for the initial volume distribution, which we refer to as *Average*, *Low* and *High* granularity. In the three settings, the initial volume is uniformly distributed within the following ranges:

– *Low*:
$$|\mathcal{C}(\sigma_i)| \in \{30, 40, 50\}$$

– *Average*:
$$|\mathcal{C}(\sigma_i)| \in \{25, 30, 35, 40, 45, 50\}$$

– *High*:
$$|\mathcal{C}(\sigma_i)| \in \{24, 27, 30, 33, 36, 39, 42, 45, 48\}$$

We remark that in this work $|\mathcal{C}(\sigma_i)|$ at $MCS = 0$ does not coincide with A_{base}, which takes value $25\mu m$ for each cell. Others properties, such as $A_{mitosis}$ and the Hamiltonian adhesion factors, are identical in each cell and set as in [10].

Lattice Population. Lattice is filled in two different configurations.

– *Completely filled lattice:*
There are no empty spaces. Each lattice site belongs to a cell σ_i.
– *Half-filled lattice:*
Once the cell height is determined, which is initially identical for each cell, we divided the lattice in many rows with that dimension. Than we filled every other row with cells.

Biomass Limitation. This configuration settings concerns the rate of biomass accumulation. Biomass accumulation is modeled as follows:

$$\mathcal{B}(\sigma_i)^{MCS} = \mathcal{B}(\sigma_i)^{MCS-1} + \gamma \cdot b_\sigma \tag{5}$$

In previous work [10], we let biomass to accumulate independently from the actual cell's density ($\gamma = 1$). This assumption may lead to an unrestrained increase in cell density $\rho(\sigma_i)$. Here we want to test if this possibility for unlimited density influences the cellular population synchronization dynamics. Thus, we conceived two configuration settings:

– *Free biomass accumulation*:
A given cell produces biomass, at each time step, taking into account only the nutrient availability ($\gamma = 1$). No other parameters are considered.
– *Limited biomass accumulation*:
The biomass accumulated at each time step $\mathcal{B}(\sigma_i)^{MCS}$ is reduced by the following factor:

$$\gamma = \begin{cases} 1, & \text{if } \rho(\sigma_i) \leq \dfrac{1}{\mathcal{F}} \\ 1 - \min(1, 2(\mathcal{F} \cdot \rho(\sigma_i) - 1))^2, & \text{otherwise} \end{cases}$$

By doing this, biomass cannot accumulate ($\mathcal{B}(\sigma_i)^{MCS} = \mathcal{B}(\sigma_i)^{MCS-1}$) if the cell density $\rho(\sigma_i)$ exceeds its initial value by 1.5 times.

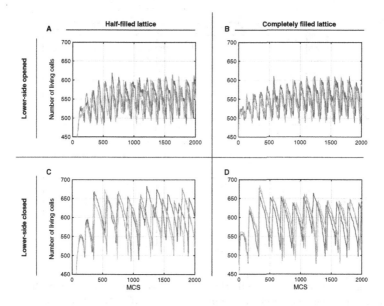

Fig. 2. (A-D) biomass can be accumulated over time steps without any limitation. Each plot shows the total number of living cells at each MCS. (A, C) The simulation started with ∼ 200 cells distributed leaving half of the overall space empty. (B, D) The simulation started with ∼ 400 cells distributed leaving no empty lattice sites. (A, B) To mimic a intestinal crypt, cells were removed from the simulation if they reached the bottom lattice side. (C, D) To increase the space competition we close all the lattice sides so that cells could leave the lattice only if mashed. Each plot shows three repetitions (Red, Yellow and Blue curves) with the same parameters. (Color figure online)

3   Results

3.1   No Sensing of Population Density

As one can observe in Fig. 2, most simulation settings are characterized by the emergence of patterns of synchronization in cell populations. More in detail, death and mitosis events appear to occur at very close time points for a very large number of cells. This phenomenon is amplified if the space is fully closed (Fig. 2 C,D). It is important to notice that the range of oscillations w.r.t. the overall number of alive cells is prominent (around 150 cells) in most cases, whereas the (average) period is a few MCSs only.

Moreover, by comparing initial configurations in which the lattice is completely filled with configurations in which only half of the lattice is filled with cells, one can still see a synchronization phenomenon, yet characterized by a certain delay, due to the time needed for cells to fill the whole lattice.

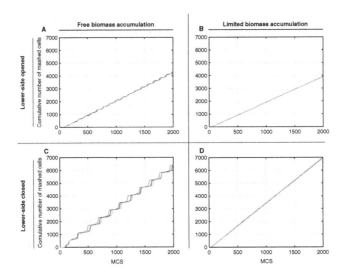

Fig. 3. Cumulative number of cells that are removed from the system after a mashed death. (A,C) Biomass can freely accumulate over the MCS. (B,C) Biomass production is limited proportionally to $\rho(\sigma_i)$. (A, B) To mimic an intestinal crypt, cells were removed from the simulation if they reached the bottom lattice side. (C, D) To increase the competition for space we close all the lattice sides so that cells could leave the lattice only if mashed. Each plot shows three repetitions (Red, Yellow and Blue curves) with the same parameters. (Color figure online)

Also, the frequency of oscillations is different when the lattice is either open or closed, mostly because the only way for a cell to leave the system in the latter case is by compression, whereas in the former case cells can be expelled when reaching the lower side of the lattice.

In this respect, one can observe a reduction of the number of cell crushed by compression of 31% by comparing open with closed experimental settings (Lower-side open: 4284 ± 17; Lower-side closed: 6402 ± 11). This result indicates that also with an open lattice the competition for space plays an important role. Furthermore, the rate of cell death is not constant in time but displays repeated peaks with almost constant frequency (Fig. 3 A,C); this effect is amplified if the space is closed.

Focusing on the open lattice setting, we investigated how the initial volume distribution affects the competition during a simulation. To this end, we simulated a lower-side opened, completely filled lattice, with the three initial granularity configurations defined in 2.1.

Comparing the blue curves in Fig. 4 B and F (Low and High granularity, respectively), one can see that the overall dynamics becomes quite similar, after around ~ 500 MCSs. In particular, the lower the level of granularity, the faster the synchronization patterns appear to emerge.

Moreover, in all simulations one sub-population (defined as cells with the same initial configuration in terms of volume and biomass) becomes predominant. In some cases, the predominant sub-population is the one characterized by the largest initial volume, yet there are exception to this phenomenon, especially in the scenarios with higher granularity (see e.g., Fig. 4).

In Fig. 4 E a zoom-in of the sub-population dynamics is shown. The red, dark blue and dark green curves appear to be synchronized, yet around 1000 MCSs the dynamics of the latter dramatically changes and the sub-population extinguishes in a very short time.

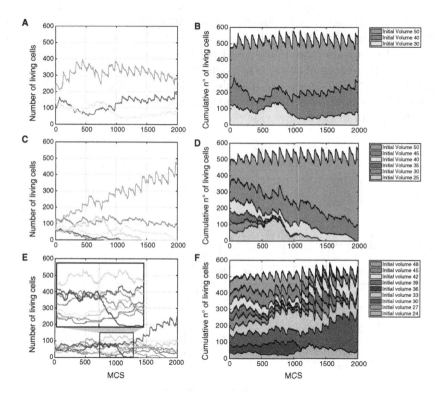

Fig. 4. Simulation settings: full lattice populated, lower-side opened and free biomass accumulation. (A,B) Low granularity: cell initial volume randomly assigned in $[30, 40, 50]$. (C,D) Medium granularity: cell initial volume randomly assigned in $[25, 30, 35, 40, 45, 50]$. (E,F) High granularity: cell initial volume randomly assigned in $[24, 27, 30, 33, 36, 39, 42, 45, 48]$. (A,C) Number of living cells grouped by initial volume values. (E) Number of living cells grouped by initial volume values, with a zoom in on the intermediate steps. (B,D,F) Cumulative number of living cells that highlights the contribution of each population (stratified by initial volume values) for the overall cell number. Color of each population groups is reported on the right of the figure. (Color figure online)

3.2   Growth Limited by Direct Biomass Production Reduction

A possible hypothesis is that an uncontrolled accumulation of biomass might be responsible for the observed synchronization effects, due to lattice overpopulation. To investigate this issue, we defined an experimental setting in which the biomass production is constrained to be proportional to cell density, which in turn depends to population density (i.e., the overall number of cells present in the lattice in a given time step).

As one can see in Fig. 5, by imposing such limitation on biomass accumulation, the synchronization phenomena seem to disappear. In particular, in Fig. 5 D one can observe an initial synchronization pattern, most likely due to a fully populated initial configuration and to a closed lattice (i.e., the most space-limited setting). Yet, after 500 MCSs the total number of cells stabilizes and the subsequent oscillations are more limited and noisy, at least with respect to the case in which biomass accumulation is not density-dependent (Fig. 2 D). Comparing Fig. 5 A-B vs. C-D, one can see that the total number of cells depends mostly on the either open or closed lattice configuration, likely because more cells can leave the system in the former case.

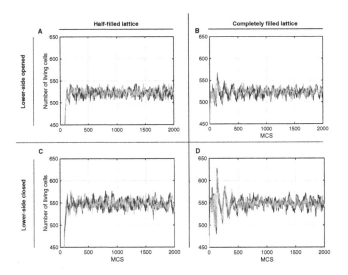

Fig. 5. Total number of living cells at each MCS, when biomass production was limited proportionally to $\rho(\sigma_i)$. (A, C) The simulation started with $\sim$ 200 cells distributed leaving half of the overall space empty. (B, D) The simulation started with $\sim$ 400 cells distributed leaving no empty lattice sites. (A, B) To mimic a intestinal crypt, cells were removed from the simulation if they reached the bottom lattice side. (C, D) To increase the space competition we close all the lattice sides so that cells could leave the lattice only if mashed. Each plot shows three repetitions (Red, Yellow and Blue curves) with the same parameters. (Color figure online)

Another interesting result is that the limitation on the biomass accumulation rate does not significantly affect the overall number of cells crushed by compression ($+10\%$ in the open lattice scenario; -11% in the close lattice scenario).

4 Discussion

Oscillatory phenomena are involved in a variety of physiological, as well as pathological, conditions in living systems [7]. Many attempts have been put forward to investigate these phenomena *in-silico*, which typically involve simulation of cell cycle dynamics, via ODEs, at the single cell and cell culture level, as e.g. [24].

We here investigated population density effects in a multi-scale model of multi-cellular system that takes into account proliferation driven by metabolic growth and competition for space (FBCA [10]).

We showed that, when we let populations of cells, starting from different cell-sizes, grow unrestrained and divide when they reach the same target-volume, oscillations phenomena emerge. On the contrary, if metabolic growth is inhibited by cell density, which in turn is a proxy of population density, synchronicity is disrupted.

Density-dependent regulation of proliferation in cell populations is a matter of fact: one may think, for example, at quorum sensing in bacteria communities. The second scenario could therefore be regarded as more realistic.

Although these results are preliminary, this study shows the potential of FBCA in investigating important population phenomena of complex biological systems, especially with regard to the investigation of cancer development.

In the next future, we will investigate more sophisticated strategies to model density-dependent regulation and we will overcome some current limitations of our model, with particular regard to the modeling of spatial diffusion of nutrients and of metabolic interactions via exchange of metabolites between cells. We finally remark that the dynamics of metabolically heterogeneous cell populations may also be investigated, as proposed in [1,3].

References

1. Damiani, C., et al.: A metabolic core model elucidates how enhanced utilization of glucose and glutamine, with enhanced glutamine-dependent lactate production, promotes cancer cell growth: The warburq effect. PLOS Comput. Biol. **13**(9), e1005758 (2017)
2. Damiani, C., Di Filippo, M., Pescini, D., Maspero, D., Colombo, R., Mauri, G.: popFBA: tackling intratumour heterogeneity with flux balance analysis. Bioinformatics **33**(14), i311–i318 (2017)
3. Damiani, C., et al.: An ensemble evolutionary constraint-based approach to understand the emergence of metabolic phenotypes. Nat. Comput. **13**(3), 321–331 (2014)
4. De Matteis, G., Graudenzi, A., Antoniotti, M.: A review of spatial computational models for multi-cellular systems, with regard to intestinal crypts and colorectal cancer development. J. Math. Biol. **66**(7), 1409–1462 (2013)
5. Di Filippo, M., et al.: Zooming-in on cancer metabolic rewiring with tissue specific constraint-based models. Comput. Biol. Chem. **62**, 60–69 (2016)

6. Glass, L.: Synchronization and rhythmic processes in physiology. Nature **410**(6825), 277 (2001)
7. Glass, L., Mackey, M.C.: From Clocks to Chaos: The Rhythms of Life. Princeton University Press, Princeton (1988)
8. Goodwin, B.: Synchronization of escherichia coli in a chemostat by periodic phosphate feeding. Eur. J. Biochem. **10**(3), 511–514 (1969)
9. Graudenzi, A., Caravagna, G., De Matteis, G., Antoniotti, M.: Investigating the relation between stochastic differentiation, homeostasis and clonal expansion in intestinal crypts via multiscale modeling. PLoS One **9**(5), e97272 (2014)
10. Graudenzi, A., Maspero, D., Damiani, C.: Modeling spatio-temporal dynamics of metabolic networks with cellular automata and constraint-based methods. In: Mauri, G., El Yacoubi, S., Dennunzio, A., Nishinari, K., Manzoni, L. (eds.) ACRI 2018. LNCS, vol. 11115, pp. 16–29. Springer, Cham (2018). https://doi.org/10. 1007/978-3-319-99813-8_2
11. Graudenzi, A., et al.: Integration of transcriptomic data and metabolic networks in cancer samples reveals highly significant prognostic power. J. Biomed. Inform. **87**, 37–149 (2018)
12. Kruse, K., Jülicher, F.: Oscillations in cell biology. Curr. Opin. Cell Biol. **17**(1), 20–26 (2005)
13. Massie, T.M., Blasius, B., Weithoff, G., Gaedke, U., Fussmann, G.F.: Cycles, phase synchronization, and entrainment in single-species phytoplankton populations. In: Proceedings of the National Academy of Sciences, p. 200908725 (2010)
14. Orth, J.D., Thiele, I., Palsson, B.Ø.: What is flux balance analysis? Nat. Biotechnol. **28**(3), 245 (2010)
15. Pikovsky, A., Rosenblum, M., Kurths, J., Kurths, J.: Synchronization: A Universal Concept in Nonlinear Sciences, vol. 12. Cambridge University Press, Cambridge (2003)
16. Rosenblum, M.G., Pikovsky, A.S., Kurths, J.: Synchronization approach to analysis of biological systems. Fluct. Noise Lett. **4**(01), L53–L62 (2004)
17. Rubinacci, S., et al.: Cognac: a chaste plugin for the multiscale simulation of gene regulatory networks driving the spatial dynamics of tissues and cancer. Cancer Inform. **14**, CIN-S19965 (2015)
18. Scianna, M., Preziosi, L.: Multiscale developments of the cellular potts model. Multiscale Model. Simul. **10**(2), 342–382 (2012)
19. Scianna, M., Preziosi, L.: Cellular Potts Models: Multiscale Extensions and Biological Applications. CRC Press, Boca Raton (2013)
20. Serra, R., Villani, M.: Modelling Protocells: The Emergent Synchronization of Reproduction and Molecular Replication. Springer, Heidelberg (2017). https:// doi.org/10.1007/978-94-024-1160-7
21. Sheppard, J.D., Dawson, P.S.: Cell synchrony and periodic behaviour in yeast populations. Can. J. Chem. Eng. **77**(5), 893–902 (1999)
22. Steinberg, M.S.: On the mechanism of tissue reconstruction by dissociated cells, i. population kinetics, differential adhesiveness, and the absence of directed migration. Proc. Natl. Acad. Sci. **48**(9), 1577–1582 (1962)
23. Szabó, A., Merks, R.M.: Cellular potts modeling of tumor growth, tumor invasion, and tumor evolution. Front. Oncol. **3**, 87 (2013)
24. Wegerhoff, S., Neymann, T., Engell, S.: Synchronization of a budding yeast cell culture by manipulating inner cell cycle concentrations. In: 2012 IEEE 51st Annual Conference on Decision and Control (CDC), pp. 1029–1034. IEEE (2012)
25. Xu, Z., Tsurugi, K.: A potential mechanism of energy-metabolism oscillation in an aerobic chemostat culture of the yeast saccharomyces cerevisiae. FEBS J. **273**(8), 1696–1709 (2006)

Dynamic DNA Damage and Repair Modeling: Bridging the Gap Between Experimental Damage Readout and Model Structure

Mathias S. Weyland[1,5](✉) , Pauline Thumser-Henner[2,3,4] ,
Carla Rohrer Bley[2,3] , Simone Ulzega[1] , Alke Petri-Fink[5,6] ,
Marco Lattuada[6] , Stephan Scheidegger[1] , and Rudolf M. Füchslin[1]

[1] Zurich University of Applied Sciences, Winterthur, Switzerland
weyl@zhaw.ch
[2] Division of Radiation Oncology, Vetsuisse Faculty, University of Zurich,
Zurich, Switzerland
[3] Center for Applied Biotechnology and Molecular Medicine (CABMM),
University of Zurich, Zurich, Switzerland
[4] Center for Clinical Studies, Vetsuisse Faculty, University of Zurich,
Zurich, Switzerland
[5] BioNanomaterials Group, Adolphe Merkle Institute, University of Fribourg,
Fribourg, Switzerland
[6] Department of Chemistry, University of Fribourg, Fribourg, Switzerland

Abstract. In this work, a method is presented to map a set of experimentally obtained, time-resolved distributions to a dynamic model. Specifically, time-resolved comet assay readouts of cancer cells after application of ionizing radiation are mapped to the Multi-Hit-Repair model, a radiobiologically motivated dynamic model used to predict DNA damage and repair. Differential evolution is used for parameter-search to showcase the potential of this method, producing a prediction close to the experimental measurement. The results obtained from the parameter search are used to characterize aspects of the repair process. The method is compared to prior attempts of finding model parameters from dose-response curves, revealing that calibration is required to render the two comparable.

Keywords: Dynamic DNA damage/repair model ·
Comet assay (single cell gel electrophoresis) · Differential evolution

1 Introduction

Radiotherapy is a cancer treatment in which tumors are targeted with high doses of ionizing radiation to eradicate the cancer cells. The treatment induces DNA damage which the cells attempt to repair in order to avoid eradication. This repair process can be characterized with the help of biologically inspired

© Springer Nature Switzerland AG 2019
S. Cagnoni et al. (Eds.): WIVACE 2018, CCIS 900, pp. 127–137, 2019.
https://doi.org/10.1007/978-3-030-21733-4_10

dynamic models. These models have parameters such as radiosensitivity, speed and efficiency of repair; the corresponding parameter values can be used to gain insights into the nature of the repair process and to characterize cancer- and normal tissue cell lines. Knowing more about these aspects of cancer ultimately leads to novel or optimized treatments for cancer.

A critical property of DNA damage in cells is that it is not deterministic: When a number of cells are irradiated, the specific damage is very different in each of the cells due to the stochastic nature of the process [3]. In consequence, damage induction in cells, as well as their individual reaction to it, will vary even when they are selected from a genetically well defined cell line and irradiated homogeneously. This variation is concealed to some extent when only mean values and standard errors are reported. Sometimes, it is of importance to consider how data are distributed, and how these distributions change over time. As explained below, DNA damage and repair is such a case. More generally, distributions are reflecting some aspects of complexity in the system: A population of genetically identical or similar entities (e.g. cells) will divide into sub-populations which start to evolve differently. When modelling such complex systems, modellers are often confronted with model parameters that cannot be determined uniquely by fitting the average behaviour of experimentally observed populations.

In this broader context, the strategy presented here can be applied not only to DNA damage and repair, but rather to any situation where data distributions in a time-resolved context are paramount. The example of DNA damage and repair chosen here to showcase the method is a good example for the following reason: If little damage is introduced to a cancer cell, the probability of a successful repair is high. After repair, this cell is able to undergo mitosis, contributing to the progression of cancer. Even if only a small number of cancer cells reach this state, the consequences may be critical and very relevant [19]. Since a few cells with little damage would hardly influence the mean damage of a cancer cell population, it is beneficial to consider the full distribution of damage within the population rather than the mean (or any other aggregate, e.g. the median damage). It is equally important to consider how this distribution changes over time. The methodology presented here has therefore been specifically designed to bridge the gap between the experimental readout and the model structure in a fashion that takes into account the damage-distribution in a time-resolved manner.

Following a model-based strategy calls for a set of tools, specifically (a) a mathematical model able to predict DNA damage and its repair; (b) a methodology to obtain DNA damage readout experimentally from irradiated cells, i.e. to quantify DNA damage; and (c) a way to map and compare the model prediction (a) to experimental results (b). The contribution of this work is as follows. First, a method (c) to map experimentally obtained DNA damage readout (b, based on comet assay) to a DNA damage- and repair-model (a, the Multi-Hit-Repair model [14]) is presented, attributing particular care to the stochastic nature of the readout. This mapping also takes into account the dynamic nature of the repair process by considering measurements taken in a time-resolved manner. Second, the properties of the model (a) and the readout (b) necessary for a successful mapping are discussed to generalize these findings to other research questions. Third, parameter search is performed on such data, showcasing the potential of this method.

2   Methods

In this section, the various methods used in this work are described. Section 2.1 outlines how the cells are treated during the experiment. Section 2.2 describes the comet assay, a method to quantify DNA damage. In Sect. 2.3, the Multi-Hit-Repair model is presented, which is the mathematical model used to predict DNA damage and repair. Section 2.4 describes how experimentally quantified DNA damage is mapped to the prediction of the model. These three sections correspond to the three key-aspects (b), (a) and (c) mentioned in the in introduction. Lastly, an approach for parameter search is presented in Sect. 2.5.

2.1   Experimental Setup

A canine osteosarcoma cell line (Abrams) is kept in culture at 37 °C. At the beginning of the experimental procedure, cells and medium are transferred to cell culture dishes. One dish is used for each time-point. The dishes containing the cells and medium are irradiated at 6 Gy with a clinical linear accelerator (Clinac iX, Varian, Palo Alto, CA, USA) operating at a dose rate of 6 Gy/min. Using the comet assay, DNA damage is quantified before, as well as 15, 30, 60, 120, 240 and 360 min after irradiation.

2.2   Comet Assay

The comet assay (also referred to as single cell gel electrophoresis assay, Trevigen, Gaithersburg, MA, USA) is a method to assess the amount of damage in DNA [13]. Cells are dispersed and suspended in agarose gel and lysed, thus dissolving cellular membranes, proteins, RNA and other cell constituents. At the end of this step, only unwound DNA is left. Then, electrophoresis is performed; DNA fragments are dragged towards the positive electrode. The smaller a fragment, the easier it can move through the gel and the farthest it has moved after the completion of the electrophoresis step. At this stage, structures resembling comets can be observed by fluorescence microscopy. The fragments form a comet tail shape, facing away from the bulk of DNA, which looks like a comet head. Sample comets are shown in Fig. 1. The standard Trevigen protocol was used for this procedure, specifically following recommendations for obtaining reliable and repeatable results [6].

Each cell embedded into the gel forms one comet. Thus, DNA damage is quantified on a per-cell basis from the resulting microscopy image by computing the relative pixel intensity of the tail compared to the total pixel intensity of the comet structure, i.e.

$$\text{Relative tail intensity} = \frac{\sum_{x,y \in \text{tail}} I(x,y)}{\sum_{x,y \in \text{head}} I(x,y) + \sum_{x,y \in \text{tail}} I(x,y)} \quad (1)$$

$I(x,y)$ denotes the pixel intensities at coordinates x and y. The Comet IV software was used to quantify the relative tail intensity of approx. 100 randomly selected cells for each of the 7 time-points.

2.3   Multi-Hit-Repair (MHR) Model

The MHR model [14] is a dynamic population model where cells are assigned to populations H_i depending on the number of radiation-induced hits they have accumulated. Cells with one or more hits have lost their ability to form clones (clonogenicity). This implies that a hit is defined as a lesion which prevents cells from undergoing mitosis. Regarding DNA, the MHR model does not impose what a hit consists of. In particular, one hit does not correspond to one DNA break, but it can be assumed that more hits generally correspond to more damage. As illustrated in Fig. 1, the populations are arranged in a chain structure. Initially, all cells are assigned to population H_0 which represents cells able to undergo mitosis – they are clonogenic. Damage is induced at a rate $\alpha R(t) H_0$ where $R(t)$ is the dose rate of irradiation. It is set to $0\,\text{Gy/min}$ prior to and after irradiation and has a value of $6\,\text{Gy/min}$ during irradiation. Irradiation starts at $t = 0\,\text{min}$, and its duration is such that the target dose of $6\,\text{Gy}$ is reached.

Population H_1 contains cells that have accumulated one hit, H_2 contains cells with two hits, etc. According to the definition of a hit, these cells cannot undergo mitosis. When a hit of a cell in population H_i is repaired, the cell is transferred to population H_{i-1}. Damaged cells in the H_i populations can also undergo cell death at a rate of $c_e H_i$, which occurs when a damaged cell fails to repair itself and dies instead. The repair rate is a function of H_i, the repair rate constant c_r and the repair inhibition due to radiation-induced protein damage (see below). These various contributors to the repair rate are all summarized in the repair function $r(H_i)$. Thus, the differential equations for population H_i is:

$$\frac{\mathrm{d}H_i}{\mathrm{d}t} = \alpha R(t) H_{i-1} - \alpha R(t) H_i - r(H_i) + r(H_{i+1}) - c_e H_i \quad (2)$$

Since radiation induces protein damage, such damage in DNA repair proteins must be cured before DNA repair can occur. This is modeled with a transient biological dose equivalent (TBDE) Γ. After irradiation, repair proteins are impaired, resulting in a high TBDE. As time progresses, these proteins are repaired, the TBDE drops and DNA repair starts to take place. This is modeled as follows:

$$\frac{\mathrm{d}\Gamma}{\mathrm{d}t} = R(t) - \gamma \Gamma \quad (3)$$

$$r(H_i) = c_r \exp\left(-\mu_\Gamma \Gamma\right) H_i \quad (4)$$

The derivation of these equation along with further discussion and validation of the model can be found in [14]. Initial conditions are $H_0(0) = 1$, $H_{i>0}(0) = 0$ and $\Gamma(0) = 0$, assuming that no damage is present before irradiation. In cases where this assumption is violated, $H_i(0)$ can also bet set according to the pre-existing damage (see Sect. 3). The full set of equations is given in Fig. 1. A summary of the model parameters is presented in Table 1.

Table 1. Summary of model parameters with their respective search space boundaries. The last column indicates the result of parameter search. For completeness, the dose rate $R(t)$ is also given. It is not determined during parameter search, but rather fixed to reflect the experimental conditions. The fit error ε (as defined in Sect. 2.5) is 0.06.

Parameter	Description	Min.	Max.	Fit
α	Radiosensitivity (Gy^{-1})	0	2	0.09
c_r	Repair rate constant (h^{-1})	0	10	0.22
c_e	Elimination rate constant (h^{-1})	0	10	0.00
μ_Γ	TBDE weighting factor (Gy^{-1})	0	10	0.00
γ	TBDE rate constant (h^{-1})	0	10	3.80
R	Dose rate (h^{-1})	$\begin{cases} 360 & 0\,h \leq t \leq \frac{1}{60}\,h \\ 0 & \text{otherwise} \end{cases}$		

2.4 Relationship Between Comet Assay Readout and Model State

At any point in time t, the state variables H_i quantify the fraction of the cell population that has accumulated i hits $(0 \leq i \leq K)$. This is a consequence of choosing the initial conditions such that 100% of the cells are in H_0 initially $(H_0(0) = 1)$. Conversely, the comet assay readout is a number d_j for each of the m cells that are quantified. Since d_j is a relative tail intensity as defined in Eq. 1, $0 \leq d_j \leq 1$.

Because of the assumption that an increasing amount of DNA damage d_j translates to a higher number of hits i, a strategy where the populations H_i are mapped to histogram frequency bins of the distribution of d_j in an ordered fashion appears to be the obvious choice. This mapping, however, implies that a specific range of DNA damage (e.g. 0%–5%) is mapped to a population (e.g. H_0). Since the model imposes that only the H_0 population can undergo mitosis, the choice of range is not arbitrary. As explained below, calibration of a scaling factor s is required to ensure a correct relationship.

More formally, the mapping is achieved as follows for every time-point t: First, the m comet assay readouts d_j are scaled with a scaling factor s, i.e. $\tilde{d}_j = s d_j$. This is done to establish the correct relationship between the DNA damage frequency bins and the model populations. Second, all $\tilde{d}_j$ are binned into $K + 1$ bins such that the ith bin r_i contains the number of $\tilde{d}_j$ with a

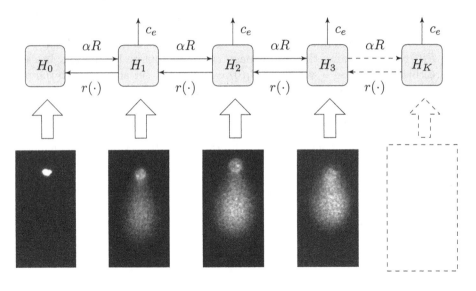

$$\frac{\mathrm{d}H_0}{\mathrm{d}t} = -\alpha R H_0 + r(H_1)$$

$$\frac{\mathrm{d}H_1}{\mathrm{d}t} = \alpha R H_0 - \alpha R H_1 - r(H_1) - c_e H_1 + r(H_2)$$

$$\dots$$

$$\frac{\mathrm{d}H_{i-1}}{\mathrm{d}t} = \alpha R H_{i-2} - \alpha R H_{i-1} - r(H_{i-1}) - c_e H_{i-1} + r(H_i)$$

$$\frac{\mathrm{d}H_i}{\mathrm{d}t} = \alpha R H_{i-1} - \alpha R H_i - r(H_i) - c_e H_i + r(H_{i+1})$$

$$\frac{\mathrm{d}H_{i+1}}{\mathrm{d}t} = \alpha R H_i - \alpha R H_{i+1} - r(H_{i+1}) - c_e H_{i+1} + r(H_{i+2})$$

$$\dots$$

$$\frac{\mathrm{d}H_K}{\mathrm{d}t} = \alpha R H_{K-1} - r(H_K) - c_e H_K$$

$$\frac{\mathrm{d}\Gamma}{\mathrm{d}t} = R - \gamma\Gamma$$

$$r(H_i) = c_r \exp\left(-\mu_\Gamma \Gamma\right) H_i$$

Fig. 1. Top: High-level illustration of the MHR model. The boxes depict the chain structure with the populations H_i; the arrows denote how cells accumulate hits (to the right), undergo cell death (to the top) or undergo repair (to the left). Below the chain, comet assay pictures conceptually illustrate how comets with increasingly high relative tail intensities are mapped to populations with increasingly high numbers of hits. Bottom: Below the illustration, the full set of system equations is given. (See [14] for details.)

damage between $\frac{i}{K}$ and $\frac{i+1}{K}$. These histogram bins r_i sum up to m and are then normalized to the bins $\tilde{r}_i$ which sum up to 1. In a third step, the cell populations H_i are normalized in the same way, such that

$$\sum_{i=0}^{K} \tilde{r}_k = \sum_{i=0}^{K} \tilde{H}_i = 1. \tag{5}$$

This normalization is necessary to overcome the fact that dead cells are eliminated in the model, thus reducing H_i, while the experimentally obtained damage readouts are always performed on approx. 100 cells.

Finally, to compare comet assay readout and model state, the normalized cell populations $\tilde{H}_i$ are mapped to the damage readout bins $\tilde{r}_i$ in a pairwise fashion. This technique allows for a comparison in distribution rather than just mean values. In general, the length of the chain K is not critical provided that it is sufficiently long [14] – in an excessively long chain, populations with a high number of hits simply remain empty. In the simulation presented here, a value of $K = 24$ was chosen. The scaling factor s was fixed to 1 for now, mapping DNA damage between 0% and 4% to H_0, damage between 4% and 8% to H_1 etc. The choice of s is non trivial and remains a challenge, thus strategies to determine s are discussed in Sect. 4.

2.5   Parameter Search

Differential evolution [16] was used to perform parameter search by minimizing the sum of squares

$$\varepsilon = \sum_{t>0} \sum_{i=0}^{K} \left(\tilde{r}_i^{(t)} - \tilde{H}_i(t) \right)^2 \tag{6}$$

where $\tilde{r}_i^{(t)}$ denotes the ith normalized histogram bin at time point t. The time-points $t \in (15, 30, 60, 120, 240, 360)$ min are considered for the minimization, but not the time-point $t = 0$ min (i.e. before irradiation) since no parameter has any effect on the model-prediction at $t = 0$ min.

The model was implemented using Python 3.6.6 and employing the `odeint()` function from version 1.1.0 of the `scipy` python package. Differential evolution was performed with the `differential_evolution()` of the same package.

3   Results

Figure 2 shows experimental results from comet assays (top) along with the model prediction (bottom) after parameter search. The resulting model parameters are listed in Table 1. Parameter search took approx. 10 min on a 2.0 GHz Intel Xeon core and reliably converged to always the same endpoints with an error of $\varepsilon = 0.06$.

As expected, the damage increases after irradiation both in the experimental readout (top half of Fig. 2) as well as in the model prediction (bottom half of Fig. 2). The violin-like structures in the plot show the statistical density of the data; when the violin is wide, a high number of values are present in the corresponding range of relative tail intensities. The violins of the model prediction are jagged due to the discrete nature of the populations. For the experimental data, the violins are generated from the readout without binning (i.e. from $\tilde{d}_j$), thus the violin outlines are smoother. The comet assay readout before irradiation suggests that the assumption of no damage prior to irradiation is false – some damage is present even before irradiation. The initial conditions for H_i were set according to the distribution of this readout.

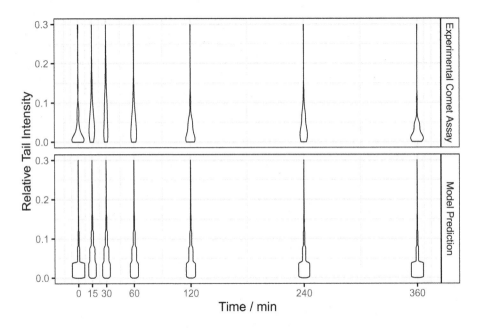

Fig. 2. Violin plots of comet assay readouts after irradiation with 6 Gy (top) and corresponding model prediction (bottom) of Abrams osteosarcoma cells. The readout at $t = 0$ min is acquired immediately before irradiation. The vertical axis is limited to the range between 0% and 30% of relative tail intensity.

4   Discussion and Conclusion

The results showcase that the MHR model is able to produce output that is in line with DNA damage readouts obtained with comet assays after irradiation. Thus, the strategy proposed in this work appears to be a viable candidate to map experimental DNA damage readout to the MHR model state and back, and more generally, to grasp the distribution of aspects of populations that change over time.

So far, most parameter searching has been performed based on clonogenic cell survival curves, i.e. dose-response curves that assess for each dose the proportion of cells which survived irradiation and were able to form clones [14,18]. This proportion corresponds to $\lim_{t\to\infty} H_0(t)$ in the MHR model, i.e. the fraction of initial cells that have fully recovered from the irradiation and have regained their ability to undergo mitosis. Thus, $H_0(t)$ is evaluated many hours after the essential dynamics have ceased. Doing so introduces an undesired ambiguity: as long as the duration of irradiation is short compared to the repair process, parameters can be scaled in the time-domain without affecting the end result. For example, reducing c_r by a factor of e.g. 10 would eventually yield the same surviving proportion provided that other parameters are scaled accordingly. The process would take longer, but this has no effect on the proportion of surviving cells since only the end-point is evaluated. In fact, such ambiguities in the prediction of cell survival curves have been found [18] and prompted for the time-resolved approach introduced here.

While such a time-resolved approach does remove the aforementioned ambiguity, the scaling factor s is required to determine the scaling in the damage/hit-domain. $s = 1$ was used for the parameters reported in Table 1, linking clonogenic cells to relative tail intensities of 0%–4%. As discussed above, other ranges are equally reasonable; the yet unknown scaling factor s is required to render the results from parameter search comparable to parameter values estimated from cell survival curves. It is critical to note that finding a suitable scaling factor would still produce the results shown in Fig. 2, but the parameter values would change, allowing for a comparison with values found and reported in the past. Unfortunately, it is not possible to calibrate s from comet assay readouts because these readouts do not carry any information on the clonogenicity of the cells. This information, however, is required because H_0 must contain clonogenic cells by definition. Hence, a parameter search with combined data from comet assay and clonogenic assay should be used instead.

Interestingly, both the elimination rate constant c_e as well as the TBDE weighting factor μ_Γ converged to 0, which was the lower bound of the search space. A possible explanation for a low c_e is that the normalization introduced in Eq. 5 in order to compensate for the fact that a fixed number of cells are examined in the comet assay, thus disregarding a reduction of the overall number of remaining living cells, conceals cells that have been eliminated. Moreover, cell death is a process that takes time, and the 6 h of simulation may simply not extend to the point in time at which cell death occurs. These findings again prompt for a combined analysis with both comet assay and clonogenic assay because the latter inherently captures cell survival.

The estimate of $\mu_\Gamma = 0\,Gy^{-1}$ is challenging to interpret, since a slow-down or even stall of repair directly after irradiation is a plausible and well established phenomenon [15], which is thought to be a combination of time required to recruit DNA repair proteins before DNA repair can start and time required to repair such proteins that may have been damaged by radiation. Setting $\mu_\Gamma = 0$ Gy^{-1} eliminates this phenomenon from the model, suggesting that efforts should be put into investigating how relevant and robust this parameter is. A potential method to achieve this could be approximate bayesian computation (ABC) [1], where parameters search does not yield point-estimates, but rather results in distributions of parameters in the search space.

For a successful application of the method presented here, the readout should reflect the quantity that is modeled. In the context of DNA damage and repair, this entails that the readout correlates well with the damage introduced by radiation. While the correlation between primary damage and radiation dose is well established [2,12], the practice of quantitatively inferring DNA damage from a microscopy image of cells subject to the electrophoresis process may appear questionable at first. However, an excellent linear relationship between the applied radiation dose and the relative tail intensity was found, with coefficients of determination exceeding $R^2 = 0.95$ [8,17]. One may generally question whether comet assay is the best technique to investigate DNA damage and response in quantitative terms. A popular alternative would be the use of γH2AX, a biomarker for double strand breaks [9]. However, the γH2AX response is delayed by up to 30 min and remains detectable after the double strand break has been repaired, and the relationship between applied dose and response is worse than with comet assay [7,11]. The first issue in particular renders γH2AX an inferior alternative to comet assay since the readout should reflect the current state of the system rather than some time-delayed state.

Similarly, one may question whether the MHR model is a suitable choice for the task at hand. Most models commonly used in radiobiology do not model DNA damage and repair kinetics. Instead, they model the observed outcome directly. For example, the linear-quadratic model [4,10] and the linear-quadratic-liner model [5] describe the relationship that is observed between dose and surviving fraction of cells. They do not relate to radiobiological principles but merely reflect the observed outcome. Thus, they cannot be used in this context. The MHR model, on the other hand, is a suitable choice because it is designed with radiobiological concepts from the ground up. In consequence, the topology of the model can be mapped to the distribution of damage-readouts, as demonstrated in this work.

In conclusion, the method presented here appears to be suitable for bridging the gap between the time-resolved comet assay readout and the MHR model because it tackles the key difficulty of the problems, which is to treat the readout as a distribution and to establish a relationship between this distribution and the model populations. In a next step, the scaling factor s should be calibrated using the proposed multi-assay parameter search, consisting of both comet- as well as clonogenic assay, followed by validation of the model and the mapping.

Funding Information. This work was supported by the Swiss National Foundation (grant number 320030_163435) – Stephan Scheidegger; Carla Rohrer Bley.

References

1. Albert, C., Künsch, H.R., Scheidegger, A.: A simulated annealing approach to approximate Bayes computations. Stat. Comput. **25**(6), 1217–1232 (2015)
2. Barnard, S., Bouffler, S., Rothkamm, K.: The shape of the radiation dose response for DNA double-strand break induction and repair. Genome Integr. **4**(1), 1 (2013)
3. Besserer, J., Schneider, U.: A track-event theory of cell survival. Zeitschrift fuer Medizinische Physik **25**(2), 168–175 (2015)
4. Dale, R.G.: The application of the linear-quadratic dose-effect equation to fractionated and protracted radiotherapy. Br. J. Radiol. **58**(690), 515–528 (1985)
5. Guerrero, M., Li, X.A.: Extending the linear-quadratic model for large fraction doses pertinent to stereotactic radiotherapy. Phys. Med. Biol. **49**(20), 4825 (2004)
6. Hartmann, A., et al.: Recommendations for conducting the in vivo alkaline comet assay. Mutagenesis **18**(1), 45–51 (2003)
7. Kinner, A., Wu, W., Staudt, C., Iliakis, G.: γ-h2ax in recognition and signaling of dna double-strand breaks in the context of chromatin. Nucleic acids research **36**(17), 5678–5694 (2008)
8. Kumaravel, T., Jha, A.N.: Reliable comet assay measurements for detecting dna damage induced by ionising radiation and chemicals. Mutat. Res./Genet. Toxicol. Environ. Mutagen. **605**(1), 7–16 (2006)
9. Kuo, L.J., Yang, L.X.: γ-h2ax-a novel biomarker for dna double-strand breaks. In vivo **22**(3), 305–309 (2008)
10. Lea, D.E.: Actions of Radiations on Living Cells. Cambridge University Press, Cambridge (1946)
11. Mariotti, L.G., et al.: Use of the γ-h2ax assay to investigate DNA repair dynamics following multiple radiation exposures. PLoS ONE **8**(11), e79541 (2013)
12. Mori, R., Matsuya, Y., Yoshii, Y., Date, H.: Estimation of the radiation-induced DNA double-strand breaks number by considering cell cycle and absorbed dose per cell nucleus. J. Radiat. Res. **59**(3), 253–260 (2018)
13. Olive, P.L., Banáth, J.P.: The comet assay: a method to measure DNA damage in individual cells. Nat. Protoc. **1**, 23–29 (2006)
14. Scheidegger, S., Fuchs, H.U., Zaugg, K., Bodis, S., Füchslin, R.M.: Using state variables to model the response of tumour cells to radiation and heat: a novel multihit-repair approach. Comput. Math. Methods Med. **2013**, 15 (2013). https://www.hindawi.com/journals/cmmm/2013/587543/
15. Schulz, N., et al.: Dynamic in vivo profiling of DNA damage and repair after radiotherapy using canine patients as a model. Int. J. Mol. Sci. **18**(6), 1176 (2017)
16. Storn, R., Price, K.: Differential evolution–a simple and efficient heuristic for global optimization over continuous spaces. J. Glob. Optim. **11**(4), 341–359 (1997)
17. Wang, Y., et al.: Evaluation of the comet assay for assessing the dose-response relationship of DNA damage induced by ionizing radiation. Int. J. Mol. Sci. **14**(11), 22:449–22:461 (2013)
18. Weyland, M., Thumser-Henner, P., Nytko, K., Rohrer Bley, C., Füchslin, R., Scheidegger, S.: Proceedings: extracting information about cellular repair processes after hyperthermia - radiotherapy by model-based data analysis - ambiguities in survival prediction as a challenge? Strahlenther Onkol **194**(5), 503–504 (2018)
19. Zaider, M., Hanin, L.: Tumor control probability in radiation treatment. Med. Phys. **38**(2), 574–583 (2011)

The Relevance of Inorganic Nonlinear Chemical Reactions for the Origin of Life Studies

Ylenia Miele[1] , Zsófia Medveczky[2], István Lagzi[2] , Marcello A. Budroni[3] ,
and Federico Rossi[4(✉)]

[1] Department of Chemistry and Biology, University of Salerno,
Via Giovanni Paolo II 132, 84084 Fisciano (SA), Italy
[2] Department of Physics, MTA-BME Condensed Matter Physics Research Group,
Budapest University of Technology and Economics,
H-1111 Budafoki ut 8, Budapest, Hungary
[3] Department of Chemistry and Pharmacy, University of Sassari,
Via Vienna 2, 07100 Sassari, Italy
[4] Department of Earth, Environmental and Physical Sciences - DEEP Sciences,
University of Siena, Pian dei Mantellini 44, 53100 Siena, Italy
federico.rossi2@unisi.it

Abstract. We discuss the fundamental role played by nonlinear inorganic chemical reactions to understand the minimal conditions for the origin of life. In particular, we propose a focus on the chemo-physical processes that modulate the interplay between self-organisation and self-assembly at the basis of important life-like functionalities. We present results about two proofs-of-concept that support this view. The first pertains the collective behaviours and patterns obtained from networks of autonomous inorganic oscillators confined in self-assembled structures and coupled *via* chemical communication. The second shows how a specific autocatalytic reaction can trigger conformational changes of self-assembled structures, giving rise to membrane self-division processes.

Keywords: Origin of life · Self-organisation · Self-assembly ·
Nonlinear chemistry · BZ oscillator · Compartimentalization ·
Replication

1 Introduction

The origin of life has always attracted attention for its important scientific, epistemological and social implications. The scientific investigation of this topic involves the interaction between different disciplines (chemistry, biology, physics, earth and planetary sciences), among which chemistry plays a prominent role [37]. Since the pioneering experiment of Miller and Urey of 1953 [22], it was demonstrated that, in proper conditions, organic molecules could originate from simple inorganic compounds similar to those found in Earth's early atmosphere.

© Springer Nature Switzerland AG 2019
S. Cagnoni et al. (Eds.): WIVACE 2018, CCIS 900, pp. 138–150, 2019.
https://doi.org/10.1007/978-3-030-21733-4_11

From an experimental point of view, many efforts have been devoted to show possible prebiotic conditions for the formation of the building blocks of living systems, namely lipids, amino acids and nucleotides. About lipids, though Hargreaves et al. in 1977 [12] demonstrated that the synthesis of phosphatidic acid and other lipids could be achieved abiotically, it is considered improbable that fatty acids, glycerol, and phosphate could have been present together in high enough concentrations on the primordial Earth. For these reasons, it is generally assumed that the primordial membranes were mainly made of fatty acids with a chemical composition much simpler compared to the modern membranes. Fatty acids and fatty alcohols could have been produced through a sort of Fischer-Tropsch synthesis, in presence of metal surfaces and at high temperatures [10,11,24]. As for prebiotic amino acid syntheses, several plausible pathways have been reported. Here we name just two: (*i*) the Strecker reaction in which amino acids are obtained from carbonyl compounds, ammonia, and HCN [19]; (*ii*) the synthesis of α-amino acids and α-hydroxy acids under possible volcanic conditions by CO-dependent carbon fixation at temperatures between $80\,^\circ$C and $120\,^\circ$C, with nickel or nickel/iron precipitates as catalysts; carbonyl, cyano and methylthio derivatives as carbon sources; calcium or magnesium hydroxide as buffering species [13]. Comprehensive reviews on the main experimental and theoretical achievements in this research activity can be found in refs [9,37].

In parallel, different approaches pointed at identifying inorganic processes and structures relying on "simple" molecules able to reproduce the minimal functionalities and traits of alive systems. The definition of an autopoietic system (from the Greek "self-production"), given by Maturana and co-workers [1,52], well summarizes these essential traits: self-organised, complex, open, dissipative, self-referential, auto-catalytic, hierarchical, far from equilibrium and autonomous systems.

Self-organisation and related topics constitute the realm of nonlinear chemistry. This area has traditionally focused on the spontaneous formation and the dynamics of chemical self-organised structures in far-from-equilibrium conditions. According to the extended formulation of thermodynamics developed by Prigogine and co-workers [23], open systems fed by a constant flux of energy and/or matter can locally decrease their entropy to favour the emergence of ordered (so-called "dissipative") structures [9,30,32]. In particular, systems governed by nonlinear kinetics can exhibit complex scenarios such as multistability, periodic and chaotic oscillations as well as stationary and dynamical spatio-temporal patterns in spatially extended systems, impossible to attain close to the equilibrium branch [5,6,8,29]. From the theoretical viewpoint, nonlinear kinetic models have acquired great plaudits for the description of symmetry breaking phenomena (e.g. the emergence of homochirality), autocatalysis in prebiotic conditions and the origin of the RNA world [16,18]. Autocatalytic cycles have been considered an essential feature in the origin of life as they exhibit the life-like property of exponential growth while being composed of relatively simple molecules. In this framework, inorganic oscillators and autocatalytic reactions have been widely used as benchmark test-tube models to get insights on metabolic oscillations observed for instance in the Krebs reductive cycle and nonlinear behaviour characterising the RNA replication and enzymatic reactions.

Another essential feature for the development of life is compartmentalisation (hierarchical structures in Maturana's sense) [41–43], i.e. the physical or chemical confinement and accumulation of relevant molecules for life-type processes in sub-domains. Different plausible mechanisms have been proposed to fulfil this task, including natural convection induced by thermal gradients combined to thermophoresis [2,4].

Nevertheless, *Self-assembly* appears the most convincing description of compartmentalisation as we observe in modern living systems. Differently from self-organisation, self-assembly is driven by the minimisation of free-energy in equilibrium conditions. This framework pertains the study of dispersed systems and addresses processes at the basis of formation and growth of thermodynamically stable structures such as emulsions, micelles and vesicles, reminiscent of those that typically characterise cellular environments.

While a rich literature exists on the study of self-organising and self-assembling systems alone, little has been done to understand the interplay between the two. Especially in the field of the origin of life, the innermost physico-chemical mechanisms ruling such a complex interplay have never been emphasised. In this work, we show how simple nonequilibrium and equilibrium systems can interact to produce emerging life-like properties in a prebiotic environment. In particular, by using relatively simple chemical systems allows one to focus on the crucial physico-chemical processes that govern the interplay between these two main levels of organisation, neglecting the role of *evolute* biological functionals.

Here we present two genuine examples of this promising perspective. The first focuses on the collective dynamics of ensembles of nano- and micro-inorganic oscillators, embedded in self-assembled supports (resin and clay micro-particles, emulsions, vesicles and double emulsions) that, thanks to different possible pathways for chemical communication, are capable to produce a variety of dynamical patterns. These dynamics are mediated by the nature of the supports, which can be tuned to selectively interact with the oscillating key intermediates and produce different global behaviours, especially synchronisation and quorum-sensing phenomena. Such systems may also provide simple models for communication in neural networks, logic implementation and possible memory architectures.

While in the first part we emphasise the influence of the self-assembled compartments on the self-organising properties of the protocells, in a second part we focus on the reverse case. In particular, based on two previous approaches, we propose a new idea where a nonlinear autocatalytic reaction is coupled to a stimuli-responsive membrane to trigger cell-like self-division phenomena, that is a key signature of living systems.

2   Self-organisation Phenomena Mediated by the Properties of the Compartments: Chemical Communication

In laboratory scale, protocells like lipid or fatty acid vesicles can be used to mimic the simplest features of living cells, while inorganic chemical oscillators and nonlinear (possibly autocatalytic) reactions are proofs-of-concept for reproducing the self-organised oscillatory dynamics typically occurring in cells during metabolic cycles or enzymatic processes.

The most familiar chemical oscillator studied in this field is the Belousov-Zhabotinsky reaction [40, 45]. This reaction involves the oxidation of an organic species such as malonic acid by an acidified bromate solution in the presence of a metal ion catalyst. The BZ reaction represents a genuine inorganic analog of living-like systems (in Maturana's sense) as it develops self-organised and autonomous complex oscillatory behaviours (including spatio-temporal patterns such as chemical waves) in far from equilibrium conditions that can be maintained for a long period thanks to a slow depletion of the initial reactants. The system shows periodic oscillations between the oxidative state n and $n + 1$ of the metal and periodic changes in the concentration of other intermediates. Various redox metal catalysts can be employed, including ferroin (i.e. the redox couple red coulored $[Fe(II)phen)]^{2+}$ and blue coloured $[Fe(III)(phen)]^{3+}$), that allow following the oscillatory behaviour from chromatic changes of the reactive solution. The reaction mechanism is quite complicated, involving more than 18 reactions and the production of 21 species. However, according to the minimal FKN model [25, 39], the complexity of the resulting dynamics can be reduced to the cyclic alternation of 3 processes: the first two steps involve the depletion of bromide ions (Br^-), the autocatalytic species $HBrO_2$ is produced and the catalyst oxidised; in a third step (the reset of the clock), the catalyst is brought back to the reduced form *via* a reaction with the oxidisable organic species (typically malonic acid) and, simultaneously, new Br^- ions are produced. The switching among the three steps is ruled by the concentration of bromides. High concentration of bromide precursor, Br_2, corresponds to the dominance of the third process and low concentration of the autocatalytic species, and it thus identifies the inhibitor in the global mechanism.

The BZ reaction has been performed in a great variety of reaction environments and media such as surfactants [7], gels [44], micelles [26, 34], water in oil reverse microemulsion [47], polymers [38], cation exchange particles [46] and clays [31]. In particular, the presence of zwitterionic surfactants dispersed in the BZ medium has been used to unveil possible breaks of symmetry in chemical patterns due to the mutual influence of self-organisation and self-assembly-induced processes [7].

When the reaction is encapsulated inside compartmentalized and self-assembled domains that are chemically coupled to build a network of micro-oscillators, different types of chemical communication can also be studied. Two characteristic behaviours are found depending on the chemical coupling:

in–phase synchronization occurs if the autocatalytic species $HBrO_2$ is the fast diffusing species and rules the communication among different compartments, and an *anti–phase* synchronization if Br_2 is the fast diffusing *messenger* species.

Figures 1 and 2 show respectively an array of cation exchange particles and an array of kaolinite microparticles. In both cases, the chemical communication is regulated by $HBrO_2$ giving rise to an *in-phase* synchronisation among the droplets (i.e. the phase difference between the different oscillatory droplets is $\Delta\phi \sim 0$).

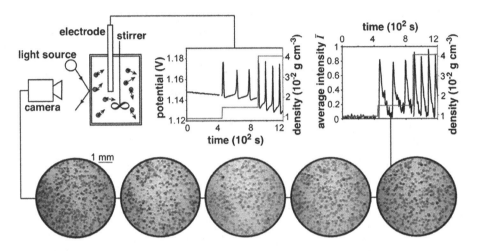

Fig. 1. Catalytic micro-particles are globally coupled by exchange of species with the surrounding catalyst-free BZ reaction medium. Electrochemical time series illustrate the change in oscillatory amplitude and period with increasing particle density (red line) for a stirring rate of 600 rpm. Reproduced with permission from [46] (Color figure online)

Figure 3 shows a network of water-in-oil droplets made of a fluorinated surfactant (PEG-PFPE amphiphilic block copolymer) separated by a fluorinated oil. In this case, the chemical oscillators confined in the droplets communicate through the exchange of the apolar bromine, giving rise to an *anti-phase* synchronization (i.e. the phase difference between confined oscillators is $\Delta\phi \sim \pi$).

In a more realistic biomimetic approach, our group proposes to substitute the synthetic surfactant introduced by Epstein and co-workers [47] with phospholipids. In this way, we can easily build an experimental model to study chemical communication in liposomes, double emulsions and emulsions made of 1,2-dimyristoyl-sn-glycero-3-phosphocholine (DMPC) [33,35,48–51]. In liposomes and double emulsions the communication among micro-oscillators is dominated by the activators (pulse transmission and *in-phase* oscillations). This is in contrast to what happens in simple emulsions where the communication between adjacent oscillatory droplets mainly exhibited an inhibitory character (*anti-phase*

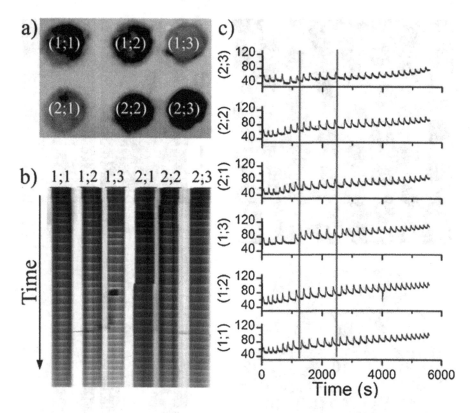

Fig. 2. Global behaviour of a 2 × 3 lattice where single ferroin-kaolinite oscillators are globally coupled through a BZ medium. (a) The 6 elements of the lattice (i;j) in different oxidation states: (1;3) and (2;1) are oxidized (bright color) while the remaining oscillators are in the reduced state (dark color). (b) ST plot of each element of the lattice. (c) Time series of the oscillatory dynamics of each element of the lattice, extracted from the ST plot. Reproduced with permission from [31]

oscillations), governed by the prominent role of Br$_2$. In the presence of mono-lamellar membranes (lamellarity is controlled by using surfactants like Sodium Tetradecyl Sulphate, STS), in fact, molecular bromine has a higher permeability with respect to the activator HBrO$_2$. This is also confirmed when bromine-blocking molecule (i.e. cholesterol) are intercalated in the membrane structure. In this case, the global dynamics results in a weakly coupled array with an erratic global behaviour (Fig. 4).

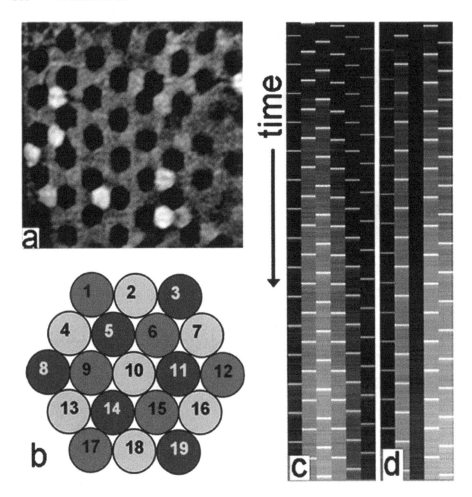

Fig. 3. Stationary and oscillatory BZ drops in 2D. (a) Hexagonally packed drops with BZ solution. The pattern arising from global chemical coupling form hexagons consisting of seven drops: each stationary drop (in black) is surrounded by six antiphase oscillatory drops. The imaged area is 0.7×0.7 mm. (b) Schematics of the pattern (stationary drops in grey). (c,d) ST plots (duration 2800 s) of drops 6, 11, 15, 14, 9, and 5 (c) and drops 1, 5, 10, 15, and 19 (d). Reproduced with permission from [47]

3   Influence of Autocatalysis on Stimuli-Responsive Compartments: Chemically-Driven Protocell Self-division

The reproduction in the laboratory of a self-division process could shed light on how the first protocells *learned* to divide and possibly to self-reproduce.

Following the pioneering work of Luisi [3] on the autopoietic behaviour of reverse micelles, the group of Szostak [53] conducted numerous studies to

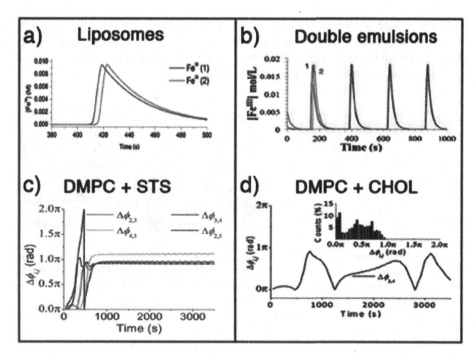

Fig. 4. (a) Signal transmission between two liposomes. At $t = 400$ s a signal is triggered in droplet 1 (black trace) and after 4 s the signal reaches droplet 2 and causes the oxidation of the catalyst (red trace); (b) Numerical simulations of the coupled dynamics of two BZ droplets in a double emulsion system. After a few cycles a perfect synchronisation is attained; (c) phase difference ($\Delta\phi_{ij} = \pi$) for the anti-phase droplets in an array of linearly coupled oscillating simple emulsions; (d) phase difference for droplets in the presence of a messenger-blocking molecule, showing uncorrelated phase behaviour over time [33]. (Color figure online)

examine how fatty acid vesicles may form, grow and divide. When fatty acid micelles are added to a solution of pre-formed vesicles, the vesicles grow rapidly. Vesicle growth is thought to occur first through the formation of a micelle shell around a vesicle. Individual fatty acids are transferred from the micelles to the outer leaflet of the vesicle membrane. Fatty acids may then flip from the outer leaflet to the inner leaflet, which allows the membrane bilayer to grow evenly. In case of multilamellar fatty acids vesicles fed with fatty acid micelles, the initially spherical vesicles turn into long thread-like vesicles, a process driven by the transient imbalance between surface area and volume growth.

Peterlin [27] also observed division in Giant Unilamellar Vesicles (GUV) of 1-palmitoyl-2-oleoyl-*sn*-glycero-3-phosphocholine (POPC) immersed in a solution of Large Unilamellar Vesicles of oleic acid/oleate (Fig. 5a). In the experiments of Szostak and Peterlin, the growth and the division of the vesicles are due to an imbalance between surface area and volume growth after the addition of fatty acids. More recently, Lagzi [17] managed to get the division of a fatty acid emulsion (2-hexyldecanoic acid) in a solution of sodium hydroxide (Fig. 5b). The main routes to induce the division of a vesicle are thus external triggers: change of the surfactant concentration (addition of micelles to vesicles or hydrolysis of oleic anhydride) or change of the external pH.

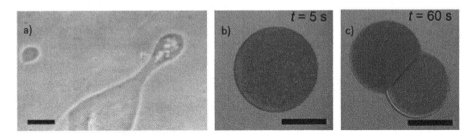

Fig. 5. (a) Image recorded upon the transfer of a POPC GUV into a 0.8 mM suspension of oleic acid in a 0.2 M sucrose/glucose solution buffered to pH 8.8. The bar represents $20\,\mu$m [27]; (b) and (c) Self-division of a mineral oil–fatty acid droplet in an alkaline solution of KOH (2 M, pH 14.3). The mineral oil–droplet contains initially 30 v% 2-hexyldecanoicacid. The scale bar represents 1 mm. Reproduced with permission from [17]

In contrast to previous approaches, the challenge is to stimulate the proto-cell division with an internal chemical trigger. This approach would make the artificial cells more similar to the natural ones where the division is governed by internal complex biochemical reaction networks. The recent progresses in stimuli-responsive materials field [36] can help to develop a self-assembled system, possibly a vesicle-like compartment, compatible with a prebiotic environment and that is prone to self-divide by a simple chemical trigger. For example, one of the simplest chemical trigger that could likely take place in a prebiotic condition is a pH change; in this respect, mixed fatty acid/lipids compartments are reliable prebiotic model [15] that can respond to pH changes of the environment [14].

Nonlinear chemical reactions, such as the oscillating Belousov-Zhabotinsky, or *clock reactions*, which show an abrupt change of their parameters after a latency period, could be employed to control the division dynamics. The encapsulation of such reactions into pH-sensitive vesicles would refine the work of Lagzi to obtain a marked biomimetic character and possibly to reproduce the basic features of a self-dividing process.

The complex interplay between the Belousov-Zhabotinsky reaction and lipids forming archaeal plasma membrane (1,2-diphytanoyl-*sn*-glycero-3-phosphocholine, DPhPC), showed that the oscillating redox behaviour can induce important changes in the lamellarity of the lipid domains [28], however, the change of the redox state is not sufficient to prompt the conformational changes needed for fission and division processes of the membranes. Autocatalytic pH clock reactions, such as the formaldehyde-sulfite [20], seem to be a more suitable candidate for this purpose. In fact, such reactions can produce a pH jump up to 5 units, a chemical shock that could drive pH-sensitive membranes out of equilibrium and ultimately to a conformational rearrangement compatible with a division dynamics.

Enzymatic clock reactions, though with a less prebiotic character, can also be employed as pH changing medium. In fact, it has been shown that the urea-urease system can be successfully encapsulated in POPC vesicles and undergo a hydrolysis reaction (producing OH^- ions) following a trans-membrane input of urea [21]. A next obvious step would be the confinement of the urease system in mixed phospholipid/fatty acids compartments.

4 Conclusions

In this work we highlighted those characteristics of nonlinear chemical systems that can help to understand the transition from inanimate to animate matter and we presented few experimental systems able to reproduce in vitro, on a laboratory scale, complex biological processes. In particular, we showed how the oscillating Belousov-Zhabotinsky reaction, a model for biochemical autocatalytic cycles, can be employed in a confined environment to model trans-membrane communication by using simple periodic chemical signals. Such trafficking among individual self-organising chemical reactions generates bio-mimicking global behaviours; when many units are free to exchange activatory or inhibitory signals, in-phase and anti-phase oscillations or quorum sensing phenomena can be attained. Such dynamics are a genuine demonstration that simple abiotic chemical systems, when properly coupled with self-assembling confining membranes (or supports), can undergo bifurcations and symmetry-breaking dynamics, also at a population level.

We also proposed a simple experimental system to induce self-division in mixed fatty acids/phospholipids vesicles. Autocatalytic pH-changing clock reactions are thus employed to induce a chemical shock and drive out of equilibrium the vesicles membranes, that, on the basis of previous systems explored, should undergo a self-division process.

In conclusion, both population dynamics and self-division processes are distinctive traits of life that can be reproduced and explored by taking advantage of relatively simple nonlinear reactions coupled to self-assembled systems.

References

1. Amoroso, R.L., Amoroso, P.J.: The fundamental limit and origin of complexity in biological systems: a new model for the origin of life. In: AIP Conference Proceedings, vol. 718, pp. 144–159. AIP (2004)
2. Baaske, P., Weinert, F.M., Duhr, S., Lemke, K.H., Russell, M.J., Braun, D.: Extreme accumulation of nucleotides in simulated hydrothermal pore systems. Proc. Natl. Acad. Sci. **104**(22), 9346–9351 (2007)
3. Bachmann, P.A., Walde, P., Luisi, P.L., Lang, J.: Self-replicating reverse micelles and chemical autopoiesis. J. Am. Chem. Soc. **112**(22), 8200–8201 (1990)

4. Braun, D., Libchaber, A.: Thermal force approach to molecular evolution. Phys. Biol. **1**(1), P1 (2004)
5. Budroni, M.A., De Wit, A.: Dissipative structures: from reaction-diffusion to chemo-hydrodynamic patterns. Chaos: Interdisc. J. Nonlinear Sci. **27**(10), 104617 (2017)
6. Budroni, M.A., Calabrese, I., Miele, Y., Rustici, M., Marchettini, N., Rossi, F.: Control of chemical chaos through medium viscosity in a batch ferroin-catalysed Belousov-Zhabotinsky reaction. Phys. Chem. Chem. Phys. **19**, 32235–32241 (2017)
7. Budroni, M.A., Rossi, F.: A novel mechanism for in situ nucleation of spirals controlled by the interplay between phase fronts and reaction-diffusion waves in an oscillatory medium. J. Phys. Chem. C **119**(17), 9411–9417 (2015)
8. Budroni, M.A., Masia, M., Rustici, M., Marchettini, N., Volpert, V.: Bifurcations in spiral tip dynamics induced by natural convection in the Belousov-Zhabotinsky reaction. J. Chem. Phys. **130**(2), 024902–8 (2009)
9. Coveney, P.V., Swadling, J.B., Wattis, J.A., Greenwell, H.C.: Theory, modelling and simulation in origins of life studies. Chem. Soc. Rev. **41**(16), 5430–5446 (2012)
10. Fiore, M.: The synthesis of Mono-Alkyl phosphates and their derivatives: an overview of their nature, preparation and use, including synthesis under plausible prebiotic conditions. Org. Biomol. Chem. **16**(17), 3068–3086 (2018)
11. Fiore, M., Strazewski, P.: Prebiotic lipidic amphiphiles and condensing agents on the early Earth. Life **6**(2), 17 (2016)
12. Hargreaves, W.R., Mulvihill, S.J., Deamer, D.W.: Synthesis of phospholipids and membranes in prebiotic conditions. Nature **266**(5597), 78 (1977)
13. Huber, C., Eisenreich, W., Wächtershäuser, G.: Synthesis of α-amino and α-hydroxy acids under volcanic conditions: implications for the origin of life. Tetrahedron Lett. **51**(7), 1069–1071 (2010)
14. Ikari, K., et al.: Dynamics of fatty acid vesicles in response to pH stimuli. Soft Matter **11**(31), 6327–6334 (2015). http://pubs.rsc.org/en/Content/ArticleLanding/2015/SM/C5SM01248A
15. Jin, L., Kamat, N.P., Jena, S., Szostak, J.W.: Fatty acid/phospholipid blended membranes: a potential intermediate state in protocellular evolution. Small **14**(15), 1704077 (2018)
16. Kitadai, N., Kameya, M., Fujishima, K.: Origin of the reductive tricarboxylic acid (rTCA) cycle-type $CO2$ fixation: a perspective. Life **7**(4), 39 (2017)
17. Lagzi, I.: Self-division of a mineral oil-fatty acid droplet. Chem. Phys. Lett. **640**, 1–4 (2015)
18. Liu, Y., Sumpter, D.: Spontaneous emergence of self-replication in chemical reaction systems. arXiv preprint arXiv:1801.05872 (2018)
19. Martins, Z., Sephton, M., Hughes, A.B.: Aminoacids, Peptides and Proteins in Organic Chemistry - Origins and Synthesis of Amino Acids, vol. 1. Wiley, Weinheim (2009)
20. McIlwaine, R., Kovacs, K., Scott, S.K., Taylor, A.F.: A novel route to pH oscillators. Chem. Phys. Lett. **417**(1), 39–42 (2006)
21. Miele, Y., Bánsági, T., Taylor, A.F., Stano, P., Rossi, F.: Engineering enzyme-driven dynamic behaviour in lipid vesicles. In: Rossi, F., Mavelli, F., Stano, P., Caivano, D. (eds.) WIVACE 2015. CCIS, vol. 587, pp. 197–208. Springer, Cham (2016). https://doi.org/10.1007/978-3-319-32695-5_18
22. Miller, S.L.: A production of aminoacids under possible primitive earth conditions. Science, New Ser. **117**(3046), 528–529 (1953). http://www.jstor.org/stable/1680569

23. Nicolis, G., Prigogine, I.: Self-organization in Nonequilibrium Systems. Wiley, New York (1977)
24. Nooner, D., Gibert, J., Gelpi, E., Oro', J.: Closed system fischer-tropsch synthesis over meteoritic iron, iron ore and nickel-iron alloy. Geochimica Et Cosmochimica Acta **40**(8), 915–924 (1976)
25. Noyes, R.M., Field, R., Koros, E.: Oscillations in chemical systems. I. Detailed mechanism in a system showing temporal oscillations. J. Am. Chem. Soc. **94**(4), 1394–1395 (1972)
26. Paul, A.: Observations of the effect of anionic, cationic, neutral, and zwitterionic surfactants on the Belousov-Zhabotinsky reaction. J. Phys. Chem. B **109**(19), 9639–9644 (2005)
27. Peterlin, P., Arrigler, V., Kogej, K., Svetina, S., Walde, P.: Growth and shape transformations of giant phospholipid vesicles upon interaction with an aqueous oleic acid suspension. Chem. Phys. Lipids **159**(2), 67–76 (2009)
28. Ristori, S., Rossi, F., Biosa, G., Marchettini, N., Rustici, M., Tiezzi, E.: Interplay between the Belousov-Zhabotinsky reaction-diffusion system and biomimetic matrices. Chem. Phys. Lett. **436**, 175–178 (2007)
29. Rossi, F., Budroni, M.A., Marchettini, N., Cutietta, L., Rustici, M., Turco Liveri, M.L.: Chaotic dynamics in an unstirred ferroin catalyzed Belousov-Zhabotinsky reaction. Chem. Phys. Lett. **480**(4–6), 322–326 (2009)
30. Rossi, F., Liveri, M.L.T.: Chemical self-organization in self-assembling biomimetic systems. Ecol. Model. **220**(16), 1857–1864 (2009)
31. Rossi, F., Ristori, S., Marchettini, N., Pantani, O.L.: Functionalized clay microparticles as catalysts for chemical oscillators. J. Phys. Chem. C **118**(42), 24389–24396 (2014)
32. Rossi, F., Ristori, S., Rustici, M., Marchettini, N., Tiezzi, E.: Dynamics of pattern formation in biomimetic systems. J. Theor. Biol. **255**(4), 404–412 (2008)
33. Rossi, F., Torbensen, K., Ristori, S., Abou-Hassan, A.: Signal transduction and communication through model membranes in networks of coupled chemical oscillators. In: Pelillo, M., Poli, I., Roli, A., Serra, R., Slanzi, D., Villani, M. (eds.) WIVACE 2017. CCIS, vol. 830, pp. 16–31. Springer, Cham (2018). https://doi.org/10.1007/978-3-319-78658-2_2
34. Rossi, F., Varsalona, R., Marchettini, N., Turco Liveri, M.L.: Control of spontaneous spiral formation in a zwitterionic micellar medium. Soft Matter **7**, 9498 (2011)
35. Rossi, F., et al.: Activatory coupling among oscillating droplets produced in microfluidic based devices. Int. J. Unconventional Comput. **11**(1), 23–36 (2015)
36. Roy, D., Cambre, J.N., Sumerlin, B.S.: Future perspectives and recent advances in stimuli-responsive materials. Progr. Polym. Sci. **35**(1), 278–301 (2010)
37. Ruiz-Mirazo, K., Briones, C., de la Escosura, A.: Prebiotic systems chemistry: new perspectives for the origins of life. Chem. Rev. **114**(1), 285–366 (2013)
38. Sciascia, L., Rossi, F., Sbriziolo, C., Liveri, M.L.T., Varsalona, R.: Oscillatory dynamics of the Belousov-Zhabotinsky system in the presence of a self-assembling nonionic polymer. Role of the reactants concentration. Phys. Chem. Chem. Phys. **12**(37), 11674–11682 (2010)
39. Scott, S.K.: Chemical Chaos. Oxford University Press, Oxford (1993)
40. Scott, S.K.: Oscillations, Waves, and Chaos in Chemical Kinetics. Oxford University Press, Oxford (1994)
41. Stano, P., D'Aguanno, E., Bolz, J., Fahr, A., Luisi, P.L.: A remarkable self-organization process as the origin of primitive functional cells. Angewandte Chemie International Edition **52**(50), 13397–13400 (2013)

42. Stano, P., Mavelli, F.: Protocells models in origin of life and synthetic biology. Life **5**(4), 1700–1702 (2015)
43. Szostak, J., Bartel, D., Luisi, P.: Synthesizing life. Nature **409**(6818), 387–390 (2001)
44. Takeoka, Y., Watanabe, M., Yoshida, R.: Self-sustaining peristaltic motion on the surface of a porous gel. J. Am. Chem. Soc. **125**(44), 13320–13321 (2003). http://pubs.acs.org/doi/abs/10.1021/ja036904c
45. Taylor, A.F.: Mechanism and phenomenology of an oscillating chemical reaction. Progr. React. Kinet. Mech. **27**(4), 247–325 (2002)
46. Taylor, A.F., Tinsley, M.R., Wang, F., Huang, Z., Showalter, K.: Dynamical quorum sensing and synchronization in large populations of chemical oscillators. Science **323**(5914), 614–617 (2009)
47. Toiya, M., González-Ochoa, H.O., Vanag, V.K., Fraden, S., Epstein, I.R.: Synchronization of chemical micro-oscillators. J. Phys. Chem. Lett. **1**(8), 1241–1246 (2010)
48. Tomasi, R., et al.: Chemical communication between liposomes encapsulating a chemical oscillatory reaction. Chem. Sci. **5**(5), 1854–1859 (2014)
49. Torbensen, K., Ristori, S., Rossi, F., Abou-Hassan, A.: Tuning the chemical communication of oscillating microdroplets by means of membrane composition. J. Phys. Chem. C **121**(24), 13256–13264 (2017)
50. Torbensen, K., Rossi, F., Pantani, O.L., Ristori, S., Abou-Hassan, A.: Interaction of the Belousov-Zhabotinsky reaction with phospholipid engineered membranes. J. Phys. Chem. B **119**(32), 10224–10230 (2015)
51. Torbensen, K., Rossi, F., Ristori, S., Abou-Hassan, A.: Chemical communication and dynamics of droplet emulsions in networks of Belousov-Zhabotinsky microoscillators produced by microfluidics. Lab Chip **17**(7), 1179–1189 (2017)
52. Varela, F.G., Maturana, H.R., Uribe, R.: Autopoiesis: the organization of living systems, its characterization and a model. Biosystems **5**(4), 187–196 (1974)
53. Zhu, T.F., Szostak, J.W.: Coupled growth and division of model protocell membranes. J. Am. Chem. Soc. **131**(15), 5705–5713 (2009)

Optimal Curing Strategy Enhancement of Epidemic Processes with Self-adaptive SBX Crossover

Clara Pizzuti$^{(\boxtimes)}$ and Annalisa Socievole

National Research Council of Italy (CNR),
Institute for High Performance Computing and Networking (ICAR),
Via Pietro Bucci, 8-9C, 87036 Rende (CS), Italy
{clara.pizzuti,annalisa.socievole}@icar.cnr.it

Abstract. Epidemic processes in networks pose sever challenges to network operators and more generally in the management of public health. One of these challenges is the research of an optimal curing policy able to suppress the epidemic. In this paper, we model the epidemic spreading in networks with a Susceptible-Infected-Susceptible (SIS) process and exploit the N-Intertwined Mean-Field Approximation (NIMFA) of the SIS model. Then, we propose a constrained genetic algorithm which assigns specific curing rates to nodes in order to minimize the total curing cost while reducing the number of infected nodes within the network. Simulating both real-world Internet backbones and Facebook networks, together with Erdős-Rényi, Watts-Strogatz and Bárabasi-Albert synthetic networks, we show that the use of a self-adaptive simulated binary crossover (SBX) improves a genetic algorithm employing a classical SBX crossover.

Keywords: Epidemic spreading · NIMFA · Complex networks ·
Genetic algorithms · Adaptive simulated binary crossover

1 Introduction

The diffusion of viruses within networks or among people has always attracted a lot of attention in many different research fields such as computer science, physics, medicine, and biology [13]. The aim of the research on this topic within these fields is mainly the characterization of the epidemic spreading in order to prevent or mitigate the diffusion of epidemics. The development of policies to control the epidemic spreading is thus a crucial problem. Epidemic models have been defined studied since the twenties [11]. Basically, these models represent the network subject to the virus spreading with a graph where nodes are the individuals and the edges the direction of the infection from an infected individual to a susceptible one. One of the most popular epidemic models is the *Susceptible-Infected-Susceptible* (SIS) where a node can be either in the *susceptible* state S, in which it can contract the infection, or the *infectious* state I,

© Springer Nature Switzerland AG 2019
S. Cagnoni et al. (Eds.): WIVACE 2018, CCIS 900, pp. 151–162, 2019.
https://doi.org/10.1007/978-3-030-21733-4_12

in which it is infected. It is assumed that an individual can be reinfected, thus repeating the transition states $S \rightarrow I \rightarrow S$ eventually forever. The SIS model is one of the simplest epidemic models, some other models like the SIR, for example, consider a *recovered* state R where a node recovered from the infection, the $SEIR$ includes also an *exposed* state E where a node has been infected but it is not yet infectious due to incubation, and so on. In general, when controlling the evolution of epidemics, the network resources are limited. Epidemic models, thus, in order to suppress the epidemic spreading, define a search problem where an objective function must be optimized. Find the minimum number of nodes to immunize, or the number of connections to remove between individuals [3,13], distribute vaccine to control epidemic outbreaks [2,20,21], allocate recovery resources at the lowest cost to prevent the indefinitely persistency of an epidemic [14] are just some examples.

In this work, we consider the problem of finding a minimal-cost curing strategy over a network able to suppress the epidemic spreading. Exploiting the *N-Intertwined Mean-Field Approximation* ($NIMFA$) of the SIS spreading process, introduced by Van Mieghem et al. [24,25], we investigate the use of Genetic Algorithms (GAs) for an optimal curing policy. Specifically, we focus on an heterogeneous setting where each node has its own curing rate and cost, and each node infects the other with a particular infection rate.

In [18], we proposed $OCPGA$, a constrained GA method which determines specific curing rates for each node able to minimize the total cost for curing the network and having all the nodes healthy. $OCPGA$ employed the *simulated binary crossover* (SBX) of Deb [4], and it has been shown to generally outperform the exact semidefinite programming solver $SDPT3$ [23]. In this paper, we investigate a self-adaptive version of SBX [5] in order to evaluate the benefits of having a *parent-centric* crossover in the creation of offsprings and a mixed *parent/mean-centric* crossover, that adapts to the evolution of the population of chromosomes, respectively. While the parent-centric crossover generates offsprings near to one of the parents, the mean-centric one creates children near to the centroid of the parents. Comparing $OCPGA$ and the modified version, named $OCPGA_{aSBX}$, with $SDPT3$ over real-world and synthetic networks, we show that the two approaches find solutions whose curing cost is lower than that obtained by the classical baseline method $SDPT3$, and that $OCPGA_{aSBX}$ sensibly improves the already good results of $OCPGA$.

The paper has been organized as follows. Section 2 describes the related work. In Sect. 3, we recall the $NIMFA$ model of the heterogeneous SIS process. In Sect. 4, we formalize the problem of the minimal-cost cure as a constrained optimization problem. Section 5 describes the GA algorithm designed to solve the problem, the representation and the variation operators. In Sect. 6, we test the method on several real-world and synthetic networks and compare the results with those obtained by the exact semidefinite solver $SDPT3$. Finally, Sect. 7 concludes the paper and points out the future developments in this context.

2   Related Work

Epidemic spreading on networks have been largely studied in the last years. Extensive surveys on the modeling of infectious diseases can be found in [13, 17]. Concerning the network type on which the virus spreads, epidemics have been mainly investigated on scale-free networks [16], random graphs [12] and contact networks [27]. Focusing on the optimization of resources over a network where a virus spreads, in the work of Gourdin et al. [7] a curing budget, given a certain level of network infection, is minimized. Prakash et al. [19] dealt with the problem of distributing a fixed amount of resources to network nodes in order to minimize the infection rate. Preciado et al. [20,21] allocated resources in presence of spreading processes by modifying the infection rates of individuals. Zhai et al. [29] analyzed several epidemic evolution models and proposed a framework optimizing of the rate of the epidemic evolution. More recently, Ottaviano et al. studied an optimal curing policy over a community network [14].

Few works dealt with genetic algorithms applied to epidemic spreading problems. In [15], a GA is used to obtain the minimum-cost number of vaccines to distribute over a network under a SIR (Susceptible-Infected-Recovered) process. In [3], a GA minimizes the infection spreading over a network by removing a specified number of connections. Lahiri and Cebrian [9] focused on information diffusion processes on social networks by proposing a *genetic algorithm diffusion model* (GADM).

3   Epidemic Spreading in Networks: The $NIMFA$ Model

In the SIS model, the viral state of a node i belonging to an undirected graph $G(V,E)$ with N nodes, is described by a Bernoulli random variable $X_i \in \{0,1\}$: $X_i = 0$ when a node is healthy and $X_i = 1$ when a node is infected. If infected at time t, a node is in the *infected state* with probability $v_i(t) = \Pr[X_i(t) = 1]$, otherwise it is in the healthy state with probability $1 - v_i(t)$. The problem in the SIS model is thus to compute $v_i(t)$ for each node in the graph. When *infection rates* per link are independent Poisson processes with rates δ and β, respectively, the SIS model is called homogeneous (Fig. 1(a)). In such setting, the *effective infection rate* is defined as $\tau = \beta/\delta$. In the heterogeneous case (Fig. 1(b)), instead, the curing rate for each node i is node-specific (i.e. δ_i), and the spreading rate denoted by β_{ij} becomes link-specific (i.e. a node can infect the other nodes j with different infection rates).

The SIS model can be expressed exactly in terms of a continuous Markov chain with 2^N states, where each state represents a possible combination in which the nodes can be infected [25]. A remarkable property of the exact SIS Markov process is the existence of a phase transition in the epidemic spreading called *epidemic threshold*, usually denoted with τ_c. Specifically, if the effective infection rate τ is higher than τ_c, the infection becomes persistent, while if $\tau < \tau_c$, the virus goes extinct and the overall healthy state is reached. In real-world networks, computing the exact solution of the SIS model requires the resolution of a system of 2^N linear differential equations. For this reason, approximations of the SIS model have been proposed [22,25]. The mean-field approximation model $NIMFA$, for example, requires the resolution of N non-linear differential equations. In the homogeneous setting, $NIMFA$ determines the epidemic threshold as the inverse of the spectral radius[1] $\lambda_{max}(A)$ of the adjacency matrix A associated with the graph G, i.e. $\tau_c^{(1)} = \frac{1}{\lambda_{max}(A)}$.

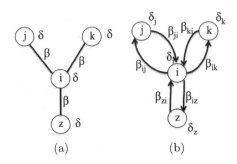

(a)   (b)

Fig. 1. 4-nodes example of (a) homogeneous SIS setting, (b) heterogeneous SIS setting.

In the heterogeneous case [24], $NIMFA$ describes the probability $v_i(t)$ for the node i of being infected as:

$$\frac{dv_i(t)}{dt} = \sum_{j=1}^{N} \beta_{ij} v_j(t) - \sum_{j=1}^{N} \beta_{ij} v_i(t) v_j(t) - \delta_i v_i(t). \tag{1}$$

These equations can be rewritten as

$$\frac{dV(t)}{dt} = \bar{A} V(t) + F(V) \tag{2}$$

where $V(t)$ is the vector $V(t) = (v_1(t), v_2(t), ..., v_N(t))$, $\bar{A}$ is defined as

$$\bar{A} = \begin{bmatrix} \delta_1 & \beta_{12} & \cdot\cdot & \cdot & \beta_{1N} \\ \beta_{21} & \delta_2 & & & \\ \cdot & & \cdot & & \\ \cdot & & & \cdot & \\ \cdot & & & & \cdot \\ \beta_{N1} & \cdot & \cdot\cdot & \beta_{NN-1} & \delta_N \end{bmatrix} \tag{3}$$

and $F(V)$ is a column vector having as i-th element

$$-\sum_{j=1}^{N} \beta_{ij} v_i(t) v_j(t) \tag{4}$$

---

[1] The spectral radius of a square matrix $A \in C^{N \times N}$ is the largest absolute value of its (real or complex) eigenvalues $\lambda_1, \ldots, \lambda_N$, i.e. $\lambda_{max}(A) = max\{|\lambda_1|, \ldots, |\lambda_N|\}$.

In [14] the epidemic threshold for the heterogeneous setting is obtained by exploiting the results of Lajmanovich and Yorke [10] regarding the real component of the maximum eigenvalue $r(\bar{A})$ of $\bar{A}$:

$$r(\bar{A}) = max_{1 \leq j \leq N} Re(\lambda_j(\bar{A})) \tag{5}$$

where $Re(\lambda_j(\bar{A}))$ is the real part of the eigenvalues of $\bar{A}$. The authors, by using the Theorem 3.1 of [10] stating that if $r(\bar{A}) \leq 0$, then the epidemic will go extinct (Theorem 2.1 in [14]), are able to identify the epidemic threshold.

4   The Optimal Curing Policy (OCP) Problem

Starting from the $NIMFA$ model in the heterogeneous setting, we tackle the problem of finding an optimal assignment of the curing rates to each node of a weighted network ensuring the extinction of the virus. In [14], this problem has been formalized as follows. Given a node i, this node is cured with rate equal to δ_i while the cost for allocating recovery resources (e.g. medicines, medical staff, etc.) to this node is c_i. The total cost for curing a network is expressed as

$$U(\Delta) = \sum_{i=1}^{N} c_i \delta_i \tag{6}$$

where $\Delta = (\delta_1, \delta_2, ..., \delta_N)$ is the curing rate vector to minimize.

For undirected weighted networks the adjacency matrix $A = (\beta_{ij})$ is symmetric since $\beta_{ij} = \beta_{ji}$. As such, the eigenvalues are real. For Theorem 2.1 in [14], if $\lambda_{max}(A - diag(\Delta)) \leq 0$ the infection disappears and all nodes are healthy. Consequently, the largest eigenvalue of $(A - diag(\Delta))$ can be considered the epidemic threshold for the network considered.

In order to find a cost-optimal allocation of curing rates, the optimization problem to solve is formalized as follows.

Problem *Optimal Curing Policy OCP.* Given a graph $G = (V, E)$, the weighted adjacency matrix A of the spreading rates with elements $a_{ij} = \beta_{ji}$, and the cost coefficients $c_i > 0, i = 1, ... N$, find the vector $\Delta \geq 0$ of curing rates which solves the nonlinear constrained problem:

$$\text{minimize } U(\Delta)$$
$$\text{subject to } \lambda_{max}(A - diag(\Delta)) \leq 0$$
$$\Delta \geq 0$$

The OCP problem can be reformulated as a semidefinite programming problem (SDP) [26] as:

$$\text{minimize } U(\Delta)$$
$$\text{subject to } diag(\Delta) - A \geq 0$$
$$\Delta \geq 0$$

since $diag(\Delta) \geq 0$ and the inequality sign in $diag(\Delta) - A \geq 0$, when $diag(\Delta) - A$ is a matrix, means that it is semidefinite positive[2]. Given this formulation, the OCP problem can be thus solved also by using an SDP solver, like $SDPT3$ [23].

5   Methods

For solving the OCP problem, we proposed $OCPGA$ [18], a constrained genetic algorithm that uses the total curing cost $U(\Delta)$ as fitness function. In this method, each individual of the population is represented by a vector $\Delta = (\delta_1, \delta_2, ..., \delta_N)$ containing the curing rates for each node. Thus the i-th gene represents the node i which is cured with rate δ_i, where each δ_i assumes values between 0 and 1. The constraints to satisfy in the OCP problem are the positiveness of the real part of the largest eigenvalue of the matrix $A - diag(\Delta)$, besides the lower and upper bound of each variable, i.e. $x_i^l \leq \delta_i \leq x_i^u$. OCPGA employed as mutation operator the *adaptive feasible* mutation, which randomly generates directions that adapt to the last successful or unsuccessful generation. Specifically, it chooses a direction and a step length satisfying the bounds and the linear constraints. Moreover, in order to generate feasible children from feasible parents, it employed the Simulated Binary Crossover of Deb [4], which controls the spread of the children around the parents using a distribution index η_c. Giving two feasible parents $x^{(1)}$ and $x^{(2)}$, the SBX operator computes the children solutions $y^{(1)}$ and $y^{(2)}$ as follows:

$$y^{(1)} = 0.5 \left[(x^{(1)} + x^{(2)} - \bar{\beta}[x^{(2)} + x^{(1)}] \right] \tag{7}$$

$$y^{(2)} = 0.5 \left[(x^{(1)} + x^{(2)} + \bar{\beta}[x^{(2)} + x^{(1)}] \right] \tag{8}$$

where

$$\bar{\beta} = \begin{cases} (\alpha u)^{1/(\eta_c+1)} & \text{if } u \leq 1/\alpha \\ (\frac{1}{2-\alpha u})^{1/(\eta_c+1)} & \text{otherwise} \end{cases} \tag{9}$$

is the *spread factor*, with u a random number between 0 and 1, $\alpha = 2 - \beta^{-(\eta_c+1)}$, and

$$\beta = 1 + \frac{2}{y^{(2)} - y^{(1)}} min[(x^{(1)} - x^l), (x^u - x^{(2)})]$$

Note that η_c can assume only nonnegative values for which small values produce children far from the parents, while large values generate solutions closer to the parents. In any case, the children stay within the fixed range $[x^l, x^u]$ of the lower and the upper bounds. The SBX crossover is by definition parent-centric since the children are close to one of the parents. However, there are also mean-centric crossover operators (e.g. BLX-α and UNDX) that generate children around the centroid of the participating parents. Deb and Jain [5] showed that using a

---

[2] A semidefinite positive matrix $A \in R^{N \times N}$ is a symmetric matrix such that $x^T A x \geq 0$ for all the $x \in R^N$. Equivalently, all the eigenvalues of A are nonnegative.

parent-centric crossover at the beginning of the simulation and then switching to a mean-centric one when the population stabilizes is more effective for a fast convergence to the global optimum. We thus implemented in $OCPGA_{aSBX}$ the *self-adaptive SBX* operator which creates two *virtual* parents

$$v^{(1)} = \frac{x^{(1)} + x^{(2)}}{2} - \lambda \frac{x^{(2)} - x^{(1)}}{2} \tag{10}$$

$$v^{(2)} = \frac{x^{(1)} + x^{(2)}}{2} + \lambda \frac{x^{(2)} - x^{(1)}}{2} \tag{11}$$

and then uses these virtual parents as parents of the classic SBX. Self-adaptation is given by the parameter λ computed as

$$\lambda = \frac{d_{best}}{d_{avg}} \tag{12}$$

where d_{best} is the distance between the best solution of the population and the centroid, and d_{avg} is the average distance between the chromosomes of the population and the centroid. For both distances, we computed the Euclidean distance. It can be observed that $\lambda > 1$ when the population approaches to the optimum, while $\lambda < 1$ when the population is close to the optimum.

6   Experimental Evaluation

In this section we compare $OCPGA$, $OCPGA_{aSBX}$, and $SDPT3$ on both real-world and synthetic networks. To run $SDPT3$ over Matlab, we used the CVX package for specifying and solving convex programs [8]. $OCPGA$ and $OCPGA_{aSBX}$ have been written using the Genetic Algorithm solver implemented in the Global Optimization Toolbox. Using a trial-and-error procedure on the benchmark datasets, the following parameter set was used:

(1) population size = 500;
(2) number of generations = 500;
(3) crossover fraction = 0.9;
(4) mutation rate = 0.2;
(5) $\eta_c = 1$;
(6) number of runs = 10;

Moreover, for setting the infection spreading rates of each node, we randomly generated rates in the range $[0, 1]$ and then multiplied them for 10^{-3}. In the following, we describe the datasets used for the simulations and the results obtained.

6.1   Datasets

We analyzed the networks reported in Table 1 which summarizes their topological features. The five Internet Backbones have been selected from the Internet Topology Zoo repository[3] containing hundreds of real-world backbone graphs. The backbones made available by the network operators have been selected within our experiments since such kind of networks are often subject to attacks such as blackholing by compromised BGP routers (i.e. incoming or outgoing traffic discard) which can severely degrade network performances. The other class of real-world networks chosen for our experiments are the Facebook friend lists[4]. Here, each network is the ego network of a user social profile with its Facebook friends. This kind of networks are interesting to analyze since are often subjects to attacks as the spreading of fake news from an hacked social profile to its friends, for example.

In conjunction with real-world networks, we tested a set of synthetic networks with $N = 128$ nodes. Specifically,

- Erdős-Rényi (ER) random graphs [6]: within such graphs each node pair is connected independently with probability p_c. In our simulations, we set $p_c = \ln(N)/N$ and checked if each resulting graph was connected. These graphs well model peer-to-peer and ad-hoc networks.
- Watts-Strogatz (WS) small-world graphs [28]: a class of graphs where nodes can be easily reached in few hops by the other nodes and the clustering coefficient is high. We generated Watts-Strogatz graphs from a ring lattice of N nodes, where each node has been connected to $k = 6$ nodes, by rewiring each edge with probability $p = 0.5$. These graphs are usually used to model Bluetooth or Wi-Fi device-to-device networks.
- Bárabasi-Albert [1] scale-free graphs: graphs where nodes tend to attach to other high degree nodes (i.e. the *preferential attachment* feature). Given an initial connected graph of m_0 nodes, a Bárabasi-Albert graph is generated connecting at each time step a new node to $m \leq m_0$ existing nodes with a probability that is proportional to the node degree of the existing nodes. In our simulations, we set $m_0 = 5$ and $m = 2$.

6.2   Results

Real-World Networks. In Table 3, we shows results obtained running $SDPT3$ $OCPGA$ and $OCPGA_{aSBX}$ over the real-world networks. The methods have been executed 10 times and the values reported in the table represent the average values of the objective function. Due to the very low values of the standard deviations, we do not report them. For equal costs for all the nodes (i.e., $C = (c_1, c_2, ..., c_N) = (1, 1, ..., 1)$), $OCPGA_{aSBX}$ always outperforms $OCPGA$, except for the Bell South network, where $OCPGA$ performs better

---

[3] http://www.topology-zoo.org/.
[4] https://snap.stanford.edu/data/egonets-Facebook.html.

Table 1. Topological features of real-world networks: number of nodes (N), number of links (L), average degree ($<k>$), average clustering coefficient ($<C>$) and density (D).

Network	ID	N	L	$<k>$	$<C>$	D
Bell South	BS	51	66	1.294	0.081	0.052
OTE Globe	OTE	93	103	1.108	0.011	0.024
ITC Deltacom	ITD	113	161	1.425	0.053	0.025
ION	ION	125	146	1.168	0.006	0.019
US Carrier	USC	158	189	1.196	0.002	0.015
Ego 3980	3980	52	146	5.625	0.462	0.11
Ego 686	686	168	1656	9.8572	0.266	0.059

Table 2. Topological features of synthetic networks. Here, the topological measures L, $<k>$, $<C>$ and D have been averaged over 10 network realizations.

Networks	ID	N	L	$<k>$	$<C>$	D
Erdős-Rényi	ER	128	627.3	5.23	0.054	0.041
Watts-Strogatz	WS	128	384	6	0.109	0.047
Bárabasi-Albert	BA	128	253.4	3.954	0.132	0.031

than $OCPGA_{aSBX}$ with an objective function value of 0.027 against 0.029 for $OCPGA_{aSBX}$. Both methods, moreover, are always able to find solutions with better $\Delta(U)^e$ than those obtained by $SDPT3$. In the case in which the vector of curing costs contains random values, $OCPGA_{aSBX}$ performs always the best on all the networks. On the Facebook Ego networks, $OCPGA$, however, obtains a fitness value worst than that returned by $SDPT3$, while with the self-adaptive SBX crossover $OCPGA_{aSBX}$ obtains values of $\Delta(U)^r$ lower than those corresponding to $SDPT3$. In general, we observe that $OCPGA_{aSBX}$ results in better objective function values over real-world networks. For equal costs, the better performance of $OCPGA$ and $OCPGA_{aSBX}$ with respect to $SDPT3$ is more evident. On the US Carrier network, for example, the total curing cost diminishes from 0.182 to 0.078 for $OCPGA$ and to 0.046 for $OCPGA_{aSBX}$, while for random costs, $SDPT3$ obtains 0.079, $OCPGA$ 0.063, and $OCPGA_{aSBX}$ 0.024. Finally, with random costs, where curing rates are lower than or equal to 1, $\Delta(U)^r$ values are lower in general. For the Facebook networks, we found that the difference between the genetic algorithms and $SDPT3$ is less marked.

Synthetic Networks. Table 4 shows the results obtained for the Erdős-Rényi, Watts-Strogatz, and Bárabasi-Albert random networks. In all the considered scenario, $OCPGA_{aSBX}$ outperforms $SDPT3$. Differently from the real-world networks, $OCPGA$ is not able to outperform $SDPT3$, hence the adaptivity in the crossover is necessary in such networks. Note also that the reduction of $\Delta(U)_{OCPGA}$ for the synthetic networks is less strong, probably due to their network topologies. Within these networks, having a higher number k of neighbors as shown in Table 2, low curing costs are more difficult to obtain since the infection can be propagated more easily. In any case, $OCPGA_{aSBX}$ finds good curing solutions with low $\Delta(U)$ values.

Table 3. Comparison between $SDPT3$, $OCPGA$ and $OCPGA_{aSBX}$ values of objective function over real-world networks for equal costs (e) and random costs (r).

Network	$\Delta(U)^e_{SDPT3}$	$\Delta(U)^e_{OCPGA}$	$\Delta(U)^e_{OCPGA_{aSBX}}$	$\Delta(U)^r_{SDPT3}$	$\Delta(U)^r_{OCPGA}$	$\Delta(U)^r_{OCPGA_{aSBX}}$
BS	0.075	0.027	0.029	0.033	0.022	0.013
OTE	0.12	0.032	0.025	0.037	0.016	0.013
ITD	0.196	0.098	0.065	0.067	0.063	0.027
ION	0.148	0.093	0.048	0.06	0.034	0.021
USC	0.182	0.078	0.046	0.079	0.063	0.024
3980	0.162	0.1244	0.104	0.062	0.064	0.053
686	1.69	1.533	0.107	0.773	0.713	0.537

Table 4. Comparison between $SDPT3$, $OCPGA$ and $OCPGA_{aSBX}$ values of objective function over Erdős-Rényi (ER), Watts-Strogatz (WS) and Bárabasi-Albert (BA) networks with 128 nodes. Each result has been averaged over 10 graph realizations.

Network type	$\Delta(U)^e_{SDPT3}$	$\Delta(U)^e_{OCPGA}$	$\Delta(U)^e_{OCPGA_{aSBX}}$	$\Delta(U)^r_{SDPT3}$	$\Delta(U)^r_{OCPGA}$	$\Delta(U)^r_{OCPGA_{aSBX}}$
ER	0.639 (0.027)	0.747 (0.355)	0.547 (0.028)	0.257 (0.015)	0.392 (0.07)	0.228 (0.011)
WS	0.394 (0.006)	0.509 (0.075)	0.274 (0.008)	0.165 (0.007)	0.215 (0.025)	0.125 (0.003)
BA	0.266 (0.006)	0.334 (0.077)	0.199 (0.019)	0.109 (0.003)	0.136 (0.015)	0.093 (0.006)

7   Conclusion

Exploiting the N-Intertwined Mean-Field Approximation $NIMFA$ of the SIS spreading process, we have proposed a constrained genetic algorithm which solves the problem of assigning proper curing rates to the nodes of a network that are able to minimize the curing cost and allows the extinction of the epidemic. We compared the exact semidefinite programming solver $SDPT3$ and the GA method $OCPGA$, implementing a classic SBX crossover operator, with a modified version of $OCPGA$ employing a self-adaptive SBX crossover. Results on real-world and synthetic networks have shown that $OCPGA_{aSBX}$ outperforms both $OCPGA$ and $SDPT3$. Thus, the introduction of the self-adaptive SBX crossover, which is parent-centric at the beginning of the simulation and then switches to a mean-centric one when the population stabilizes, is more effective than the classic parent-centric SBX. Future work will focus on the implementation of a more specialized mutation operator and on the extension of the method to networks with community structure.

References

1. Albert, R., Barabási, A.L.: Statistical mechanics of complex networks. Rev. Mod. Phys. **74**(1), 47–97 (2002)
2. Borgs, C., Chayes, J., Ganesh, A., Saberi, A.: How to distribute antidote to control epidemics. Random Struct. Algorithms **37**(2), 204–222 (2010)
3. Concatto. F., Zunino, W., Giancoli, L.A., Santiago, R., Lamb, L.C.: Genetic algorithm for epidemic mitigation by removing relationships. In: Proceedings of the Genetic and Evolutionary Computation Conference, pp. 761–768. ACM (2017)
4. Deb, K.: An efficient constraint handling method for genetic algorithms. Comput. Methods Appl. Mech. Eng. **186**, 311–338 (2000)
5. Deb, K., Jain, H.: Self-adaptive parent to mean-centric recombination for real-parameter optimization. Technical report, Indian Institute of Technology Kanpur (2011)
6. Erdős, P., Rényi, A.: On the evolution of random graphs. Publ. Math. Inst. Hung. Acad. Sci. **5**, 17–61 (1960)
7. Gourdin, E., Omic, J., Van Mieghem, P.: Optimization of network protection against virus spread. In: Proceedings of the 8th International Workshop on Design of Reliable Communication Networks (DRCN), pp 659–667 (2011)
8. Grant, M., Boyd, S., Ye, Y.: CVX: MATLAB software for disciplined convex programming (2008)
9. Lahiri, M., Cebrian, M.: The genetic algorithm as a general diffusion model for social networks. In: AAAI (2010)
10. Lajmanovich, A., Yorke, J.A.: A deterministic model for gonorrhea in a nonhomogeneous population. Math. Biosci. **28**(3), 221–236 (1976)
11. McKendrick, A.: Applications of mathematics to medical problems. Proc. Edin. Math. Soc. **14**, 98–130 (1926)
12. Newman, M.: Spread of epidemic disease on networks. Phys. Rev. E **66**(1), 016128 (2002)
13. Nowzari, C., Preciado, V.M., Pappas, G.J.: Analysis and control of epidemics: a survey of spreading processes on complex networks. IEEE Control Syst. **36**(1), 26–46 (2016)
14. Ottaviano, S., De Pellegrini, F., Bonaccorsi, S., Van Mieghem, P.: Optimal curing policy for epidemic spreading over a community network with heterogeneous population. Inf. Inference J. IMA (2017). https://doi.org/10.1093/imaiai/drn000
15. Parousis-Orthodoxou, K., Vlachos, D.: Evolutionary algorithm for optimal vaccination scheme. J. Phys. Conf. Ser. **490**, 012027 (2014). IOP Publishing
16. Pastor-Satorras, R., Vespignani, A.: Epidemic spreading in scale-free networks. Phys. Rev. Lett. **86**(14), 99–108 (2014)
17. Pastor-Satorras, R., Castellano, C., Mieghem, P.V., Vespignani, A.: Epidemic processes in complex networks. Rev. Mod. Phys. **87**(3), 925–979 (2015)
18. Pizzuti, C., Socievole, A.: A genetic algorithm for finding an optimal curing strategy for epidemic spreading in weighted networks. In: Proceedings of the Genetic and Evolutionary Computation Conference, GECCO 2018, Kyoto, Japan, 15–19 July 2018 (2018)
19. Prakash, B.A., Adamic, L., Iwashyna, T., Tong, H., Faloutsos, C.: Fractional immunization in networks. In: Proceedings of the SIAM Data Mining Conference, pp. 659–667 (2013)

20. Preciado, V.M., Zargham, M., Enyioha, C., Jadbabaie, A., Pappas, G.J.: Optimal vaccine allocation to control epidemic outbreaks in arbitrary networks. In: Proceedings of the 52nd IEEE Conference on Decision and Control, CDC 2013, Firenze, Italy, 10–13 December 2013, pp. 7486–7491 (2013)

21. Preciado, V.M., Zargham, M., Enyioha, C., Jadbabaie, A., Pappas, G.J.: Optimal resource allocation for network protection against spreading processes. IEEE Trans. Control Netw. Syst. **1**(1), 99–108 (2014)

22. Sahneh, F.D., Scoglio, C., Van Mieghem, P.: Generalized epidemic mean-field model for spreading processes over multilayer complex networks. IEEE/ACM Trans. Netw. **21**(5), 1609–1620 (2013)

23. Tütüncü, R.H., Toh, K.C., Todd, M.J.: Solving semidefinite-quadratic-linear programs using SDPT3. Math. Program. **95**(2), 189–217 (2003)

24. Van Mieghem, P., Omic, J.: In-homogeneous virus spread in networks (2013). arXiv:13062588

25. Van Mieghem, P., Omic, J., Kooij, R.: Virus spread in networks. IEEE/ACM Trans. Netw. **17**(1), 1–14 (2009)

26. Vandenberghe, L., Boyd, S.: Semidefinite programming. SIAM Rev. **38**(1), 49–95 (1996)

27. Wang, Y., Chakrabarti, D., Wang, C., Faloutsos, C.: Epidemic spreading in real networks: an eigenvalue viewpoint. In: Proceedings of International Symposium Reliable Distributed Systems (SRDS), pp. 25–34 (2003)

28. Watts, D.J., Strogatz, S.H.: Collective dynamics of small-world networks. Nature **393**(6684), 440 (1998)

29. Zhai, X., Zheng, L., Wang, J., Tan, C.W.: Optimization algorithms for epidemic evolution in broadcast networks. In: 2013 IEEE Wireless Communications and Networking Conference (WCNC), pp. 1540–1545. IEEE (2013)

Author Index

Printed in the United States
By Bookmasters